Hide and Seek

VERITAS
Series Introduction

". . . the truth will set you free" (John 8:32)

In much contemporary discourse, Pilate's question has been taken to mark the absolute boundary of human thought. Beyond this boundary, it is often suggested, is an intellectual hinterland into which we must not venture. This terrain is an agnosticism of thought: because truth cannot be possessed, it must not be spoken. Thus, it is argued that the defenders of "truth" in our day are often traffickers in ideology, merchants of counterfeits, or anti-liberal. They are, because it is somewhat taken for granted that Nietzsche's word is final: truth is the domain of tyranny.

Is this indeed the case, or might another vision of truth offer itself? The ancient Greeks named the love of wisdom as *philia*, or friendship. The one who would become wise, they argued, would be a "friend of truth." For both philosophy and theology might be conceived as schools in the friendship of truth, as a kind of relation. For like friendship, truth is as much discovered as it is made. If truth is then so elusive, if its domain is *terra incognita*, perhaps this is because it arrives to us—unannounced—as gift, as a person, and not some thing.

The aim of the Veritas book series is to publish incisive and original current scholarly work that inhabits "the between" and "the beyond" of theology and philosophy. These volumes will all share a common aspiration to transcend the institutional divorce in which these two disciplines often find themselves, and to engage questions of pressing concern to both philosophers and theologians in such a way as to reinvigorate both disciplines with a kind of interdisciplinary desire, often so absent in contemporary academe. In a word, these volumes represent collective efforts in the befriending of truth, doing so beyond the simulacra of pretend tolerance, the violent, yet insipid reasoning of liberalism that asks with Pilate, "What is truth?"—expecting a consensus of non-commitment; one that encourages the commodification of the mind, now sedated by the civil service of career, ministered by the frightened patrons of position.

The series will therefore consist of two "wings": (1) original monographs; and (2) essay collections on a range of topics in theology and philosophy. The latter will principally be the products of the annual conferences of the Centre of Theology and Philosophy (www.theologyphilosophycentre.co.uk).

Conor Cunningham and Eric Austin Lee, *Series editors*

Not available from Cascade

Deane-Peter Baker — *Tayloring Reformed Epistemology: The Challenge to Christian Belief.* Volume 1

P. Candler & C. Cunningham (eds.) — *Belief and Metaphysics.* Volume 2

P. Candler & C. Cunningham (eds.) — *Transcendence and Phenomenology*

Marcus Pound — *Theology, Psychoanalysis, and Trauma.* Volume 4

Espen Dahl — *Phenomenology and the Holy.* Volume 5

C. Cunningham et al. (eds.) — *Grandeur of Reason: Religion, Tradition, and Universalism.* Volume 6

A. Pabst & A. Paddison (eds.) — *The Pope and Jesus of Nazareth: Christ, Scripture, and the Church.* Volume 7

J. P. Moreland — *Recalcitrant Imago Dei: Human Persons and the Failure of Naturalism.* Volume 8

Cascade

[Nathan Kerr — *Christ, History, and Apocalyptic: The Politics of Christian Mission.* Volume 3]¹

Anthony D. Baker — *Diagonal Advance: Perfection in Christian Theology.* Volume 9

D. C. Schindler — *The Perfection of Freedom: Schiller, Schelling, and Hegel between the Ancients and the Moderns.* Volume 10

Rustin Brian — *Covering Up Luther: How Barth's Christology Challenged the* Deus Absconditus *that Haunts Modernity.* Volume 11

Timothy Stanley — *Protestant Metaphysics After Karl Barth and Martin Heidegger.* Volume 12

Christopher Ben Simpson — *The Truth Is the Way: Kierkegaard's* Theologia Viatorum. Volume 13

Richard H. Bell — *Wagner's Parsifal: An Appreciation in the Light of His Theological Journey.* Volume 14

Antonio Lopez — *Gift and the Unity of Being.* Volume 15

Toyohiko Kagawa — *Cosmic Purpose.* Translated and introduced by Thomas John Hastings. Volume 16

Nigel Zimmerman — *Facing the Other: John Paul II, Levinas, and the Body.* Volume 17

1. Note: Nathan Kerr, *Christ, History, and Apocalyptic*, although volume 3 of the original SCM Veritas series, is available from Cascade as part of the Theopolitical Visions series.

Hide and Seek

The Sacred Art of Indirect Communication

BENSON P. FRASER

CASCADE *Books* · Eugene, Oregon

HIDE AND SEEK
The Sacred Art of Indirect Communication

Veritas

Cascade Books
An Imprint of Wipf and Stock Publishers
199 W. 8th Ave., Suite 3
Eugene, OR 97401

www.wipfandstock.com

PAPERBACK ISBN: 978-1-5326-7058-9
HARDCOVER ISBN: 978-1-5326-7059-6
EBOOK ISBN: 978-1-5326-7060-2

Cataloguing-in-Publication data:

Names: Fraser, Benson P.
Title: Hide and seek : the sacred art of indirect communication. / Benson P. Fraser.
Description: Eugene, OR: Cascade Books, 2020. | Series: Veritas. | Includes bibliographical references and index.
Identifiers: ISBN 978-1-5326-7058-9 (paperback) | ISBN 978-1-5326-7059-6 (hardcover) | ISBN 978-1-5326-7060-2 (ebook)
Subjects: LCSH: Kierkegaard, Søren, 1813–1855. | Jesus Christ—Parables. | O'Connor, Flannery, 1925–1964. | Lewis, C. S. (Clive Staples), 1898–1963. | Communication
Classification: B4377 F73 2020 (paperback) | B4377 (ebook)

Manufactured in the U.S.A.   07/15/20

For Cameron and Aaron,
who continually remind me that life is a gift.

"In the dark all cats are gray—"

—SØREN KIERKEGAARD, *PRACTICE IN CHRISTIANITY*

Contents

Preface

THE GENESIS OF THIS book lies in the understanding that Søren Kierkegaard has much to say to college and university students, artists, writers, and professional storytellers. He anticipated the crippling influence modernity would have on telling the truth of the gospel. As well as anyone, he recognized that direct forms of communication had lost their ability to awaken our modern audience to the uncomfortable challenges of the gospel. Perhaps better than anyone else Kierkegaard understood that if a people of faith privileges direct over indirect communication, it would diminish the ability of the church to be heard in any positive way, and that it would ultimately succumb to the ironic scandal of a belief without life, bones without flesh.

This book suggests that if a generation of storytellers and artists can learn to balance the modern penchant for direct communication with various forms of indirect communication, then it will be able to speak more powerfully and sensitively to the culture. An indirect approach to communication assumes that people are human storytellers and that we fashion our life in and through the telling and hearing of stories. In this way, indirect communication is not as much concerned with the transfer of knowledge but the conveyance of capability (the ability to do, to live the truth, rather than just knowing the truth). The indirect approach does not guarantee that one will come to belief, but it provokes the hearer in a way that is engaging and creative, causing the audience to question their preconceived beliefs. In learning from the indirect approach of Kierkegaard, Jesus, C. S. Lewis, and Flannery O'Connor, artists with Christian concerns might move hearers from mere knowledge to capability.

Acknowledgments

THIS STUDY BEGAN YEARS ago at Fuller Theological Seminary while I was taking a class with Lewis Smedes. In his class I was introduced to the works of Søren Kierkegaard. Several years later after I began teaching a graduate class on communication and theology, I, along with my graduate students, began to seriously consider Kierkegaard's influence on the field of communication. I cannot thank them enough for their scholarly insight and encouragement. Therefore, I wish to thank Harry Argo, Hanisha Besant, Kevin Crawford, Jeff Gardner, Laura Groves, Andrew Harris, Elizabeth Hornsby, Michael Jeffers, Shannon Leinen, Sheri Parmelee, Lorie Porter Mark Paustian, Pam Robles, Danny Roman-Gloro, Andrew Rosbury, Dana Sleger, Naaman Wood, and Robert Woods. Kevin Crawford was especially helpful in the early development of this project.

I want to acknowledge the assistance of several talented and supportive friends. First, I would like to thank Steve Halliday who not only read over the entire manuscript and suggested several important changes but also counseled and encouraged me through one of the most difficult seasons of my life. Second, the spiritual insight and editorial support of Michael Di Fuccia was extremely insightful and encouraging. His contribution and insight into the philosophy and theology of the church help me grow as a person and a scholar.

The faculty and administration of Virginia Wesleyan University have been very encouraging and supportive. I owe a special debt of gratitude to Steven Emmanuel, Kathy Merlock Jackson, Lisa Lyon Payne, and Craig Wansink. Furthermore, I have had the support and encouragement of a unique community of people who have been a positive force for good and encouragement in my life during the past two years as I was finishing this book. I am especially grateful to the community of support and intellectual stimulation I found in teaching classes at Westminster Canterbury.

Over the years several colleagues have contributed to my growth as a writer. I wish to thank Dennis Bounds, John Lawing, Michael Graves, Andrew Quick, and Mark Steiner for their friendship and support. Also, I wish to thank Mitch Land from The King's University for his support and friendship. Furthermore, I was bolstered by a community of friends who contributed to my life and development is various ways. Bill Harris never ceased to call me and encourage me in my work and Jim and Bobby Ward were also a strong source of inspiration and help.

My faith community, Galilee Episcopal Church, has been a continual source of strength, especially under the leadership and sermons of our rector, Rev. Dr. Andrew Buchanan. Also, I am especially grateful for a small group of men who meet weekly to study Scripture and share our lives. Therefore, I want to thank Robert Berndt, Andy Fox, Jock Freese, Stewart Goldwag, Tom Kleine, Dave Lindfors, Hugh Patterson, Tim Robertson, Steve Scoper, David Stewart, Bob Tata, Ben Unkle, David Wilkins, and Bobby Woodard.

The people at Cascade Books have been extremely helpful, and I am thankful for their extraordinary work and commitment to scholarship. I owe a special thanks to Eric Lee for editing the manuscript and providing several important insights and changes.

In addition, I am fortunate to have two close friends who I meet with regularly to discuss our writing projects and to goad each other into finishing them. William Brown has been a close friend and colleague with whom I have spent countless hours discussing and refining the manuscript. Without question he has left his imprint on this work. Furthermore, Terry Lindvall has been a friend and colleague for longer than I care to remember. We have taught together and discussed the ideas found in this work for several years. He has been a continual thorn in my side, heckling me until I finished this text. Well, now it is finished; but I have little hope that the heckling or mocking will stop.

Finally, I am grateful for my family and for their support. My brother Ken and his wife Marty have consistently shown me love and support throughout the writing of this book as they have through all the ebbs and flows of life. Moreover, I am grateful for my two sons for the support and joy they bring to my life. They keep me honest and have been a constant source of inspiration and love. In many ways they are responsible for much of the good found in this work.

Introduction

We are beginning to realize that an impoverishment of the imagination means an impoverishment of the religious life as well.

—FLANNERY O'CONNOR, *MYSTERY AND MANNERS*

W
E ARE ALL STORYTELLERS and artists. Reynolds Price reminds us that people have "a need to tell and hear stories."[1] We come to know who we are and what our world is like through our use of symbols and our symbolic interaction with others. The New Testament church was a storytelling church that conveyed the revelation of God through the telling of sacramental stories.[2] Since the enlightenment, however, our culture has gradually changed and has come to favor more rational approaches to communicating the gospel. At the same time, the church has marginalized the role that storytelling and the imaginative arts perform when communicating transcendent truth. As Eugene H. Peterson states, "A widespread practice in our postbiblical church culture is taking the story and eliminating it by depersonalizing it into propositions or 'truth' or morals or ideas."[3]

This emphasis on abstract thought, argument, and proposition can be clearly seen among many of those attempting to communicate the transcendent truth of God. For example, Jacob D. Myers states, "In some traditions, preaching has become less about embracing an encounter with God through the Spirit and more about pushing dogmatic conformity."[4]

1. Price, *Palpable God*, 3.
2. Peterson, "Foreword."
3. Peterson, "Foreword," viii.
4. Myers, *Preaching Must Die!*, 8.

1

The church has repeatedly adopted communication strategies that privilege an unmediated (direct or rationalist) form of revelation, thereby diminishing the imaginative impulse that God has placed within us. Peterson's critique of this approach asserts that so called "Godtalk—depersonalized, nonrelational, unlistening, abstract language—kills."[5] Instead of bringing to life the passionate love and work of God in Christ present within our world, it strives for doctrinal conformity.

Reason and science, which are so useful and valuable to our economic progress and lifestyle, are nevertheless imperfect ways of knowing. Thus, we should be careful not to continually elevate them above other ways of knowing. The influence of modernity on our culture led artists with Christian concerns[6] to privilege reason over imagination and proposition over narrative. In so doing the church today has forgotten just how varied, imaginative, and storied is Scripture.

The language we use has a way of defining us. We inhabit our language. We come to know what is real by the language we create, adopt, and use. Rather than embracing both imagination and reason in our communication behavior, we have allowed the language of science and reason to dominate our understanding of self and society. The Christian truth, so richly presented in Scripture and so varied in language and style of writing, has, in our generation, been constrained and limited by influences and interests of the larger culture. Unfortunately, when communicating the gospel, artists and practitioners with Christian concerns have all too often neglected their artistic giftings and chosen instead to favor direct approaches. It is argued that when dealing with an illusion or with someone who thinks they know the truth when they do not, indirect communication strategies such as "defamiliarization" or "making strange" is necessary.[7]

God's message was originally given to those living in an oral culture that emphasized narrative truth. Today we live in a culture that is primarily visual; hence, the appropriate mode of communication for both the past and present is that which conveys both images and emotion.

5. Peterson, "Foreword," xi.

6. I am using the phrase "artists with Christian concerns," which was used by Flannery O'Connor in *Mystery and Manners*, 33. My reason for using this term is that it seems more accurate than the phrase "Christian artists," which is difficult to define and unclear at best.

7. See Milbank, "Apologetics and the Imagination" and Kierkegaard, *Concluding Unscientific Postscript*, 2:275. The English translation uses, "make it strange."

However, recent attempts at presenting the gospel are influenced, at least in the West, by key characteristics of our culture: modernism, individualism, and technology. In this vein a gospel message presented principally through direct means of dogma, proposition, and argument—communication strategies that devalue narrative, symbolic, and visual forms of communication—appear anomalous when compared to the breadth of Christian history. The cultural privileging of objective ways of communicating neglects our innate desires for stories and more subjective (affective) ways of understanding and appropriating truth. The propositional or rational approach to communication favors the mind and undervalues the body or heart, the affective or emotional part of a person. Humans are every bit embodied, imaginative beings as they are rational ones. Moreover, narrative and imaginative approaches to communication access the emotions and bring about, not merely a change in belief, but an inhabited, behavioral change.

All men and women are made in the image of God and as such are artists with a holy calling. Christians as witnesses and storytellers are, in fact, artists who are to present or provoke truth within those who hear or attend to their stories. As Ambrose states, "God has no desire to save His [sic] people through argument, the kingdom of God is found in simple faith and not in verbal disputes."[8] To be clear, in sharing the gospel there is room for both reason and revelation, proposition and imagination, objective and subjective ways of knowing. Perhaps another way of saying this is that when communicating the gospel, there are occasions to use both direct and indirect forms of communication.

Today there appears to be a need to return to the creative and revelatory force God has placed within the church to communicate Christ to a culture that is driven by images and craves narrative truth. The gospel can be powerfully presented by employing stories and other imaginative styles of communication that depend upon the visual and narrative arts. Unfortunately, Christian leaders and artists with Christian concerns often feel that these artistic and narrative approaches to communicating the gospel are inferior to the more didactic or propositional approaches to communicating faith. However, Fred B. Craddock, a former distinguished professor of preaching and New Testament at Emory University, reminds us that "Art is not a gift which a few people are given, but rather

---

8. As quoted in Myers, *Preaching Must Die!*, 8.

it is a gift which most people throw away."[9] We can no longer throw away opportunities to communicate God's truth imaginatively and creatively; rather we must learn to speak truth in all its forms: sometimes directly with strong logic and clear reason and sometimes indirectly through imaginative and provocative art or stories.

We have so far discussed two communicative approaches: 1. *direct*, which conveys truth by way of logic, reason, and doctrine; and 2. *indirect*, which conveys truth by way of story, narrative, and symbol. While direct communication is a valuable and necessary form of communication, an overemphasis and preference for the direct approach has unintentionally, and in some cases intentionally, sloughed off the indirect approach. This work is meant to challenge and encourage artists with Christian concerns to recover the incarnational power of indirect strategies of communication.

It was the Danish philosopher, Søren Kierkegaard (1813–1855) who first articulated what we might call a philosophy of indirect communication. His extraordinary insight was that it is primarily indirect communication that conveys what he called a realization or "capability,"[10] i.e., indirect communication moves the hearer from abstract belief (that which is conveyed through direct communication) to action, habit, and incarnational embodiment. It is Kierkegaard's philosophy of indirect communication that serves as the ground for the present work. Following this, the thesis of this book is remarkably simple: if we are to convey Christian truth in a way that makes people "capable" of living a Christian life (i.e., not merely "believing") we must recover the sacred art of indirect communication.

Drawing largely on the work of Søren Kierkegaard, we intend to convey effective strategies to communicate the gospel to a culture that is reluctant to hear the truth (directly). In examining how to communicate the truth today we discover that Kierkegaard addressed the same question over a hundred and fifty years ago. In fact, it can be argued that much, if not the whole of his work as an author, is related "to the problem 'of becoming a Christian,'" that is, how we might embody a Christian existence.[11] We will focus on Kierkegaard's use of both direct and indirect communication and then try to adapt these concepts for communicating

9. Craddock, *Overhearing the Gospel*, 13.

10. Kierkegaard, *Søren Kierkegaard's Journals and Papers*, 1:282.

11. Kierkegaard, *Point of View*, 6.

Christ in today's postmodern world. We argue that Kierkegaard's grasp and use of direct and, in particular, indirect communication, serves as a unique and useful contribution to communicating the gospel today. Due to the profound changes that have taken place in the last two centuries, however—such as the influence of technology, science, religion, globalization, celebrity culture, and sweeping developments in the economic and political environment—we need to modify, adapt, and contextualize these strategies if we are to effectively communicate the gospel. While there are many different types of indirect communication, this study focuses primarily on the importance of story as a form of indirect communication.

The book begins by explicating Soren Kierkegaard's philosophy of communication. Drawing upon this philosophy, we then underscore the need to recover the sacred art of indirect communication. Finally, we examine the indirect strategies of Jesus, C. S. Lewis, and Flannery O'Connor, all in the hopes of restoring a robust and balanced philosophy of communication that involves the whole person, forming Christians who, like Christ, embody the Truth. Section 1 explains the need to recover the role of indirect communication in the life of the church and in the work of artists with Christian concerns. The section begins by identifying and explaining the problems facing the Danish church in the early part of the nineteenth century and then articulates Kierkegaard's remedy in addressing these difficulties. It goes on to identify and examine the challenges facing the church today that are similar to the church in Kierkegaard's day. The first section concludes by suggesting how we might employ reason, revelation, and imagination to confront the illusions we face in our culture and in the church when communicating one's faith.

Section 2 of the book carefully articulates Kierkegaard's development of indirect communication in creating stories, narrative, and other communication devices to awaken those who are resistant to or ignore the implications of the gospel in the Christian life. This section identifies man as a *homo narrans* (human storyteller), that is, a being that lives by and creates stories.

The final section of the book examines three storytellers who illustrate the use of indirect communication: Jesus, C. S. Lewis, and Flannery O'Connor. These three artists speak in carefully created and veiled ways about the truth found in Scripture.

God Plays Hide and Seek

If Scripture informs our patterns of communication, we find a variety of artistic communication styles and strategies available to us when conveying the truth. Far too often, however, those within the church attempt to make communication as easy and direct as possible. Kierkegaard, however, took a different approach, especially when communicating spiritual truth or when communicating Christ. There is nothing easy or straightforward about Christ. He did not intend it to be so. Kierkegaard tried to make communication harder to awaken a person to a serious choice that must be made when deciding if one would follow Christ or to go one's own way. In Christ, God is hidden and revealed. So, too, Christ hid spiritual truth in story or narrative form so that those who wanted to know the meaning would need to seriously think or reflect upon the truth. Christ hides the truth in order that it will be found, or better yet, acted upon.

In the Gospels, Christ indicates that if we really want to know the truth and not some comfortable or titivated version of the truth, we can know the truth if we seek it (Matt 7:7–8). Sometimes truth is hard and uncomfortable and at other times it is found in unusual or uncomfortable places—say as a first-century Jewish man hanging on a cross. Nowhere, it seems, is God more hidden than on the cross, yet nowhere is he more clearly revealed. This truth, of course, is best told as a story, not as some sort of abstract fact or doctrine. The truth of Christ is best grasped when we engage the mind and the heart, reason and imagination. We must not forget, in following Christ's example, that Truth can be conveyed indirectly.

Isaiah the prophet once exclaimed, "Truly you are a God who hides himself, O God and Savior of Israel" (Isa 45:15). And what does it mean to be hidden? What is revealed when things are hidden? An old Hebrew story attempts to address these questions: "Several students questioned Rabbi Pinhas of Koretz [about] why the Lord is always hidden. The rabbi answered: 'The Lord plays hide-and-seek, but nobody goes looking for Him. However, once you know that someone is hiding, he is no longer completely hidden.'"[12] Paradoxically, God hides to reveal himself. He disappears for a bit to be ultimately known and seen. Jer 29:13 says, "You will seek me and find me when you seek me with all your heart." God hides. He is not found where we would like to find him. He hides

12. Abicht, "Laughing in," 115.

so that we might seek him, and he chooses when and where he will be found—where he will reveal himself. In Matthew 7:7 Jesus says, "Seek and you will find."

It may be difficult to comprehend, but sometimes the best way to reveal something is to hide it. There are some who believe that logical proof or a miraculous display is the best way to know or understand something and sometimes it is, but more frequently it is not. In fact, this sort of display or "evidence" leaves people indifferent and unconvinced. Just like the instructions that accompany a child's toy, "some assembly is required," so, too, is some effort required to hear and understand God. We cannot come to believe in God's grace and then continue life just as if nothing has happened or that we are not changed. Grace is free, but it is costly. When Jesus calls someone, he calls them to come and die.[13] Another way Jesus said this is "pick up your cross and follow me."

If you have ever played hide-and-seek you know that the fun is looking for what (or who) is hidden. When they were young, I used to hide Easter egg baskets for my boys to find on Easter morning. I would hide clues all over the house and they would move from place to place trying to unravel the clues and find their Easter basket. The baskets were nice, but the real fun was in seeking. The excitement was never about whether they would find the basket. Even though they could not see the basket, nor did they know where it was, they had no doubt that there was a basket hidden somewhere in the house. Likewise, if we hide the truth in our stories or art, we find that people will be more passionate seekers of the truth hidden within the story and they will take the process of finding the meaning more seriously. In part, this is because they are involved in the process of seeking and finding. In using an imaginative approach, we will attract hearers who would never think of or listen to our well-reasoned proofs or logical arguments. Effective communication, no matter how true, is much more demanding than just providing information or quoting Scripture. This says something about how the indirect strategy of concealment makes us "capable" of embodying the belief we encounter in the direct proof or miracle.

To communicate Christ today, we need to present truth in a form that appeals to a person's emotion and imagination as well as their mind and intellect. Kierkegaard challenges us to provoke our readers or viewers into thinking for themselves and in helping them ask essential

---

13. Bonhoeffer, *Cost of Discipleship*.

questions about their own life and how they should live. Indeed, in *Fear and Trembling*, he actually uses the metaphor of "Hide and Seek" to challenge his listeners to take stock of their lives and seek out the truth.[14] In order to achieve a more effective communication method, Kierkegaard sometimes writes using a different name. As an example, Kierkegaard used the pseudonym Johannes de Silentio for his book, *Fear and Trembling*. In some cases, he employs this method in order to write from an alternate viewpoint that is not his own. As a result, some readers inaccurately attribute certain opinions to Kierkegaard when in actuality they are strategically selected to challenge the thinking of the reader. Keep in mind, while many of the opinions expressed in the pseudonymous works do reflect Kierkegaard's views, at other times they do not. He offers a unique approach (i.e., unique for our day but one that was familiar to the followers of Jesus), one that is imaginative and provocative rather than simply dependent upon crafting new arguments and parroting doctrines.

In the early part of the nineteenth century, Kierkegaard articulated this indirect approach, which he drew from Scripture, and applied to his understanding of the needs of the church of his day. He felt the church adopted the label of Christianity and structured itself like any other organization. The church was under the illusion that lip service ("I believe") was all that was required to follow Christ. He had a word for the disembodied Christianity of his time. He called it, pejoratively, "Christendom," while he called true Christians, those who embodied the teachings of Christ, "Christians." He scathingly remarks,

> Christendom is an effort of the human race to go back to walking on all fours, to get rid of Christianity, to do it knavishly under the pretext that this is Christianity perfected. . . . The Christianity of Christendom . . . takes away from Christianity the offense, the paradox, etc., and instead of that introduces probability, the plainly comprehensible. That is, it transforms Christianity into something entirely different from what it is in the New Testament, yea, into exactly the opposite; and this is the Christianity of Christendom, of us men. . . . In the Christianity of Christendom, the Cross has become something like the child's hobby-horse and trumpet.[15]

Kierkegaard clearly was concerned with both knowing *and* doing God's will. It is not enough to believe apart from following. The church,

14. Kierkegaard, *Fear and Trembling*, 74.

15. Kierkegaard, *Kierkegaard's Attack*, 160–65.

while certainly not perfect, must embody Christ's teachings. According to Kierkegaard, many in the church in Copenhagen were mouthing the truth but not living it. They thought they were Christians simply because they believed the doctrines and rituals of the church, but they failed to live what they believed.

As already alluded to, Kierkegaard believed that a different communication approach was required to help birth a new person who would live in accordance with what Christ taught. Providing information was not enough. Kierkegaard wanted to assist his fellow churchgoers to really experience Christ and to become aware of just how precarious was their own faith. He sought to help them become aware of the illusions harbored within their own lives. To do this, he used a different communication approach, one that helped them realize who they really were and provoked them to examine their own life when considering the life of Christ. This approach he called indirect communication. It was created to help people unearth their own erroneous perceptions and defamiliarize their old ways of knowing. He contrasted this approach with the direct approach. The direct approach is a straightforward strategy of communication and can be used effectively when a person is open to the gospel (i.e., does not emotionally resist following Christ) and simply needs to become aware of what Christ asks of a person.

In his book, *The Subversion of Christianity*, Jacques Ellul brings this forward. He states that the church today has a problem. Ellul's assessment of the church in modern times is much like the assessment Kierkegaard made of the church in his day. Ellul asks, "How has it come about that the development of Christianity and the church has given birth to a society, a civilization, a culture that are completely opposite to what we read in the Bible, to what is indisputably the text of the law, the prophets, Jesus, and Paul?"[16] His work asks: How do we speak to a generation that has turned a deaf ear to the church or chosen to listen selectively to the gospel so that they only hear what they want to hear? How can we speak the truth in ways that unsettle specious or flawed meanings? How can we awaken a man who is asleep and doesn't even know it? By drawing on Kierkegaard's explanation of direct and especially indirect communication, we will begin to address this question.

Part of the answer to these questions can be found in reimagining the role of the arts and the artist for people with Christian concerns. The

---

16. Ellul, *Subversion of Christianity*, 3.

arts have been neglected and under-supported by the church in recent years. Also, so many within the church fail to realize that we are called to be artists and storytellers. It is not just *reason* but also the *imagination* that is needed for men and women to be aware of the truth of God's presence in the world. The arts are a natural medium for imaginative and indirect forms of communication. This work suggests that in turning to the imagination and the arts without forsaking the rational gifts God has given us, we can usefully address and awaken men and women to the work of Christ.

With a brief introduction to the philosophy of indirect communication behind us, we now to turn to section 1. In chapter 1 we examine the indirect approach more fully and place it within Kierkegaard's own cultural context.

Section One

Indirect Communication and the Cultural Context

Chapters 1–3

.

1

Why Indirect?

*It is naturally the error of the modern period that all communi-
cation is direct, that it has forgotten that there is such a thing as
indirect communication.*

—SØREN KIERKEGAARD

Introduction

IN THIS CHAPTER, WE examine more deeply both direct and indirect
communication and provide an impetus for artists and leaders with
Christian concerns to recover indirect communication strategies. We then
examine the church in Kierkegaard's day and in our own and pinpoint some
important similarities. Next, we explore Kierkegaard's definition and use
of indirect communication and pay close attention to the use of story and
narrative as key forms of indirect communication. Finally, we cite several
examples of indirect communication and note their usefulness when
communicating to someone resistant to direct forms of communication.

Direct and Indirect Communication

How best can artists with Christian concerns and other people of faith communicate truth in this era? That's the question posed by this book. When communicating the truth of Christianity, it makes a great difference if the kind of communication we create is understood as a set of propositions (theology or dogma) or if it is a story or narrative that portrays a new way of living one's life. Church leaders and apologists with Christian concerns generally follow the modernist penchant for reason, argument, and persuasion and characteristically neglect literary and imaginative strategies.[1] The church typically underestimates or undervalues narrative and artistic approaches to communication.[2] Apparently, many within the church have forgotten how essential the narrative structure of the gospel is for communicating truth. Furthermore, much of the church has not followed the biblical example of drawing from a wide number of literary and imaginative strategies in creating stories and communicating Christ. It seems clear that those striving to communicate Christian concerns to this generation have greatly favored proposition above narrative, fact over testimony, science more than art, and mind above body. Tim Keller contends that there are many "books that provide excellent, detailed, substantial evidence and arguments for the Christian faith."[3] He then claims, "It is rationally warranted to believe that God exists."[4] However, many inside and outside the community of faith would question this naked assumption. Although this may be true for a person who is predisposed to believe in God, it is much more difficult for a person who does not believe, or those who are part of Christendom, that cultured disembodied form of Christianity that Kierkegaard loathed.

A great number of people, especially those in the West who are steeped in a worldview that privileges objectivity and science, and look for rationally warranted proofs, require some preparation of their hearts before one can speak to their minds, particularly as it regards transcendent truth. For them, God, apart from faith, is not a given nor is he easily or objectively verifiable. Very often the church has not done due diligence when trying to find ways to communicate Christian concerns to such people, frequently the soil of their hearts is not prepared to enable them

1. See Davison, *Imaginative Apologetics* and Guite, *Faith, Hope and Poetry*.

2. See Boersma, *Heavenly Participation*.

3. Keller, *Making Sense of God*, 216.

4. Keller, *Making Sense of God*, 216.

to hear the gospel unencumbered by various cultural assumptions and distractions. In fact, an impassive argument often leads to emotional and intellectual resistance to that which is being offered or suggested. Instead of such direct forms of communication, it seems prudent to begin with a gentler or less combative approach. Such methods involve beguiling the heart through story or some sort of artistic device that is less intent on making a point and more interested in raising provocative questions that stir the imagination and challenge one to think more carefully and deeply about the significant or ultimate concerns that affect one's life. Amy-Jill Levine asserts that this approach was often used by Jesus when facing the religious leaders of his day. She argues that his mysterious parables "challenge us to look into the hidden aspects of our own values, our own lives."[5]

Moreover, Hans Boersma makes an important assessment on the communication behavior of young evangelicals when he asserts that "propositional truth, once a hallmark of evangelicalism, is making way for more elusive means of expression, such as narrative, image, and symbol."[6] He argues that younger evangelicals who are concerned about absolute truth claims and have voiced doubts about "our ability to capture the essence of absolute truth have placed in question the legitimacy of the scientific method," and this is especially true when dealing with questions regarding ultimate matters.[7] He states, "Both the nature of theology and the interpretation of Scripture are experiencing the effects of our postmodern cultural mindset."[8] These are formidable concerns that influence how one might consider communicating the gospel in our age. With the legitimacy of the scientific method to capture the essence of absolute truth in question one may well ask if the church should be turning primarily to empirical analyses and reason alone to advance their beliefs. On the other hand, there is the valid concern that giving up on this mode of scientific rationality would be to compromise the gospel to send it down the slippery slope of relativism. The claim of this work is that it does not need to be an either-or situation.

Indeed, truth is both objective and personal; it is not only about knowing objective information but is a way of living in communion with

---

5. Levine, *Short Stories by Jesus*, 3.

6. Boersma, *Heavenly Participation*, 1.

7. Boersma, *Heavenly Participation*, 1.

8. Boersma, *Heavenly Participation*, 2.

Christ. Consequently, Christian truth is about embodying a new way of
life that imitates Christ. We strengthen or sustain our faith through rituals and doctrines; but when truth in this sense is resisted, misunderstood,
or lightly held in the merely objectivist sense, it tends to devolve into
ready-made formulas or doctrines. Such a situation requires the artist or
storyteller to restore or reiterate truth using a more challenging, personal
approach to create or awaken faith within an individual. Likewise, there
must be a willingness and ability or, as we shall see, a "capability" to see
oneself honestly before truth can be appropriated.

As *homo narrans* (human storytellers) living in an age that privileges empirical ways of knowing and communicating, we often mistakenly
think that communication is easy and straightforward. After all, we have
countless powerful communication tools available to us. It also makes
sense that the better and clearer the argument and the more often it gets
presented, the better one can communicate truth. This, of course, assumes that the audience includes ready and attentive listeners, interested
and inclined to accept the truth. As it turns out, this is increasingly not
the case.

Communication tends to be much more difficult than most people
want to believe. For those within the church, telling the truth about spiritual matters is not simply a matter of presenting the facts or good rational arguments, nor is it simply referencing Scripture. Today's audiences
are not ready listeners; they make their own sense out of the messages
available to them within a context crowded with competing voices. In
our media-saturated culture, most men and women feel suspicious, even
defensive, of any "truths" presented to them, especially if the message
is challenging or uncomfortable. In a post-Nietzschean culture, truths
often appear as a form of power or oppression wielded by the speaker
over the hearer. In our time, if we are to cut through such prejudices, we
must learn to be more creative and adopt a different and disarming form
of communication.

Just presenting "the facts" or articulating an argument, no matter
how true, oversimplifies the process of communication and totally dismisses the variety of ways by which Scripture itself imparts truth. If one
takes the time to carefully read the Bible, it becomes clear that the authors
utilize a variety of different ways to communicate truth, both verbally
and visually. If the audience knowingly agrees with the message and that
message is both anticipated and desired, then the communication task
is likely to be much easier and perhaps direct communication may be a

useful strategy of communication. But today's audience is often skeptical of any religious message, any claims to metaphysical truths, as Christians no longer have the highest reputation for being honest and forgiving.[9] In such an environment, telling the truth in a direct manner only perpetuates and in some cases embodies the presupposed dynamic of power over the other; one need only to think of this manifestation of power in our contemporary division of left-right politics, religious extremism and religious pluralism, nationalism and globalization, radical democracy and fascism. A more useful approach, especially for artists and media professionals, may be to hide or veil that truth in indirect and provocative stories or in other artistic expressions.

Kierkegaard's Context: Denmark

We now turn to our primary interlocutor, Søren Kierkegaard. The culture in which he lived provided the impetus of his indirect approach. As one of history's most creative and engaging communicators, a man who used both images and stories that are almost impossible to ignore, Kierkegaard reminds us of what Socrates told us long ago: as communicators, we "could not give birth but could only be a midwife" to new ideas or behaviors.[10] Kierkegaard explains that this is how "the Christian rebirth enters in—as a relationship not between man and man but between God and man, a new creation."[11] Consequently, the "audience," the people making sense out of a message or a work of art, can never become too dependent on the "truths" conveyed by artist or communicator, as if they somehow "have" the truth, because both artist and audience are ultimately united with the Truth. The artist and audience stand before God, and to us only by extension of what Christ has done. We are all his disciples and his alone. Hence, the artist's job is to lead people to the Truth, not to convince or tell them they "have" it.

As a gifted writer and scholar, Kierkegaard used many different literary, artistic, and intellectual resources to communicate his ideas. Prominent among his many techniques were direct and indirect communication. Although Kierkegaard believed that both direct and indirect communication have an important role in communicating truth, he saw

9. Kinnaman and Lyons, *UnChristian*.
10. Kierkegaard, *Søren Kierkegaard's Journals and Papers*, 1: 273.
11. Kierkegaard, *Søren Kierkegaard's Journals and Papers*, 1: 273.

indirect communication as the more effective strategy or method of communication in his day. Following his lead, most Kierkegaard scholars today emphasize indirect communication. It is fair to say that Kierkegaard gave meager attention to direct communication and frequently favored indirect communication. In this same vein, we will address both direct and indirect communication but will spend the greater amount of time on indirect communication. These two concepts are related, and one needs to discuss both to understand fully the purpose and usefulness of each. Before moving along, it is important to state that we should not think of these two concepts as entirely distinct, or one wrong and one right, but rather, they should be thought of as on a continuum, from direct to indirect. There are both good and bad forms of indirect and direct communication.

To help us understand our own contemporary dilemma, it may help first to understand the nature of the illusion that Kierkegaard identified in his own time. For Kierkegaard, the illusion was that Denmark was a Christian nation, a country in which all or most were Christians. They lived under the illusion that they themselves were Christian, when in fact all "Christian" really meant was that one was born in Denmark and, perhaps, attended the organized church.

Kierkegaard thought that the members of his audience should know better than to think of themselves as Christian just because they lived in Denmark and had been baptized in the church. Kierkegaard believed they became so comfortable with their lives, and had called themselves Christian for so long, that they began to think of their understanding as true without knowing what it really means to be a Christian and certainly what it means to inhabit a Christian way of being. They had not fallen into ordinary ignorance, but into a gradual and troubling permanent posture whereby they had become comfortable calling their way of life Christian and believing their conviction to be true. They should have known better than to call the way they were living Christian but they did so anyway.[12] Kierkegaard pinpoints the illusion of the watered-down, cultured form of Christianity that he called "Christendom" using a witty analogy:

> Imagine a kind of medicine that proposes in full dosage a laxative effect but in a half dose a constipating effect. Suppose someone is suffering from constipation. But—for some reason or other, perhaps because there is not enough for a full dose

---

12. Aumann, "Kierkegaard on Indirect Communication."

or because it is feared that such a large amount might be too much—in order to do something, he is given, with the best intentions, a half dose: 'After all, it is at least something.' What a tragedy!

So it is with today's Christianity. As with everything qualified by an either/or—the half has the very opposite effect from the whole. But we Christians go right on practicing this well-intentioned half-hearted act from generation to generation. We produce Christians by the millions, and are proud of it—yet have no inkling that we are doing just exactly the opposite of what we intend to do.[13]

Kierkegaard often accused pastors of encouraging this illusion, as he argued in *Judge for Yourself!*: "The people want to be deceived."[14] Such an audience did not "want to overcome their confusion, their inconsistency, and their misuse of language. They want[ed] to maintain a lack of clarity about themselves and their lives."[15] They did so, he suggested, so they could live as they pleased and only superficially follow Christ as his disciples.

According to Kierkegaard, the church in Denmark thought they understood Christianity and thought they were living as Christians, when in fact they were living a sort of watered-down form of Christianity that ignored the difficulties of surrender to God and sacrifice of living the way of Christ. They were following a counterfeit image of Christ, even if that image had been constructed from the pictures, teachings, doctrines, and experiences they received in the church and in the larger culture. They had substituted a kind of religious knowledge, a certain mode of truth, for sacrificial living in commitment to the Christ.

Kierkegaard lived in a time of great political and philosophical upheaval. Most importantly and for our purposes, elements of an "enlightened" world were taking hold of the academic and theological communities. One consequence of the enlightenment was the diminishment of the role of revelation as a way of understanding.[16] Kierkegaard rejected the common assumption of the modernist philosophers, particularly Georg Wilhelm Friedrich Hegel, a renowned German philosopher, and his Danish followers, who thought that "human rationality was sufficient

13. Kierkegaard, *Provocations*, 16.

14. Aumann, "Kierkegaard on Indirect Communication," 23.

15. Aumann, "Kierkegaard on Indirect Communication," 24.

16. See Roberts, *Emerging Prophet*.

for cultural progress and—more importantly—for individual human fulfillment (or becoming a self). For Kierkegaard, the age of reason had forgotten the necessity of divine revelation."[17] The culture and church of early-nineteenth-century Denmark were strongly influenced by Hegel, who believed that the "historical development of art, religion, and philosophy" gave us insight into "the Divine Mind of the Universe."[18] Backhouse explains,

> The revelation of God was not to be found in a person or a holy text but in the development of a culture's history. The unfolding Spirit is first encountered in a society's art. This artistic expression is then given meaning and explanation in the society's religion. Finally, it is philosophy that explains the religion. The Spirit is ever developing and thus the Divine is revealed in mankind's highest achievements. To see the latest and best manifestation of the Divine Mind in the world, all one has to do is look at the latest and best manifestation of the world's civilization.[19]

By the 1830s, Hegel had become extremely influential among the literary and academic figures of Denmark. Another of Hegel's more compelling ideas was that "one could approach a subject without presuppositions and attain some sort of neutral, objective point of view."[20] Kierkegaard took a critical approach to Hegel, and unleashed a fierce attack on his disciples, who became Kierkegaard's primary target of contempt.

On the one hand, Enlightenment thinkers were rejecting the tradition of the historical narrative in which we live (Kant), and on the other hand, they entirely succumbed to an historical process (Hegel), both of which Kierkegaard loathed. Contrary to the dominant views purporting forms of objective rationale in his day, Kierkegaard insisted that reason alone was limited, which meant that human beings were incapable of discerning "the truth of Christianity by means of reason (that is, objectivity)."[21] Roberts argues that Kierkegaard "was against the classical apologetic approach; using 'objective reason' to attempt to rationally prove the validity of Christianity or the existence of God."[22]

17. Roberts, *Emerging Prophet*, 15.

18. Backhouse, *Kierkegaard*, 66.

19. Backhouse, *Kierkegaard*, 66.

20. Backhouse, *Kierkegaard*, 67.

21. Turnbull, "Reason," 194.

22. Roberts, *Emerging Prophet*, 36.

This does not mean that reason plays no part or has no positive role in Kierkegaard's thinking, but that reason must be tempered, one must know one's limitations. For Kierkegaard, both reason and philosophy are useful but limited. As Turnbull argues, it is through an individual's "rational capacity to discern that the nature of the Incarnation is absolutely paradoxical that human beings can enter into a proper relationship with God. Reason thus has a fundamental role to play in leading human beings to choose between faith and offense."[23] Yet paradoxically for Kierkegaard, the basic choice that every person must make, "mainly, that God and man are absolutely different, is not a matter of rational demonstration."[24] Consequently, Kierkegaard understood Christianity to be motivated by love and compelled to embrace its centripetal reality—Jesus Christ, the God-man, whom he called the "absolute paradox." It is in this way that for Kierkegaard the rational and personal, direct and indirect, must be held in a paradoxical tension.

Clearly the cultural context in which Kierkegaard lived helps to explain why he felt so strongly about the importance of indirect communication. Kierkegaard believed that many people in Denmark had fallen under the spell of an illusion that they were in a right relationship with God, just because they were officially Lutheran (the state-supported religious belief system in Denmark and Norway). Consequently, his work as an author focused on what it means to be a Christian in a culture enveloped in the illusion he calls "Christendom," and what it means to be "against the illusion that in such a land as ours all are Christians of a sort."[25] He believed that in Denmark, "the greater number of people in Christendom who call themselves Christian only imagine themselves to be Christians."[26] For this reason, he sought to employ indirect strategies of communication in order to awaken his fellow countrymen to the illusion they'd been living and perhaps make them capable of inhabiting a true Christian existence.

23. Turnbull, "Reason," 195.
24. Turnbull, "Reason," 196.
25. Kierkegaard, *Point of View*, 6.
26. Kierkegaard, *Point of View*, 25.

Our Context: The Church in the West

We can learn from Kierkegaard's theory of indirect communication to effectively communicate truth in our own era. To communicate the truth of Christianity, it makes a great difference if the kind of messages or art we create are understood as a set of propositions, beliefs, and practices, or if they are understood as stories. Both proposition and story can communicate truth. Both methods of communication can shape our reality and the way we live. Each has its strengths and weaknesses. The argument here is that there are times when one should be preferred over the other depending on such considerations as the audience, culture, occasion, and nature of the message. We live in a time that privileges reason, doctrine, and proposition and neglects story and imagination. Ours is an age where the church has forgotten the power of the story, imagination, and arts to make people aware and to present people with the true dimensions of human existence.

Although the contemporary western church differs from the Danish church of Kierkegaard's day, in many ways it calls for a similar response. For example, Fred B. Craddock believes that contemporary preaching and other forms of communication by both clergy and laity has become too much of an intellectual exercise, a formulaic experience. He contends that our communication of faith is often scholarly and informative yet lacks a passionate authenticity. If artists or leaders with Christian concerns cease to be prophetic, if they cease to awaken the hearer, and if their art and message become overly predictable and stereotypical, they risk becoming irrelevant to the culture. In such cases, their message will not be heard, noticed, or understood. Such circumstances require a work of art or message that awakens the hearer or viewer to communicate in an understandable or useful way.

Unfortunately, in the church today, artists and leaders with Christian concerns often favor direct and rational approaches to communication and thus neglect or underutilize the various forms of imaginative indirect communication. This is especially important today when so many within the church are trying to communicate with younger audiences. Contemporary audiences are technologically savvy and visual. Therefore, they are often more influenced by images than by arguments. Webber contends that a cultural shift has taken place and "that the use of reason and science to prove or disprove a fact is questionable."[27] He claims that a new

27. Webber, *Younger Evangelicals*, 84.

understanding has emerged, influenced to a large extent by postmodern thinkers, claiming that believers and nonbelievers alike understand that all facts are to be interpreted. "A believer looks at creation and speaks of God as the Creator. That's an 'interpreted fact.' The nonbeliever may look at the creation and assumes the world derived from chance. That, too, is an 'interpreted fact.'"[28] It turns out that, both the believer and the nonbeliever are people of faith. As he states, "One has faith in the story of the Bible; the other has faith in the story of reason, science, some other religion, or the god of his or her own making. The case for the Christian faith is no longer reason against reason but faith against faith in opposing stories."[29] Clearly, story plays a larger role in communicating faith today. The twenty-first-century world has a need for and sees a value in stories that speak to the heart and not just to the mind.

Paul Elie reflects on fictional works that struggle with depicting Christian faith and life. He warns that writers who reference "sacred texts and themes see the references go unrecognized."[30] He laments that "a faith with something like 170 million adherents in the United States, a faith that for centuries seeped into every nook and cranny of our society, now plays the role it plays in Jhumpa Lahiri's story 'This Blessed House': as some statues left behind in an old building, bewildering the new occupants."[31] He also regrets that fiction writers with Christian concerns have gone where "belief itself has gone. In America today, Christianity is highly visible in public life but marginal or of no consequence in a great many individual lives."[32] What a poignant commentary on the role of the artist and the church today!

A similar sentiment can be found in the work of Michael Warren. Warren suggests that part of the challenge to "the church in our time is that of offering a compelling imagination of life in the face of other agencies offering attractive alternative imaginations."[33] Consequently, the church today needs to be awakened from its artistic slumber. It must begin to encourage artists with Christian concerns to create stories and art that speak to this age. Unfortunately, our culture in its contemporary

28. Webber, *Younger Evangelicals*, 84.
29. Webber, *Younger Evangelicals*, 84.
30. Elie, "Has Fiction Lost Its Faith?"
31. Elie, "Has Fiction Lost Its Faith?"
32. Elie, "Has Fiction Lost Its Faith?"
33. Warren, *Seeing Through the Media*, 10.

expressions has marginalized a clear understanding of good and evil, let alone salvation and sin. The church functions as only one among many influences, and in many cases, a weak one.

Among myriad social and economic influences in our world today, perhaps the most influential is human attention. Television, computers, films, video games, social media, and other popular arts grab the attention of this generation and tell the most powerful and compelling stories. At the same time, the church is failing to adequately engage the culture with disarming stories and images that provoke serious interests in a life of faith. For the most part, the church is still trying to craft rational arguments that may be intellectually defensible, but which fail to engage the imagination or provide a vision of life that interests most people today. Although stories affect the heart and influence the soul, we neglect to provide real and compelling stories.

So often, storytellers with Christian concerns create stories of faith and other messages that are too affable and easily grasped. To reveal Christ, we often over-explain and do not allow a place or time for the Holy Spirit to work in an individual. Furthermore, a single work of visual art, just as a single story, cannot present the whole of the Christian narrative. In our haste to achieve our desired ends, we often hurriedly present a version of Christ or the Christian life that is unreal and that does not leave time or space for God to work. Therefore, we fail to allow the audience to seriously consider the consequences and implications of the decision they are pondering. In so doing, we truncate the decision-making process and do not grant enough time for the individual to fully consider or reflect upon just what he or she is doing.

Bagdikian asserts that the "crisis of the human spirit in our time is, in part, a crisis of knowing what matters are worthy of our attention."[34] We assume that humans are primarily thinking beings, and in so doing, we ignore the imaginative and embodied aspects of our being. As James K. A. Smith states, "Our worldview is more a matter of the imagination than the intellect, and the imagination runs off the fuel of images that are channeled by the senses."[35] If Smith is right, we need to provide the images, stories, films, and other artistic expressions that focus on gaining the attention of the heart and the mind. We need stories that move us to act in accordance with our emotions *and* our reason. Wilder argues

34. Warren, *Seeing Through the Media*, 25.
35. Smith, *Desiring the Kingdom*, 57.

that the arts can most effectively make this kind of imaginative appeal.[36]
Unfortunately, most artists with Christian concerns are not engaging our
culture in such a forceful and provocative way. They have perpetuated the
myth that art is something extra or over against rationality.

Robust stories and inspired art cast spells that work on us over a
long period of time, and like a good movie or book, they linger in our
memory. Their images stay with us and move us in ways that textbooks
and doctrinal statements simply cannot. Not all stories are created equal,
however, and it is necessary to develop compelling and entertaining images to carry the meanings intended. It should be obvious that too much
effort has been spent on "what" is communicated and too little on "how"
it is communicated.

Much ink has been spilled about the inexcusable problems of "Christian" storytellers in all their varied forms: novels, short stories, films, etc.
Unfortunately most of the so-called "Christian" stories end in neat reso-
lutions, are populated with one-dimensional characters, and are overly
sentimental. These kind of saccharine stories are especially irksome in
that overblown sentimentality distorts reality, prompting the audience
to distrust stories written or created by so-called "Christian artists." Like
pornography, overly sentimental stories generate an unearned passion.

Neither life nor Scripture is neat and tidy. The authority of Scripture
comes, in part, from the integrity of the storyteller in recording events in
a surprisingly honest and unvarnished way. Woven within the pages of
the sacred text we see not only those who try to follow God but also a host
of unscrupulous characters. We see all of them in their volatile humanity:
Cain, Noah, Abraham, Sarah, Jacob, Moses, Rahab, Samson, David, Solomon, Judas, Mary Magdalene, Peter, and Paul. All had multiple instances
of erratic deeds and less than heroic behavior. All these characters were
flawed, yet most were forgiven, even though their wretched behavior was
never excused or passed over.

Most of us can identify with the parables of Jesus because everyone
knows a few devious servants or reckless sons. So often we want sudden and painless solutions to the problems vexing our characters, but
we should know better than that. The limits of great storytelling and
the limits of the media do not necessarily lend themselves to telling the
whole truth in one story, film, or artistic expression. Maybe we need to be
content in taking the longer view. Changing one's way of life is a serious

36. See Wilder, "Church's New Concern."

and profound event that takes time and serious consideration. This kind of change will most likely happen in increments, and storytelling should account for this by allowing God to work over the course of several incidents and perhaps even through multiple stories. Much of this change in the character remains out of the storyteller's control and in the hands of God.

Webber reminds us that "classical Christianity knew nothing of the concept of propositionalism as held by Christianity after the Enlightenment."[37] The early church interpreted the Christian faith more as a story than as a set of doctrines or propositions. To recognize this fact in no way backs away from or waters down the Christian faith. Reason plays a part, but so does the imagination, beauty, and story. As artists and storytellers, we are embodied beings who create meaningful stories that speak of the power and love of God. We are still image bearers to the truth of Scripture. The question then becomes, how does this take place?

Craddock, like Kierkegaard before him, calls the church to a new vision of truth telling—one that engages both the speaker and the listener, the artist and the audience, the writer and the reader—to an active, authentic faith. As we have noted, the church has been too concerned with *what* we are to believe and has largely ignored *how* we believe or communicate truth. For Kierkegaard and for us, both the *what* and the *how* are essential elements for effective communication and art. *How* one communicates cannot be divorced from the truth; just as *how* one lives cannot be separated from *what* one believes.

In sum, truth is not merely a fact to be examined, nor is it merely personal. Truth must be embodied. Truth is a Person; it does not exist apart from Christ and the way of life he models. Christ is an uncomfortable Truth; in exceeding both our rational and personal capacities, he is like no other person we have ever encountered. He comes to interfere with and transform our way of life and rationality; he awakens in us the desire to live for something beyond ourselves—to live for God. He is not just an interesting person we come to know, like a celebrity or even a hero; he is someone who challenges us to live a life set apart. He is a mystery who can only be conveyed through a strategy of indirect communication.

37. Webber, *Younger Evangelicals*, 84.

Kierkegaard's Notion of Direct and Indirect Communication

Before beginning to define more carefully direct and indirect communication, we need to turn our attention to understanding what Kierkegaard believed to be a crucial aspect of the communication process: knowledge and capability.

When Kierkegaard distinguished between two different forms of communication—direct and indirect—he was adamant that his readers recognize these forms by their function: communication of knowledge and communication of capability, respectively. Since this distinction is fundamental to Kierkegaard's notion of communication, we need to look more closely at how he understands these two types of communication.

For Kierkegaard, the object or topic of communication is either "knowledge about something . . . or self-knowledge."[38] Andrew F. Herrmann explains that Kierkegaard was interested primarily in self-knowledge, "particularly ethical and religious self-knowledge."[39] As we saw, many in the church in Denmark were under the illusion that faith was what one knew, believed, or understood rather than how one actually acted or lived. For Kierkegaard, knowledge of or knowing about Christ was useless unless one actually lived for Christ. Herrmann suggests, "self-knowledge is existential, as it involves the type of character one should develop, the way one maintains relationships, and how one comes to understand living the good life."[40] Thus, Kierkegaard saw self-knowledge as a corrective to the illusion that hindered the Christianity of his day. He believed that people had forgotten what it means to live or exist.

Roberts explains that the kind of human existence that Kierkegaard espoused can be understood as a sort of becoming. Kierkegaard understood sin, for example, not merely as a rational awareness of some sort of personal moral lapse, but more deeply as a fundamental alienation of the individual from self and society. Kierkegaard takes sin seriously but in so doing understands it relationally. As Roberts argues, "[For] Kierkegaard, sin is less something we do (as it is in moralism) and more a descriptor of who we are—or at least, who we inevitably become."[41] According to Roberts, Anti-Climacus, a pseudonym of Kierkegaard's, implores a sinner

---

38. Kierkegaard, *Søren Kierkegaard's Journals and Papers*, 1: 270.

39. Herrmann, "Kierkegaard and Dialogue," 76.

40. Herrmann, "Kierkegaard and Dialogue," 76.

41. Roberts, *Emerging Prophet*, 91.

confronted with a choice of whether to follow Christ to see the choice as "a journey of a radical reorientation toward God, oneself, and others."[42] People require more than knowledge, Kierkegaard insisted, they require what he expressed by the word "inwardness," brought about by the communication of "capability."[43]

We cannot understand Kierkegaard's concept of indirect communication without grasping what he means by "capability." For Kierkegaard, this term has to do with how a person lives, how one behaves and acts— capability is passionately living one's beliefs and convictions. This concept is especially difficult to communicate to others if they are under the illusion that they already know what is required to live the Christian life, or if they think they are living already in accordance with these requirements, when in fact they are not. Brian Gregor observes, "Christianity cannot be understood as an object by a detached observer; it must take hold of and transform the life of the subject," and in this way change his or her whole life.[44] Kierkegaard confronted a church that had "knowledge" of the truth but was not "capable" of living out this truth. "Christendom" lacked the ability or "capability" to live in accordance with the truth it already knew. Therefore, the church did not need more knowledge, but the capability (ability or inner strength) to first become aware of the difference between knowing and existing, and then the ability to change and live before God as it should, or at least attempt to do so. As we already implied, Kierkegaard believed that knowledge and capability correspond to two different types of communication—direct and indirect, respectively. Thus, as Kierkegaard sees it, "The communication of capability is in the medium of actuality."[45] Consequently, "All communication of capability is indirect communication."[46]

Indirect communication is a strategy that brings many literary elements to bear on communication and self-reflection. We find it throughout the Bible and see it used by many, if not all, the writers of the holy Scriptures. Jesus scarcely used any other form but indirect communication. Indirect communication is much more an art than a science and focuses primarily on the heart or emotions. As previously mentioned,

42. Roberts, *Emerging Prophet*, 92.

43. Hans Boersma makes a similar argument in suggesting that theology is more interested in participating in the truth than in simply comprehending it.

44. Gregor, "Thinking Through Kierkegaard's Anti-Climacus," 455.

45. Kierkegaard, *Søren Kierkegaard's Journals and Papers*, 1:282.

46. Kierkegaard, *Søren Kierkegaard's Journals and Papers*, 1:282.

indirect communication involves concealing the message in some way, using a veiled or provocative form of expression instead of presenting a simple and straightforward propositional message. This approach to communicating the truth requires the communicator or artist to help birth self-reflection by masking or hiding the truth within the communicative act or symbols. The primary purpose of indirect communication is to effect a fundamental change in the way of life of his or her hearers or viewers as they seek to understand the meaning of the artistic or communicative act. This, of course, can be done in several ways. Stories often use various strategies of indirect communication, including humor, questions, hinting, satire, irony, and many other literary and communication devices. We will discuss such devices in sec. 2.

Kierkegaard maintained that the communication of knowledge comes by way of direct communication. This is blunt talk that seeks to avoid deceptive, ironic, and elusive speech. For Kierkegaard, direct communication deals with the objective world of facts and figures. It intends to provide just the content of what is meant. Its meanings are not hidden; they are explicit and lie on the surface.

The direct approach is quite effective when no prior awareness or knowledge of Christ already exists. Kierkegaard argued that in his day, however, the situation was different. People were very familiar with the stories and doctrines of the church, yet they no longer moved the people. Therefore, rather than simply retelling these stories or doctrines, Kierkegaard chose to help empower or inspire a person to reevaluate the stories by giving them a new perspective. He proposed that instead of simply providing information through direct communication, a new hearing of the truth was possible through indirect communication.

If the hearer is open to and seriously interested in the ethical or religious quality of his own life, then a direct strategy may be quite useful. If, on the other hand, one is unaware of the importance of the message, simply uninterested in the ethical or religious message, is resistant to the message, or even predisposed to believe they already know and understand the message someone is trying to communicate when in fact they do not, then a different approach is needed.

As we saw, what people know or think they know is of little consequence for Kierkegaard if they cannot act or live in accordance with the knowledge they possess or think they possess. Thus, there comes a time when each person must unlearn, defamiliarize, or make strange what they erroneously understand or only weakly understand before

new understandings and action can be realized. Only then can they be
awakened to new possibilities and dismiss current understandings, so
that they can decide and then begin to act in accordance with the new
insight they have gleaned. As Kierkegaard states, "The object of [indirect]
communication is consequently not knowledge but a realization."[47]

Thus, as Kierkegaard saw it, the church was communicating *knowledge*—information—when it should have been communicating *capability*—ability to act in accordance with the gospel. Christ intends for his
people (Christians) to live or exist in a true and decisive way. Christians
do not simply know, learn, or talk about Christ. Christians are to act—
they are to live in and through Christ.

Because Kierkegaard was not consistent in how he used the term
"indirect communication," scholars studying this issue do not agree on
its exact definition. In fact, there are almost as many ways of defining
indirect communication as there are scholars studying the topic. Most
scholars agree, however, that indirect communication is in some way
veiled, hidden, or deceptive communication whose meaning is not immediately obvious.[48] Although Kierkegaard scholars have various ways of
defining this term, I will discuss only three.

One common conception of indirect communication, advanced by
Aumann, asserts that indirect communication should be identified with
the aforementioned Socratic midwifery. Aumann argues that Kierkegaard
did not encourage entering a confrontational dialogue with someone
by asking questions about their beliefs. Rather, he often used the more
creative strategy of not explicitly telling learners the truth but strove instead to help them discover or "give birth" to the truth for themselves.
This Socratic approach promotes active learning and self-discovery and
leads to self-realization.[49] In so doing, the "responsibility for learning is
transferred" to the audience or person trying to make sense of the art
or message with which they are engaged.[50] The learner takes ownership
of the sense that he or she has constructed. Saeverot suggests that this
approach "leads to an individualized understanding of responsibility,
where each and every student shall cultivate themselves and also develop

47. Kierkegaard, *Søren Kierkegaard's Journals and Papers*, 1:272.

48. See Kierkegaard, *Søren Kierkegaard's Journals and Papers*, and Pannenberg,
Revelation as History.

49. Aumann, "Kierkegaard on the Need."

50. Saeverot, *Indirect Pedagogy*, 3.

their skills."[51] In his *Journals*, Kierkegaard argues that the midwife helps others "to stand alone—by another's help" in the learning process.[52] The individual is engaged in untying the Socratic knot and constructing his or her own meaning.

One caution to this approach is worth mentioning, as not all active learning comes about through indirect communication. Aumann argues, "indirect communication occurs only if the learner actively reflects on the implications and ramifications for his or her own life on the knowledge he or she acquires."[53] Such reflection Kierkegaard's pseudonym Climacus calls "the reflection of inwardness" or "double-reflection."[54]

In *Practice in Christianity* Anti-Climacus argues that indirect communication can be viewed as an art of redoubling the communication. "The art," he insists, "consists in making oneself, the communicator, into a nobody, purely objective, and then continually placing the qualitative opposites in a unity."[55] Anti-Climacus explains how this can happen in the art of storytelling. He states,

> For example, it is indirect communication to place jest and ear-
> nestness together in such a way that the composite is a dialecti-
> cal knot—and then to be a nobody oneself. If anyone wants to
> have anything to do with this kind of communication, he will
> have to untie the knot himself. Or, to bring attack and defense
> into a unity in such a way that no one can directly say whether
> one is attacking or defending, so that the most zealous supporter
> of the cause and its most vicious foe can both seem to see in one
> an ally . . . [56]

Aumann argues that Anti-Climacus maintains that "the indirect communicator does not tell the learner exactly what the outcome of the learning process is supposed to be. Instead, the indirect communicator provides the learner with a puzzle or problem that the learner must figure out for himself or herself."[57] Nevertheless, Aumann asserts that "the read-

---

51. Saeverot, *Indirect Pedagogy*, 3.

52. Kierkegaard, *Søren Kierkegaard's Journals and Papers*, 1:280–81.

53. Aumann, "Kierkegaard on Indirect Communication," 6.

54. Kierkegaard, *Concluding Unscientific Postscript*, 1:73.

55. Kierkegaard, *Practice in Christianity*, 133.

56. Kierkegaard, *Practice in Christianity*, 133.

57. Aumann, "Kierkegaard on Indirect Communication," 8.

ers are not left completely without guidance," as hints and suggestions are delicately placed or hidden in the art or communicative event.[58]

A second way of defining indirect communication refers to the use of specific artful literary devices. Chief among the relevant devices, for Kierkegaard, is pseudonymity. However, as Aumann explains, "It is not the only device Kierkegaard has in mind. For example, he also includes deception, humor, irony, ambiguity, fictional narratives, and 'imaginative constructions.'"[59] One does well to remember that the distinction between these two ways of talking about indirect communication often gets obscured in Kierkegaard's writings. Aumann draws attention to the fact that Kierkegaard "sometimes applies the label in question to the use of artful literary devices in contexts where the midwifery method is simply not under discussion."[60] The main limitation with this form of indirect communication is that it is difficult to develop a precise and complete description of "artful literary devices."[61] It is not the purpose of the present work to solve this problem, nor is it necessary to view the variety or open-ended use of literary devices as a problem.

A third way places capability as the key to Kierkegaard's use of indirect communication. Drawing largely from Kierkegaard's unpublished lectures found in his journals, Mark A. Tietjen contends that although such tools as humor, irony, and pseudonymity capture common yet important facets of indirect communication, something else is of even greater importance to Kierkegaard's understanding and use of indirect communication. That something, Tietjen tells us, is "a kind of involved knowledge, a holistic understanding that includes not only the cognitive grasp of some idea but a deeper, existential realization of that idea in one's life."[62] This form of essential knowing aims at actualizing or eliciting a realization of a truth claim on one's life. As Climacus states, "Truth becomes appropriation, inwardness, subjectivity, and the point is to immerse oneself, existing, in subjectivity"[63]—that is, to become an actual person and exist.

58. Aumann, "Kierkegaard on Indirect Communication," 9.

59. Aumann, "Kierkegaard on Indirect Communication," 9.

60. Aumann, "Kierkegaard on Indirect Communication," 10.

61. Aumann, "Kierkegaard on the Need."

62. Tietjen, *Kierkegaard, Communication, and Virtue*, 50.

63. Kierkegaard, *Concluding Unscientific Postscript*, 1:192.

According to Kierkegaard, modern theologians often communicate truth in an inappropriate way because they have misdiagnosed the communication problem by confusing the communication of knowledge (propositional knowledge) rather than communicating the appropriation of knowledge (capability). Tietjen argues that according to Kierkegaard's lectures, "indirect communication does not in the first-place concern literary devices like pseudonymity or irony. Rather, the salient factor of indirect communication involves what Kierkegaard calls a 'communication of capability,' as opposed to a 'communication of knowledge.'"[64]

For Kierkegaard the indirect communication strategy was exactly the kind of antidote the church of his day required. Almost everyone in Copenhagen attended church because it was both socially advantageous and culturally expected. Most citizens therefore knew the creeds, rituals, and stories of the church. They were aware of its doctrine and could present themselves as loyal to the organized church. As previously mentioned, Kierkegaard distinguished between members of the church organization ("Christendom") and those who expressed a passionate faithfulness to Christ ("Christian"). He was convinced that "Christendom is nothing but a lifeless outer shell of mediocrity."[65] In short, individuals in the Danish church possessed some outward "knowledge" of God and of the church, but inwardly they held their cognitive or intellectual beliefs apart from the way they lived their lives. They lacked the passion and decisive action, or "capability," needed in order to bring their beliefs into their daily existence. As Kierkegaard understood this situation, they thought that because they participated in church activities and reflected on the issues of the church, God required nothing more of them. To them, faith was social and intellectual, not personal and vital. Such an abstract faith did not prepare them to live like Christ.

Kierkegaard understood that Christian truth cannot be reduced to an object of observation. Gregor states,

> When I attempt to observe Christian truth in a detached, objective way, I suddenly find it looking back at me, observing me, asking me "whether I am doing what it says I should do." As a result, I am unable to observe Christian truth impersonally. Insofar as I make contact with the genuine claim of Christ, I find myself called into question; I am pulled out of my objectivity and called into subjectivity—not the subjectivity of an epistemic

64. Tietjen, *Kierkegaard, Communication, and Virtue*, 54.

65. Kierkegaard, *Provocations*, xxix.

subject-object relation, but the subjectivity of responsibility. I am responsible, i.e., answerable, for what I do with this truth. And try as I might, in this moment I can no longer take refuge in detachment.[66]

Kierkegaard's pseudonym, Johannes Climacus, writes, "Because everyone knows the Christian truth, it has gradually become such a triviality that a primitive impression of it is acquired only with difficulty."[67] Again, Climacus states, "In our day, things seem actually to have gone so far that although we are all Christians and knowledgeable about Christianity, it is already a rarity to encounter a person who has even as much existing inwardness as a pagan philosopher."[68]

Confronted with the problem of knowing about truth but not living the truth—which Kierkegaard viewed as a problem of existence—it is little wonder that he saw the "flaw of this age . . . [as a] teaching which leaves a person's inwardness completely secure," yet radically hollow.[69] His remedy to this sort of false security was to recommend not more teaching but rather an unsettling kind of communicative capability that provokes thought, awareness, and action. Kierkegaard concludes that "a direct attack only strengthens a person in his illusion, and at the same time embitters him. There is nothing that requires such gentle handling as an illusion, if one wishes to dispel it. If anything prompts the prospective captive to set his will in opposition, all is lost."[70]

M. Mamie Ferreira explains that, for Kierkegaard, direct communication has its place "where the content of communication can be completed and encapsulated."[71] This description draws comparisons to the conduit metaphor of human communication.[72] Raymond E. Anderson elaborates on the distinction between direct and indirect communication by observing that "a direct form of discourse is useful . . . if one is communicating objective content or if the listener already has a serious interest in the ethical or religious quality of his life."[73] Of course, using the

---

66. Gregor, "Thinking Through," 454.

67. Kierkegaard, *Concluding Unscientific Postscript*, 1:275 (see footnote).

68. Kierkegaard, *Concluding Unscientific Postscript*, 1:279.

69. Kierkegaard, *Søren Kierkegaard's Journals and Papers*, 1:265.

70. Kierkegaard, *Point of View*, 25.

71. Ferreira, *Kierkegaard*, 102.

72. Grady, "'Conduit Metaphor Revisited.'"

73. Anderson, "Kierkegaard's Theory," 5.

direct approach with someone who expresses an interest in the content of the message still brings no assurance that the message will be understood. Effective communication is difficult at best, and sometimes almost impossible, even in the most ideal situations. Sometimes the best we can do is to limit the number of problems or "communication accidents" that make our communicative activity unproductive. Communication accidents abound, both with direct and indirect communication. Furthermore, a metaphorical element exists in all symbolic activity and language games, and if a person is only marginally interested in the information, or if they have no interest at all, then an indirect communication strategy is needed. Benjamin Nelson describes Kierkegaard's thinking about this situation:

> Early in the course of his authorship, he insisted, he had become convinced that entirely new resources would need to be developed if his contemporaries were to be converted from the normal religion hardly different from paganism, which they professed—mainly Christendom—to the Christianity proclaimed by Christ and Luther. He saw clearly that none of the inherited direct methods of quickening Spirit's—not friendly counsel, neighborly admonitions, learned explanations, moral censure, canonical penalties, not even the personal suffering of a martyr ("immediate pathos")—sufficed any longer in dialogue with contemporaries from their havens of self-satisfaction and indifference.[74]

Kierkegaard believed that a rational, well-reasoned, and clearly articulated argument about biblical truth, though sometimes desired, was not the most effective strategy for helping his contemporaries come to genuine Christian faith and practice. When the individual felt interested and motivated to apprehend the truth, but lacked knowledge of the truth, then direct communication might be useful. If, however, the individual was in any way skeptical, lacked interest, felt confused, or was under the illusion that he or she already knew the truth when he or she really didn't, then indirect communication was necessary.

Finally, Herrmann argues that indirect communication is fundamentally a dialogical approach to communicating. Even when using mass media, the communicator tries to draw the audience into dialogue through an artistic endeavor. Art can be dialogical and can stir the imagination without directly confronting the audience, but by placing jest and

---

74. Nelson, "Preface to the Torchbook Edition," x.

earnestness together, everyone in the audience can contend with his or her own life. One cannot coerce the other to his or her way of belief, as one can only induce the "other" to become aware.[75] Buber explains that dialogical communication "begins no higher than where humanity begins. There are not gifted and ungifted here, only those who give themselves and those who withhold themselves."[76] In this approach, we see the strength of openness, vulnerability, and dialogue.

Perhaps the transformative power of dialogue has the potential to serve as an alternative to some unproductive strategies of communicating Christ today. Many within the church today use various forms of rhetorical strategies to try to persuade others to come to know Christ. Christians often employ what Sonja K. Foss and Cindy L. Griffin call patriarchal perspectives in communicating the gospel—aggressive strategies based on efficiency and effectiveness as defined by a modernist sensibility. These strategies generally understand rhetoric as a means of persuasion, influence, and power. As Foss and Griffin argue, "Embedded in efforts to change others is a desire for control and domination, for the act of changing another establishes the power of the change agent over the other."[77]

Although "invitational rhetoric" as articulated by Foss and Griffin, makes an important contribution in emphasizing the role of the audience in the communication process, the authors seem to have overstated the argument that behind all efforts to change others is a desire for control and domination. If their argument were completely true, it would reduce witnessing to a post-Nietzschean power struggle over control of another's life, which should never be, as the power to free a man from sin and transform him is in the hands of God alone. The strength of indirect communication is that it makes individuals aware while still allowing them to make up their own minds. The best we can do is to try to make each person aware of God's call on his or her life.

Indirect communication focuses primarily on a person's feelings or heart. Those using indirect communication conceal their message in some way, using a veiled or provocative form of expression instead of presenting a simple and straightforward message. This approach to communicating the truth requires the communicator or artist to help birth self-reflection by masking or hiding the truth within the communicative

75. Herrmann, "Kierkegaard and Dialogue."

76. Buber, *Between Man and Man*, 35.

77. Foss and Griffin, "Beyond Persuasion," 2.

act. As we have seen, the primary purpose of indirect communication is to effect a fundamental change in the way of life of hearers or viewers as they seek to understand the meaning of the artistic or communicative act, which, of course, can be done in several ways. We saw that Kierkegaard used various strategies of indirect communication, including humor, questions, hinting, satire, irony, and many other literary devices. As noted, Kierkegaard was not systematic or even especially consistent with his definition of direct and indirect communication. He makes a strong argument for the use of both.

Now having acknowledged my debt to his work, I will advance my own understanding and definition of direct and indirect communication, in terms best suited for our present purposes. Direct communication is a straightforward or blunt approach to communicating objective knowledge. It is generally referred to as rational, propositional, and didactic. As Kierkegaard states, "All communication of knowledge is direct communication."[78] As suggested earlier, direct communication is forthright and tries to avoid deceptive, ironic, and elusive communication. In so doing, it comfortably deals with facts and figures, as it intends to communicate unambiguous and apparent meanings (not obscured), from which one gains knowledge.

As suggested earlier, direct and indirect communication are not mutually exclusive. All language and stories have a metaphorical quality to them, and this is especially true when dealing with transcendent or spiritual issues. No story, art, or message can be completely unambiguous or apparent. Nor can rational, propositional, and didactic messages be completely objective—hence, a continuum. Just as in music consonance and dissonance produce a structural dichotomy defining each other, so too does direct and indirect communication. With these limitations in mind, we advance this definition.

Indirect communication is veiled or hidden communication. Often it is entertaining and at times intentionally ambiguous so that the audience or person making sense of the message or artistic creation must determine the meaning for him or herself. It is intended to communicate capability rather than knowledge (nevertheless, some knowledge is assumed). Its purpose is to provoke thought, stir emotions, and engage the imagination, rather than impart objective information. Crucially, indirect communication intends to help the audience or person trying to

---

78. Kierkegaard, *Søren Kierkegaard's Journals and Papers*, 1:282.

make sense of the symbols or artistic expression become self-aware and come to a new perspective or commitment, which one becomes capable of living out. It is in this way that indirect art or communication conveys more than is said or shown, more than mere knowledge, but also the capacity or the capability to act. This definition of indirect communication does not dismiss the Socratic approach, or any of the artful, literary, or other communication devices so far advanced. In part, this is because indirect communication is not seen as a communication *theory* but as a communication *strategy* that can draw from various theoretical sources.

Pannenberg suggests that direct communication has an immediate way of attempting to present "just that content that it intends to communicate."[79] Conversely, indirect communication is not immediate, nor does it communicate without a break in the path of the sense-making process. With indirect communication, "the path is broken: the content first reveals its actual meaning by being considered from another perspective. Indirect communication is on a higher level; it always has direct communication as its basis but takes this into a new perspective."[80] If a person is persuaded that he or she is right or if the person has an emotional investment in his or her beliefs or behavior, then the direct approach will usually cause him or her to become defensive and resist any effort toward creating an open space for inward thought and understanding. Clearly, there are times when the direct approach is not productive. In those cases, the indirect approach compliments the direct. It is helpful to speak of the three tiers of direct and indirect communication:

1. Direct communication is useful to communicate objective truth or knowledge.

2. Direct communication faces a serious obstacle to helping people out of self-deception.

3. Indirect communication provides a way to overcome this obstacle.

The lingering question about using indirect communication is just how indirect one's choice of communication ought to be, which we will address in a subsequent chapter.

---

79. Pannenberg, *Revelation as History*, 14.
80. Pannenberg, *Revelation as History*, 14.

Three Reasons to Use Indirect Communication

There are three specific reasons for using the indirect communication strategy. First, God has communicated with us indirectly in the person of Jesus Christ. As Craddock states, "God in human form is a paradox, an indirection, eliciting rather than overwhelming faith."[81] Christ as both man and God is a difficult paradox for modern, rational man to accept. An artist with Christian concerns may use the paradox of the incarnation as a "model for word and action."[82] In the incarnation Christ did not come as the religious leaders expected. He looked weak on the cross, yet he was strong. The paradox or offence of the cross and of the life of Christ was difficult for people of his day to comprehend. No one expected the Messiah to be so humble and to die. As Frederick Buechner states, "Not only does evil come disguised in the world of the fairy tale but often good does too."[83] God himself is hidden in the ordinary, the unexpected, the impossible, or even in the joke. Alison Milbank reminds us that the ending of the story in *The Lord of the Rings* finds Frodo as "one in which lack and woundedness is opened to fullness and excess. And his destiny being hidden from the reader opens our desire."[84]

Second, the indirect approach to communicating may be used where there is a glut of religious or spiritual information, which most often is considered useless and offensive to the hearers or viewers. The advantage of the indirect approach in this situation is that the message can be veiled so as to entertain while at the same time enabling the individual to reflect on the meaning of the message as it relates to his or her own life. In this situation, the communication is intended to provoke thought and self-reflection. Buechner illustrates this approach by commenting on the communicative behavior of Christ. Buechner states, "He [Christ] suggests rather than spells out. He evokes rather than explains. He catches by surprise. He doesn't let the homiletic seams show. He is sometimes cryptic, sometimes obscure, sometimes irreverent, and always provocative. He tells stories."[85]

Third, the indirect approach may be preferred when those who already know some of the truth—or think they know the truth—will

81. Craddock, *Overhearing the Gospel*, 70.
82. Craddock, *Overhearing the Gospel*, 70.
83. Buechner, *Telling the Truth*, 79.
84. Milbank, "Apologetics and the Imagination," 43.
85. Buechner, *Telling the Truth*, 63.

perceive the direct approach as making a direct attack on their beliefs and person. The direct approach therefore will create only opposition and serve to entrench current beliefs, as well as cause the hearer or viewer to take a defensive posture, all of which serves only to strengthen the illusion. Therefore, the indirect approach may be used in situations where the content is known but not inwardly appropriated. In such a situation, more knowledge may only feed the illusion that one already understands the Christian faith or that one is already a Christian. By rejecting the indirect approach and attempting to communicate directly, one would run the risk of forcing a direct confrontation with the listener or viewer, who may not be emotionally or intellectually ready to receive such a message, thus planting in the listener's mind yet another negative impression of faith.

In the presence of information but no inward realization of the truth, supplying more information is often unnecessary and unhelpful, as the message will not be heard as interesting or inviting. Rather, it will be viewed as confrontational or as personal judgment. In such a situation, the hearer or viewer is not able to effectively consider new information, or to reconsider their previous beliefs, and will more likely respond negatively and emotionally to a perceived attack on their convictions or identity. In a sense, the direct approach is perceived as exerting a new level of hegemonic control over the hearer's or viewer's experience. And in that case, truth is not served, nor is it even heard.

Contexts that Require Indirect Communication

The following are three distinct communication contexts wherein one may prefer to use an indirect communication strategy. First, the indirect communication strategy is useful in helping people become aware of currently held misconceptions or misapprehensions to which they hold passionately, but erroneously. A person might think he or she is a likable and tolerant person, for example, but in fact may be a perfectionist with whom no one wants to work. Just telling the person, "You are difficult and demanding," will not usually help the person gain a new understanding of himself or herself. Another approach is needed.

By provoking or creating a space or opportunity for individuals to construct new meaning, they may be able to view themselves in a new or different way. When someone is taken by surprise and helped to look at themselves from a different direction, they may be helped to discover a new meaning regarding a previously held belief, doctrine, or story. This occurs because the indirect approach creates distance between the communicator and the message, allowing the individual to construct new meaning. It does so by engaging the imagination of the individual interacting with the story, art, or other symbolic creations, and thus allows the space and freedom to create an alternative meaning. This approach therefore gives greater responsibility to the listener or viewer to create meaning, rather than to let it be dictated. By sneaking past preconceived intellectual and emotional resistance, this indirect approach opens up the hearer or viewer to the possibility of greater ownership of the meaning of the story or message.[86] It does so, in part, through imaginative reflection of a perceived nonthreatening situation (nonthreatening to the individual hearer or viewer) in order to allow the hearer or viewer to apply the message to his own unique situation.

Part of the strength of the indirect approach is that, by using a veiled strategy that engages the emotions through the imagination, it strives to awaken individuals and give them space and time to consider new meanings that, to some extent, remain unpolluted by previous understandings and emotions. In this way, the old stories or words heard time and time again can gain new connotations. The message therefore can become more efficacious because it moves one's attention from well-worn facts, propositions, stories, and songs to potent emotional encounters through provocation and art.

The preeminent art form of story is often used in indirect communication. A narrative or story can avoid a direct assault on the listeners' or viewers' beliefs, because a good story invites the hearer or viewer to imagine the world differently. Only later, after their attention and emotion is captured, will they discover the implications the story has for their own life. This may happen with those already attending church, or with people who have heard the stories many times before, but who, due to familiarity, fail to fully engage with the familiar story. In effect, the familiarity distances them from truly engaging with the story. For these, the story must be "defamiliarized."

The second situation concerns individuals who are *not* people of faith and who have no intention to believe, yet who have some interest in the faith because they live in a culture that is, as Flannery O'Connor

---

86. Lewis, "Sometimes Fairy Stories," 37.

suggests, Christ-haunted if not Christ-centered.[87] Many people who have never darkened a church door nor spent time reading Scripture may still hold strong beliefs they have gleaned from the larger culture's interpretation and communication of what Christianity is and how Christians behave. This can happen totally apart from confessing Christians or the church. People who fall into this group have already been exposed to a particular Christian story or message and think they really understand the message, when in fact, they too are under an illusion and do not truly know what is being offered or presented by Christ. Their encounters through the media with a variety of so-called Christian behaviors, and their brief exposures to enthusiastic believers who recite scriptural or ethical propositions divorced from their original context, have jaded their understanding and left them with a distorted view of Christ and Christianity. For the most part, they have chosen not to attend to the predictable stories and messages presented to them by people speaking pious words and often orchestrated by marketing strategies. Any straightforward attempt to communicate with these people will be repelled, just as salesmen and politicians often get rebuffed. Significant emotional and possibly intellectual barriers are raised against these supposedly familiar messages.

Western culture itself presents an unflattering image or persona of the Christian faith that many in the culture resist. People who do not attend church but who have strong opinions of the church can be found in almost any western culture where Christian stories and faith are still communicated, whether inside or outside the gathered church community. Furthermore, weak or erroneous ideas of the Christian faith populate almost every area of our culture. Christian images and stories cut off from the true source of the Christian faith are empty and misguided symbols of truth and hold little sway in helping people embrace the truth of the gospel. The gospel, separated from Christ, no matter how beautiful the story or rational the argument, is nothing but an attractive lie.

On the other hand, many in our culture no longer believe doctrinal arguments, in part because they feel our age has moved beyond the age of superstitious knowledge and progressed into a more rational or scientific age. We live in an era that privileges reason and dismisses other ways of knowing, especially revelation—now errantly understood as opposed to reason, not the perfection of reason. If our society were eager to find and

---

87. O'Connor, *Mystery and Manners*.

look for reasons to follow Christ, that would be one thing; but we live in a very different age. We live in an age of doubters and searchers, an age captured by momentary whims and electronic illusions.

In this situation, modern or even postmodern ideas have captured the popular imagination and distract people from truly attending to serious questions regarding our world and their place in it. As Charles Taylor suggests, many people today no longer seriously consider God as necessary to live a fulfilled life. "Modernity brings about secularity, in all its . . . forms."[88] Furthermore, "Most religious people, even very fervent ones, operate within a secular discourse in important areas of their lives."[89]

The third situation references a group that includes non-Christians who have been taught that the stories of Scripture are not true, or that the Christian faith and the stories of faith as understood by Christians are false. These people are under an illusion that the stories told them by their cultural or religious leaders, who either dismiss Christ or challenge the church's understanding of Him, are true. This, of course, is a serious illusion that needs to be dealt with before one can begin to help others see their need for Christ. This category of individuals is not secular but holds to a belief in some sort of God—just not the Christian God. In fact, many have been told explicitly that the Christian faith is false and a lie.

I remember overhearing a conversation where a person called herself a "recovering Christian." I thought she meant that she was a Christian and had turned away from her former life as a non-Christian, and now was trying to live a Christian life. I soon learned, however, that she really meant she no longer followed Christ; she was "recovering" from a belief in Him. The path she now followed told her that Christianity was a lie and Christ a false teacher. She knew of the stories of faith, but they no longer held meaning for her. It is likely that she was inoculated against the true gospel.

Many people of other faiths have a jaundiced view of Christ and Christianity, as well as negative feelings toward Christ. All these need to be understood and dealt with before the individual becomes open to hear the truth about Him. Clearly the misinformation and misunderstanding that exists needs to be addressed before they will even consider the meaning and purpose of Christ. Since they will view a direct approach as an attack on their current beliefs, an indirect approach may help the

88. Taylor, *Secular Age*, 21.

89. Berger, *Many Altars of Modernity*, x.

individual become open to learn more. Indirect communication can open a space for individuals to examine their lives without shame or judgment, which can in turn create space for Christ to work.

In our context, where some level of knowledge already exists, the indirect approach is preferred. This is true even if the audience imperfectly understands the biblical stories and does not clearly know Christian values. In fact, if one is creating art or some other form of communication for people from a culture where Christ is not proclaimed, but false teaching and spurious information is communicated about Him, then indirect communication is often the most useful approach. One cannot begin by confronting the "other" with what one may view as a negative message. Instead, as Kierkegaard suggests, we must approach "from behind," helping the other to upend their inadequate understanding and encouraging a new awareness of Christ, even if he is not initially named. Through this gentler and less threatening approach, one may encounter a new dimension of the truth.

Ethically, the indirect method implies complete respect for the listener. The listener is respected for what is already known and for the One in whose image he or she is made. Listeners are respected for their mental capacity, for their capacity to understand what is being communicated, and for their yearnings and faculties for living fully. Craddock suggests that we appeal "to the full range of human faculties for joy, anxiety, love, purpose, meaning, and longing for eternity."[90]

Story and Narrative as Forms of Indirect Communication

As previously suggested the majority of this work will focus on the indirect communication form of story. Stories by their very nature are indirect. As Peterson contends, "Storytelling creates a world of presuppositions, assumptions, and relations into which we enter. Stories invite us into a world other than ourselves, and if they are good and true stories, a world larger than ourselves."[91] Storytellers with Christian concerns invite us into a world of God's creation, and they, by way of invitation and imagination,

---

90. Craddock, *Overhearing the Gospel*, 78.

91. Peterson, "Foreword," viii.

show us rather than tell us the truth. They satisfy our "narrative hunger" to hear and ultimately tell good stories.[92]

In his book *Planet Narnia*, author Michael Ward argues that C. S. Lewis understood "the importance of 'hiddenness' in literature."[93] Lewis often talked about the "hidden" or "cryptic" element in a story. In fact, in his essay "On Stories," Lewis asserts that in storytelling the hidden thing is a major concern.[94] As a medievalist, Lewis was interested in the important features of literature of that period. Ward observes,

> Spenser disguised Venus in the *Faerie Queene* (so Lewis argues in *Spenser's Images of Life*) because he was drawing on the tradition of neo-Platonic thought which deemed it proper that "all great truths should be veiled," should "be treated mythically (*per fabulosa*) by the prudent." It is for the same reason that the god "is (usually) hidden" in Spenser and that the *Faerie Queene* is "dangerous, cryptic, its every detail loaded with unguessed meaning."[95]

Furthermore, Ward argues convincingly that "Lewis praised the indirect approach in communication," as "he believed that success in writing comes about by 'secretly evoking powerful associations.'"[96]

Story is a powerfully indirect influence primarily because it is not seen as being directed at the listening or viewing individual. As veiled communication, stories "evoke rather than articulate Christian doctrine," leaving the spiritual meaning hidden.[97] This form of communication ignites the imagination of the receptive reader or viewer and can capture their emotions before they are fully aware of what is happening to them. In this way stories do not put the hearer or viewer on guard against any theological issues involved but are left to contemplate the meaning of the story by themselves. Stories allow storytellers with Christian concerns to provoke thought and provide a degree of distance to the listener or viewer. As they are confronted with the plot, characters, images, and atmosphere found in the story, they are free to decide on the meaning of the story as it relates to their own life. Stories are powerful indirect

92. Price, *Palpable God.*

93. Ward, *Planet Narnia*, 7.

94. Lewis, *On Stories*, 15.

95. Ward, *Planet Narnia*, 19.

96. Ward, *Planet Narnia*, 21.

97. Hans, "That Hideous Strength," 23.

contrivances because they work on an individual on two levels at once. They have a surface level of meaning, but they also have a hidden meaning that often escapes the immediate attention of the reader or viewer, and only on reflection does that second meaning become evident.

Stories are essential to our identity and to understanding who we are as human beings. As such, stories are a form of indirect communication. Not only do the stories we hear and tell nurture our social life, but they define who we are as people of God. The stories we hear and the stories we create inform and empower our lives. Stories bring a sense of meaning and coherence to our existence. To know ourselves is to know our own stories and to know others is to know their stories. We inhabit our stories and they shape our understanding of who we are and what we believe. As Dan P. McAdams states, "We are all tellers of tales."[98]

A story can even save your life. Søren Kierkegaard loved the old tale, *A Thousand and One Nights*. In the story, a young woman named Scheherazade saves her own life by telling stories. The sultan, betrayed by an unfaithful wife, decides to prevent such a thing from ever happening again by spending a single night with an unlucky woman, whom he then puts to death the very next day. He therefore spends every night with a new woman. When Scheherazade's turn comes to spend a night with the sultan, she tries to avoid the fate of her predecessors by telling a story—but she stops her tale before she comes to the story's end. When the sultan begs to hear the end of the story, she explains that that night they have run out of time. The sultan therefore spares her life so that he can hear the end of the story. The next evening, she finishes the story and begins a new one, but again, stops in the middle. The sultan again spares her life; and so it goes, night after night. In the end, the sultan falls in love with Scheherazade and makes her his queen.

As a storyteller Kierkegaard found great strength in this story. He stated, "I so often have said of myself, that as Scheherazade saved her life by telling stories, I save my life or keep alive by being productive."[99] For Kierkegaard, the most important characteristic of a person is not reason but passion—and passion comes to us through story. Kierkegaard's emphasis on subjectivity fills his stories of human existence with realism. Stories can give form to an existence that resists the traditional boundaries of our being. Stories, especially fantasies—unlike our everyday, referential

98. McAdams, *Stories We Live By*, 11.

99. Kierkegaard, *Søren Kierkegaard's Journals and Papers*, 6:72.

language—are not obliged to refer to a determinable reality to sustain meaning. Yet they give "us access to vivid and sensory rich worlds."[100]

All of us are storytellers, and as such we are artists and image-bearers. Art, especially the art of storytelling, is a gift that all people have; yet few keep and develop it. James Hillman suggests that "art is dedicated to beauty; it's a way to let beauty into our world by means of the artist's gifts and sensibilities."[101] Both beauty and metaphor are necessary elements of art in general but are especially necessary for the art of storytelling. As men and women made in the image of God, we are artists and storytellers who make people aware of the transcendent, to help them recognize God's presence in our world. In this way, beauty and art can serve to create and nurture both community and faith.

Unfortunately, we live in a time that has devalued art and story, especially regarding communicating our faith in Christ. Holly Ordway, a Catholic scholar and Christian apologist at Houston Baptist University, explains how we have turned instead to "the analytical detached view point over the experiential one."[102] We focus on the mind and often ignore the imagination. Ordway warns against thinking of "the rationalistic idea of conversion as making an intellectual decision."[103] We need, instead, to recognize that reason, imagination, and the will are all important to our existence and life in Christ.

Walter Fisher's narrative paradigm of human communication suggests that we are all *homo narrans*, that is, human storytellers.[104] The narrative paradigm synthesizes two strands of rhetoric or communication: argumentative or persuasive with the literary or aesthetic. Fisher, an accomplished communication scholar from the University of Southern California, draws on Stanley Hauerwas when he argues that the "meaning and significance of life in all of its social dimensions requires the recognition of its narrative structure."[105] As storytellers and artists, we can "get around" a person's intellectual and emotional prejudices by telling good stories.

100. LeNotre, "Flannery O'Connor's 'Parker's Back,'" 336.
101. Gablik, "Nature of Beauty."
102. Ordway, *Apologetics and the Christian Imagination*, 162.
103. Ordway, *Apologetics and the Christian Imagination*, 168.
104. Fisher, *Human Communication as Narration*.
105. Fisher, "Narration," 3.

After examining several studies regarding the use and effects of literature, Maja Djikie and Keith Oatley concluded that "reading literary fiction can prompt personality changes."[106] Djikie and Oatley's inquiry suggests that consuming literary fiction can spark significant improvements in the hearers' or viewers' abilities to empathize with others. Likewise, the authors argue that "literature can facilitate self-change" and that "this is especially impressive, given the stability of the personality system and the difficulties people encounter in attempting to change that system."[107] Furthermore, Djikie and Oatley imply that art, particularly fiction, can bridge the gap between the seen and the unseen. They assert, "art involves the nondirective property of inviting those who engage with it to experience their own emotions and thoughts."[108] Stories and other forms of indirect communication can assist in navigating our self-development by transcending our present self, while at the same time recommending to us a variety of possible future selves. Djikie and Oatley argue,

> A striking feature of self-change through literature is that the effects are not direct, as occurs with persuasion, where an author intends the reader or listener to think, feel, or be disposed to act, in a way he or she desires. The art in fiction is a social influence, but one that helps people to understand and feel, and even change their selfhood, in their own ways. The influence is what Kierkegaard called "indirect communication."[109]

Specific Examples of Indirect Communication

Finally, let's briefly consider a familiar story found in the Old Testament as an example of the power of story as a form of indirect communication, followed by a few contemporary anecdotes. The "source material" for this powerful story comes from an ancient throne room. The tale begins when the prophet Nathan was directed by God to challenge the criminal activity of David, king of Israel.

As a military hero, accomplished musician, and poet, David possessed both political power and celebrity status, which together allowed him to do almost anything he wanted—or so he thought. Consequently,

106. Djikie and Oatley, "Art of Fiction," 498.
107. Djikie and Oatley, "Art of Fiction," 498.
108. Djikie and Oatley, "Art of Fiction," 503.
109. Djikie and Oatley, "Art of Fiction," 498.

Nathan had no small job when God led him to confront King David about his adultery and murder. Of course, David did not want to hear what Nathan had to say. He already knew with full certainty that he had displeased God through his affair and subsequent successful murder plot. Nathan had to ask himself very carefully, "How can I bring up such atrocities to the one in power? Especially when he does not want to hear the truth?"

Nathan realized that David did not lack information on this matter, nor was the king misinformed about his actions. David knew he had done wrong. So, when God told Nathan to confront David, the prophet clearly found himself in a very difficult and dangerous position. No doubt, Nathan spent a long time pondering how to approach the king, judiciously considering his most effective approach. Nathan had deduced that his royal friend's lapse in judgment was a failure to act on the truth—not a lack of knowledge. We might say the king had a "heart" problem rather than a "head" problem.

At times, all of us are faced with a similar challenge. In these moments what we need most is not a new discovery or a new idea, but a different slant. We need a tactical or strategic modification in our way of perceiving the situation "on which attention is already fixed."[110] This describes Nathan's confrontation with David, exactly.

Therefore, on the fateful day, the prophet approached David carefully—one might even say with some holy deception—in order to tell him a story aimed at the heart. Nathan did not initially confront David with the bald facts or lay out the whole purpose (or truth) of that day's engagement. Instead, Nathan told the king the following story:

> There were two men in a certain town, one rich and the other poor. The rich man had a very large number of sheep and cattle, but the poor man had nothing except one little ewe lamb he had bought. He raised it, and it grew up with him and his children. It shared his food, drank from his cup and even slept in his arms. It was like a daughter to him.
>
> Now a traveler came to the rich man, but the rich man refrained from taking one of his own sheep or cattle to prepare a meal for the traveler who had come to him. Instead, he took the ewe lamb that belonged to the poor man and prepared it for the one who had come to him.

110. Barfield, *Saving the Appearances*, 11.

> David burned with anger against the man and said to Na-
> than, "As surely as the LORD lives, the man who did this deserves
> to die! He must pay for that lamb four times over, because he did
> such a thing and had no pity."
>
> Then Nathan said to David, "You are the man!" (2 Sam
> 12:1–7).

Now comes the point of decision. How would David react? The king realized his sin was exposed, stood guilty of this great wrong, chose to confess his immoral behavior, and plead his case before God. By using the indirect approach, Nathan had succeeded in assisting David to face up to the true meaning of his improper behavior. Nathan faithfully and effectively communicated this difficult message to David through indirect means.

Two things immediately become clear in this account. First, Nathan did not provide any new information to the king, as David did not require new information. Second, Nathan did not begin by directly launching into the matter at hand. Rather, he veiled his full purpose and hid his primary intent. Some may even say that he acted deceptively by not making clear his true purpose from the beginning. But by taking this indirect approach, Nathan gave David both time and distance from the evil he had done so that he might see his own destructive behavior in a new way. When Nathan first approached David, the king likely regarded him warily, ready to defend himself. When the two men began their discussion, David was far from ready to be confronted with the ugly truth. David needed the opportunity to approach the situation from a different vantage point, one that could enable him to see his behavior in a new light.

By appealing to David's emotions before appealing to his intellect, Nathan placed David in the position of a judge rather than the one being judged. Since David knew well this position of authority, he was quickly engaged in the story without suspecting that the prophet would soon call him to account. Only after David had emotionally connected to the characters in the story—and made his harsh judgment on the rich man spoken about in the story—did Nathan reveal the true meaning of his tale. By this time, David had clearly immersed himself in the sentiment of the story; by then, only a slight emotional distance remained between the unlawful behavior of the rich man and that of David himself. Nathan's story clearly provoked thought while stirring David's emotions, ultimately bringing the king to repentance.

Indirect communication has value in many different areas of communication activity, but in this context we want to focus primarily on its use by Christian leaders and artists with Christian concerns. As we have seen, a clear example of capability comes through indirect communication in the Old Testament story of Nathan confronting the adultery of King David. This example shows how one can effectively speak truth even in the face of worldly power. That is, it gives us a way to speak to those who are more powerful and hold greater social capital, but who need to hear and live the truth.

Before we close, let's have a look at two contemporary examples that exhibit the proper use and influence of indirect communication. A former student of mine teaches at a small college. One afternoon in class he found himself with an irritating problem. His freshmen students in a speech course had almost uniformly ignored some important instructions about how to submit an assignment. He had given the instructions verbally several times over several class periods and had repeatedly called the students' attention to the written instructions in the syllabus. Nevertheless, on the day his students had to turn in the assignment, only two out of twenty-one students had followed his instructions.

Rather than respond with threats, lectures, or pleas, my friend decided to take a page out of the book of an Old Testament prophet named Nathan.

"You all know I work with several book publishers on a number of writing projects," he said to them. "Well, I need your advice on a project that's gone wrong. I'm not quite sure how to address the problem."

The students all perked up and nodded their heads, eager to help.

"Here's the deal," he continued, "on this book, I'm working with a team of young writers and editors. I think a number of them are about your age, because the book is intended for undergraduates. About five times already I've sent corrections for the first chapter, but each time the pages come back to me from the publisher without any corrections. It's very frustrating. What do you think I should do?"

The whole class, almost in unison, replied, "Fire them!"

"Are you sure?" he asked.

"Yes!" they answered cheerfully.

My friend smiled. "You are the man!" he said, quoting 2 Sam 12:7. "Actually, you're the young people in my story. You're the ones who failed to listen to my instructions. Although I've told you repeatedly how to submit the assignment that is due today, only two out of twenty-one of you did what I asked. So, what should I do? You just told me that I should fire those young people. I can't fire you, but I could give you all Fs. Should I?"

The room got very quiet.

My friend then used the opportunity to remind them that their next assignment, a much bigger one, needed to be submitted on time and according to instructions. And you know what? The next time, he got 100 percent compliance.

We find indirect approaches in countless contexts, not merely in a classroom or in a palace. Consider the experience of another former student who at the time was taking a class on indirect communication.

The young son of this student had resisted all his parents' attempts at potty training. My student and her husband had tried all sorts of behavior modification from trying to bribe their toddler with M&Ms, to buying a small potty chair for him to sit on, to getting an attachment to the toilet, all to entice him to relieve himself on the toilet. Nothing worked—neither threat, nor reward, nor praise, nor shame. They finally decided to try an indirect approach.

Since this child loved pirates and pirate stories, one night they told him a story about pirates. They explained how the pirates engaged the enemy and boarded the other ship and won the battle. After his triumph, the pirate captain climbed to the top of the ship and sat on his throne. Then he made it rain.

This couple had agreed not to mention anything about the throne being another word for "potty," or what it meant to "make it rain." The little boy loved the story and the next day wanted to hear it again. The following day, at some point the boy found his father and led him into the bathroom. He pointed his little finger toward the toilet and said, "Is that the throne?"

"Yes," the father replied.

The next day, after hearing the story again, the little boy wanted to sit on the throne. And yes, he made it rain. And from that day on, he was potty trained.

I am not a child rearing expert and I don't mean to suggest this story or method as a new form of potty training, but the incident does illustrate how indirect communication can be used quite effectively, especially when direct communication has proven unsuccessful. Let's briefly unpack what happened.

First, the little boy did not lack information. He knew what was expected of him and how to comply with his parents' wishes; he just didn't want to do it. Second, this approach allowed the boy to become aware of and experience a new way, a creative way, and a more fun and interesting way of thinking about the challenge presented to him. Third, no one told him the meaning of the story; he had to figure it out for himself. This story gave him an opportunity to reflect on his own life and to decide for himself how he wanted to proceed, without feeling judged or deprived of his freedom.

Conclusion

This chapter introduced both direct and indirect communication and contends that artists and leaders with Christian concerns need to pay more attention to indirect communication strategies, precisely because, unlike the direct communication of *knowledge*, indirect communication conveys *capability*. We examined the church in Kierkegaard's day and in our day and concluded that an indirect means of communication might awaken "Christendom"; that is, it could provoke Christians with *knowledge* of Christianity to be *capable* of living it out. We then explored Kierkegaard's definition and use of indirect communication and paid close attention to the use of story and narrative as key forms of indirect communication. Finally, we cited some examples of indirect communication.

To the degree that we ignore, forget, underutilize, or neglect the strategy of indirect communication, we become less effective communicators. If we wish to become better communicators, we must learn to effectively use both direct and indirect approaches. Let us now turn our attention to those illusions we must overcome.

2

Illusions, Culture, and Christendom

But for the present age, which prefers the sign to the thing signified, the copy to the original, representation to reality, appearance to essence . . . truth is considered profane, and only illusion is sacred. Sacredness is in fact held to be enhanced in proportion as truth decreases and illusion increases, so that the highest degree of illusion comes to be the highest degree of sacredness.

—LUDWIG FEUERBACH, PREFACE TO
THE ESSENCE OF CHRISTIANITY

Introduction

No COUNTRY FOR OLD Men is not a reflection on our nation's retirement plan, but a grotesque and disturbing film that has sparked several conversations in the Christian community about the nature of art. This Oscar-winning film is violent, to be sure, perhaps one of the most violent and bleakest films I have ever seen. Its dark, flat Texas landscapes and almost iconic characters lend an unusual sense of evil to the film that feels both troubling and revealing. The Coen brothers' film, based on a Cormac McCarthy novel, casts a tragic vision of a culture tired and vexed by its own unhealthy vices, a culture not so much in decline as one that has hit rock bottom and cannot find a way out of its own pit of despair. The discussion of this film and other films like it leads ultimately to the question of whether the film has enough redemptive value to serve any meaningful artistic purpose.

Films or stories like this one speak powerfully to our modern sensibilities because they identify some of the distortions and illusions prevalent within our communities. Their artistic critiques of our cultural landscape serve a useful purpose in stirring viewers to examine their lives and reflect upon the false illusions existent within our culture. While some view these exaggerated and difficult films or stories as useful and redemptive, others consider them to be depressing or depraved—stories lacking any kind of useful purpose or redemptive value.

Although several of these stories are graphic, even shocking or exaggerated in their depiction of the social or moral evil existent within our culture, it can be argued that they cannot be anything less if they are to help us see, feel, and connect the proper sentiment to the proper behaviors. This film and stories like it resist the temptation to dress up the truth in order to make our communities look more beautiful or more respectable than they are.

Perhaps we can see these kinds of stories or films as potentially useful in awakening an audience to the challenge our modern culture presents. Through story and art of this kind, one no longer feels comfortable ignoring the truth or dismissing the real challenges confronting our culture. In my view, this film and the book that inspired it present artistically and compellingly a culture that has seriously deluded itself, a culture that refuses to look at the problems facing it. The film may not tell the whole truth, but it does tell the difficult truth that we so often refuse to face: the truth found in our existence.

Illusions

The illusions of our age—the entertainment industry, prescription and nonprescription drugs, materialism, economic wealth, social media, and a host of other diversions—have so preoccupied us that we, as Socrates suggests in Plato's *Apology*, seem unable to live an "examined life." We live in a time of unprecedented scientific and technological advancement, yet often we have used this new knowledge to avoid, cover up, or bury our real concerns. Rather than facing our problems, whether alienation, loneliness, or meaninglessness, we use the media or some other form of diversion—including various forms of self-medication—to distract ourselves from facing the tangible and difficult issues life presents.

Fred B. Craddock, like Kierkegaard, called the church to a new vision of truth telling—one that engaged both the speaker and the listener, the artist and the audience, and the writer and the reader to an active, authentic faith. This engagement of our mind and our emotions is exactly why indirect communication is so powerful. For Kierkegaard, Christ is an uncomfortable truth because he is like no other truth we have encountered and because he comes to enter and transform our lives. He stirs within us the uncomfortable desire to live for something beyond ourselves. He is not just an interesting personality we come to know— like a celebrity or even a hero—but someone who challenges us to live a life set apart. In encountering him, we come to experience life as a gift from God. Therefore, our lives are not to be seen as self-created products determined by our own whims; they gifts from God. We are made to serve the one who gave us life and not our own ends. Our existence is entwined with his; our purpose or identity is found in him.

In this chapter we examine the illusions found in our culture. First, we will look at the storytellers of our age, primarily the media and the new technology that have captured the attention and fancy of so many people in our culture. Our technological society has fostered a belief that communication is primarily a commodity or form of social capital. In so doing it has significantly diminished, but not completely severed, our understanding and use of communication as primarily a means to establish and maintain relationships. Rather, it has fostered an understanding of communication as abstract and disembodied forms of symbolic exchange. This, in turn, cultivates an understanding of one's will against our God-given nature and hence the natural world. Second, we look at the influence that media and technology have had on our communication behavior, both mediated and interpersonal, and how these changes have influenced the church. Finally, we examine the need to address these illusions primarily through indirect communication. Indirect communication stimulates our need to reimagine our religious sensibilities and in so doing awakens us to the need to reconnect our ways of existing or being in the world to our Christian beliefs. The indirect approach helps reshape individuals by encouraging them to move beyond simply knowing and toward inhabiting a more fully embodied or incarnational mode of existence—one that is connected to his or her natural sensibilities. We begin this exploration with a brief look at our culture.

Secularism

Charles Taylor tells us that we are living in "a secular age." Earlier in human history, he explains, the distinctions we so often make about various aspects of human life—economic, political, religious, and social, etc.— were not so easily distinguishable. In these earlier societies, religion was everywhere, interwoven with everything else.

Taylor identifies three ways in which we can understand what is meant by "living in a secular age." First, he suggests, we can understand secularity in terms of political spaces and that these political spaces have been allegedly cleared of any reference to God or to any mention of an alternate reality. Thought of in another way, "we function within various spheres of activity—economic, political, cultural, educational, professional, recreational—the norms and principles we follow, the deliberations we engage in, generally don't refer us to God or to any religious beliefs; the considerations we act on are internal to the 'rationality' of each sphere—maximum gain within the economy, the greatest benefit to the greatest number in the political area, and so on."[1]

A second sense in which we use the term secularity has to do with the waning of religious belief and practice; that is, when people turn away from God and no longer attend church. By this logic, most of the countries of Western Europe have become secular, even those which retain vestigial reference to God in public spaces. "This," Taylor suggests, "is the issue that people often want to get at when they speak of our times as secular, and contrast them, nostalgically or with relief, with earlier ages of faith or piety."[2]

Taylor identifies a third use of the term, related to the second and not without some connection to the first, but which for the most part focuses on the conditions of belief. He states, "The shift to secularity in this sense consists, among other things, of a move from a society where belief in God is unchallenged and indeed, unproblematic, to one in which it is understood to be one option among others, and frequently not the

1. Taylor, *Secular Age*, 2.
2. Taylor, *Secular Age*, 2.

easiest to embrace."[3] Taylor further explains that it seems plausible that significant differences exist between those societies in terms of *what it is to believe*. These difference stem in part from the fact that belief is an option, and in some sense an embattled option in the Christian or post-Christian society, and not in those societies where this is not yet the case.

Carefully and with keen insight, Taylor examines our society in this third sense of secularity. Consequently, he traces and defines "secular" as that

> which takes us from a society in which it was virtually impossible not to believe in God, to one in which faith, even for the staunchest believer, is one human possibility among others. I may find it inconceivable that I would abandon my faith, but there are others, including possibly some very close to me, whose way of living I cannot at all honestly just dismiss as depraved, or blind, or unworthy, who have no faith (at least not in God, or in the transcendent). Belief in God is no longer axiomatic. There are alternatives. And this will also likely mean that at least in certain milieu, it may be hard to sustain one's faith. There are people who feel bound to give it up, even though they mourn its loss. This has been a recognizable experience in our societies, at least since the mid-nineteenth century. There will be many others to whom faith never even seems an eligible possibility. There are certainly millions today of whom this is true.[4]

Secularity as recognized in this "sense is a matter of the whole context of understanding in which our moral, spiritual, or religious experience and search takes place."[5] Taylor argues that the secular emerges amid the religious. For example, the Protestant Reformation, by breaking down the political structures of the Roman Catholic Church, provided the starting point down the road to our secular age. The presence of religious aspects of life has not been lost in Western culture; rather, it has become one among many stories striving for acceptance. This gives artists and storytellers of faith an opportunity to speak into this cultural setting.

Through Taylor's examination of the rise of unbelief in the nineteenth century, we are reminded that religious influences remain part of our present view of the meaning of secularity—and, by extension, part of the fabric of the world in which we communicate. Peter L. Berger

3. Taylor, *Secular Age*, 3.
4. Taylor, *Secular Age*, 3.
5. Taylor, *Secular Age*, 3.

contends that the notion that modernity inevitably brings about a decline of religion "can no longer be maintained in the face of the empirical evidence."[6] He argues that a new paradigm of pluralism might be a better way to make sense of modernity and religion. Whatever the case, the secularization hypothesis—people are more areligious or atheist than in the past—is today seriously questioned, if not completely discredited. Nevertheless, certain illusions of the "secular" are still felt within our modern culture. As Berger states, "All of life becomes an interminable process of redefining who the individual is in the context of the seemingly endless possibilities presented by modernity."[7]

Secularity, of course, is the arena to which we are called. The challenges facing men and women in this circumstance is the context in which we are called to live and witness to the presence of the divine in our world. So, let's consider how we come to know, understand, and live as men and women of faith in the technologically saturated world in which we now live.

The New Storytellers

We live in an era when spiritual formation has taken a back seat to comfort and entertainment, an age where an abundance of information gets confused with wisdom and personal economic wealth conflated with happiness. Our time is awash with "mediated reality" that has so encroached upon our lives that we have no idea we are living with "a deficit of wonder."[8] The entertainer Tom Waits echoes the sentiment of several artists and scholars when he suggests that "we are buried beneath the weight of information, which is being confused with knowledge."[9] Years ago, Herbert A. Simon, in his book *Administrative Behavior*, predicted that the sheer amount of information from developing technologies would tax our ability to grasp their meanings. From his perspective, an information-rich world creates a wealth of knowledge that in turn produces a scarcity of whatever that information consumes. In this case, that "whatever" is our attention. Simon argues that in our enthusiasm for unlimited information "we sometimes lose sight of the fact that a new

6. Berger, *Many Altars of Modernity*, ix.

7. Berger, *Many Altars of Modernity*, 5.

8. Tom Waits, in Hoskyns, *Lowside of the Road*, 489.

9. Tom Waits, in Hoskyns, *Lowside of the Road*, 489.

scarcity has been created: the scarcity of human time for attending to the information that flows in on us."[10] Evidently, this wealth of information creates a poverty of time and attention. Unquestionably, this has become a reality today. The over-diffusion of opinion and argument has created a deterrent for individuals to remain open to many sources of information or to actively seek out new points of view. The unfortunate result is that individuals have grown weary of almost anyone attempting to persuade them, fearful of becoming a mere object of persuasion. In essence, many people feel like non-beings who are identical to every other willing listener.

Amid all these social and technological changes, we are distancing ourselves not only from one another but from ourselves. We have created a society where meditation, contemplation, and silence no longer play a vital role in our existence. We long for the spectacle and to "join in" as imagined participants as we gather around the technological inventions we have created. Living in a technological age that is marked by abstract and disembodied knowledge makes it incredibly difficult for an individual to engage in self-examination and to contemplate the possibility of change.

Technology and the New Self

Since Aristotle technology has been understood to be a certain form of human making that is analogous to but lesser than the making of nature. That is, for Aristotle, our making is not about the willful projection of one's desired ends or of one's self, but a natural expression of what is already naturally given, a participation in the natural processes. In this way works of art or technological inventions tell us something about the virtuous nature of the artist or craftsman. The nature of the maker is seen in his or her making as an effect resembling its cause. Of course, the highest achievement of humankind is the most natural: the begetting of children. The child most closely resembles his or her "makers," the parents. This ontology of human making suggests that good or respectable non-natural making—that which is not begetting—such as technology and art, ought to be analogous to the given or fixed reality of the craftsman or artist. It is not until the modern period that technology and art are determined not by intrinsic ends and purposes of the craftsman or artist,

10. Simon, *Administrative Behavior*, 22–23.

but by a "free" human will—"free" meaning free from naturally given and intrinsic ends. This new form of freedom underlying a selfish form of technological making has been linked to the ecological crisis (e.g., in Heidegger) and to post-humanism. The natural intrinsic purposes are now seen merely as limits the individual should strive to overcome. With no intrinsic purposes and/or natures, the human will, now unbounded, is free to "make" whatever it wishes of nature and of self.

Celebrity culture and social media are simply the logical outworking of a technological ontology, a form of making that unties the willed self from its given natural ends—the creating of the self over against the self that is true to one's nature. Such are the false images of the self we loathe yet feel the pressure to keep up. We want desperately for ourselves and others to be "true to ourselves," all the while we are constantly placed in a position where the very forms in which we communicate and the technological ontology we've adopted suggest otherwise. We now seem incapable of recovering our true natures. It is in this way that today's technological ontology or "tech-knowledge"—knowledge disconnected from higher ends, purposes, moral, and/or ethics—leaves us incapacitated. With no higher ends we are left only to make false images into which we craft our own identities.

Advertisers draw on these false images, knowing that today's youth, with no given identities to which to cling, feel increasingly concerned with self-image and are susceptible to all sorts of media influence. Emma Brockes suggests that one such influence is "the corrupting influence of celebrity culture."[11] Nudged on by the media, both children and adults seem increasingly absorbed with celebrity behavior, despite its frequent degradation and the flawed example of healthy human conduct. For some, the view of the person as performer carries a sense of entitlement in at least two ways. First, we construct our world as a spectacle—we live to be watched. Second, we organize our lives in narcissistic ways, and as such we find meaning and define beauty or the beautiful by their mere appearance rather than in their ontological reality.[12] As John Durham Peters suggests, "The most subject-like of all objects is an image of a subject."[13] He asserts that we often treat mediated human images as incarnations of the divine. A shift occurs, wherein the image becomes the reality—more

11. Brockes, "I Want to Be Famous."

12. Lasch, *Culture of Narcissism.*

13. Peters, "Beauty's Veils," 9.

real than reality itself—and we imagine a social relationship with the mediated other.[14] This disconnection from the self helps explain why so many people enter so-called "parasocial" relationships with media celebrities such as Elvis, Beyoncé, Justin Bieber, Kim Kardashian, Kanye West, etc. "Iconoclasm," Peters suggests, "is the protest against the confusion of subject and object . . . It unmasks an imagined mutual relationship as a unilateral product of the worshiper's own longing."[15]

Unfortunately, we have few iconoclasts today, as evidenced by the success of such shows as *American Idol*, *The Voice*, *If I Can Dream*, *Battle of the Bods*, and a host of other "reality" shows that attempt to create instant celebrities out of normal people. We do not seem to clearly understand that only certain kinds of virtues ought to be elevated. For example, Peters states that "Only certain kinds of beauty can be reproduced. The beauty gradually disclosed through the time of a shared life—mortal beauty—cannot show itself to strangers."[16] Furthermore, he argues that in entering imagined relationships, we privilege the outer surface over the internal nature of one's being. Peters reminds us that modernity privileges "our access to images of instantly beautiful others, inviting an attitude of neglect toward beauty's less flashy kinds that escape reproduction by the image. The danger of the mechanically reproduced image, in short, is beauty without history." Peters harkens back to the prophet Isaiah who "complained: 'Their land is full of idols; they worship the work of their own hands, that which their own fingers have made.'"[17] We live in a media age and sometimes it envelops almost every part of our life and world: school, church, social life, economics, entertainment, and family.

It seems that everyone is a performer—or wants to be—and the distinction or distance between actor and audience has almost disappeared as performance and masking one's identity through the media, especially social media, has leaked out into the conduct of our everyday lives; although now we seem almost unaware of the difference between mediated and unmediated reality—between performance and life. In the article "Hail the Amateur, Loved by the Crowd," Douglas McLennan suggests the crowd is taking over positions once held by skilled professionals. Advocates of crowdsourcing believe the talents of the many can match or

14. See Schindler, "'Till We Have Facebook.'"
15. Peters, "Beauty's Veils," 9.
16. Peters, "Beauty's Veils," 12.
17. Peters, "Beauty's Veils," 9.

surpass the talent of the skilled few.[18] "People simultaneously feel [they are] members of an audience and that they are performers; they are at once watchers and being watched."[19] Since everyone is an actor *and* an audience member, "cultural consumers become cultural producers and vice versa."[20] The romantic science-fiction movie *Her* articulates the logical conclusion of this kind of association as a lonely and depressed man, Theodore Twombly, played by actor Joaquin Phoenix, develops a romantic connection with an artificially intelligent virtual assistant—man and machine in love.

The collapsing of distance between professional artist and audience results in the slow prioritizing of knowledge over capability, deeming both artist and audience incapable of recognizing the very ground from which they arose. Once the reality of the given and true self is sloughed off, we are left only to make ourselves in our own image. Such "freedom" of choice leads to anxiety of all types, as Kierkegaard argued.[21] The self-made man is the ironic illusion of today.

In addition to celebrity distractions and technological abstractions, we self-medicate with an inundation of easy-to-acquire drugs, whether pharmaceutical or recreational. All these "enhancements" are supposed to help us enjoy life, feel safe, and be comfortable with the abundance of gewgaws our culture provides. In fact, our attention gets drawn more and more not to our true selves but to the pursuit of our own pleasure. Forgetting that life is a gift from God and that we are not our own but are made in his image for his purpose, we choose to make ourselves into our own image. Certainly, these holy compounds of consumption have deeply affected our religious practices.[22] Our culture has turned to "enhancement technologies" not merely to cure disease or manage a disability, but to upgrade or enrich our capacities. Prozac, Viagra, cosmetic surgery, and sex-reassignment surgery all are available for "self-improvement." These "medical interventions that could be used to improve a person's abilities or appearance" are in many cases "used to form one's identity."[23] These modern products and services are supposed to enrich "self-invention,"

18. McLennan, "Hail the Amateur."
19. Abercrombie and Longhurst, *Audiences*, 75.
20. Abercrombie and Longhurst, *Audiences*, 75.
21. Kierkegaard, *Concept of Anxiety*.
22. Possamai, *Handbook*.
23. Elliot, "New Way."

much like Walker Percy's Ontological Lapsometer, described in his famous novel, *Love in the Ruins*. Percy's device served as a sort of stethoscope of the human soul, used to diagnose and treat existential problems and address anxiety, alienation, or loneliness.

Carl Elliott says that those who use these new "enhancements" believe the use of these products makes them "feel fulfilled . . . feel like themselves"; that is, in using these products, their lives gain meaning.[24] Elliott reminds us that this is the language of identity and authenticity, which at one time came from one's religious beliefs. Now, however, it comes from the person's association with various cultural products. These, Elliot claims, "are not just ways to look and feel better."[25]

Often our favorite medications coddle us and distract us, but in our unguarded moments, we cannot quite escape the thought that we are missing something important. Unfortunately, we juxtapose our lives to the carefully assembled lives found on social media or to the lives of the celebrities we adore, and in so doing our lives frequently appear inadequate, tawdry, and inauthentic by comparison.

Our need for entertainment seems insatiable and our longing to be known almost unquenchable. We live in a time when talent and hard work is not enough, and we feel the need to enhance our accomplishments through popularity. Our age yearns for attention. It is no longer enough to be a good athlete; now our sports figures must draw attention to themselves, both on and off the field, and celebrate after every ostensibly successful play. Guinness asserts, "everyone is in the business of relentless self-promotion—presenting themselves, explaining themselves, defining themselves, selling themselves, or sharing their inner thoughts and emotions as never before in human history."[26] Reality TV in its various incarnations can instantly make a contestant a star who draws on our heart strings and vies for our attention. Our global village is technologically saturated. It is no longer suitable just to *be*; now we must create an image or illusion that presents us as somebody or something. Our mediated world has become our reality. We are connected to everyone superficially and to no one profoundly. We now live in a world where seemingly everyone is talking, but no one is listening. Ours is a world where technological advances have provided a "democratized" platform for disseminating

24. Elliot, "New Way."
25. Elliot, "New Way."
26. Guinness, *Fool's Talk*, 15.

messages on a scale unprecedented in human history—but without talent or gift—only one's expressions carry some weight, no matter how good. We have mountains of knowledge at our fingertips, yet we cannot think deeply about our closest friends and family.

All of this may suggest that we "pay too much attention to the ways technology can fix problems and too little attention to the way technology works on our own sensibilities."[27] Often, we do not recognize the changes taking place within our own culture or within our own lives, as the changes happen so gradually and become so familiar to us that they come to be invisible to us. Elliott asserts that in using these products, "many people living in the late modern age don't expect to find the meaning of their lives by looking to God, truth, or any other external moral framework. And they don't think of their identities as fixed entities, determined by their place in a social hierarchy and ratified by God and nature."[28] Instead, they believe they can invent their own self, totally apart from God; or if God does exist, then he has given them the right to decide just who they are and how they are to live. God, it seems, matters little.

This new ontology of technology, that separates nature from cultural constructs and the gift of human existence from one's identity, has had an immense influence on our communication behavior and stories produced by our culture, especially those coming from today's most powerful media architects. In *Empire of Illusion: The End of Literacy and the Triumph of Spectacle,* Chris Hedges warns that "the problems of existence are domesticated and controlled," through entertainment, media and other forms of communication.[29] He states, "We measure our lives by those we admire on the screen or in the ring. We seek to be like them. We emulate their look and behavior. We escape the chaos of real life through fantasy. We see ourselves as stars of our own movies."[30] In *Life: The Movie: How Entertainment Conquered Reality,* Neal Gabler asserts that we are "all becoming performance artists in and audiences for a grand, ongoing show."[31] More than fifty years ago, Daniel J. Boorstin warned, "we risk being the first people in history to have been able to make their illusions

---

27. Elliot, "New Way."

28. Elliot, "New Way."

29. Hedges, *Empire of Illusion,* 16.

30. Hedges, *Empire of Illusion,* 16.

31. Gabler, *Life: The Movie,* 4.

so vivid, so persuasive, so 'realistic' that they can live in them."[32] This is far truer today than in his day.

Hedges, commenting on Boorstin's book, states, "in contemporary culture the fabricated, the inauthentic, and the theatrical have displaced the natural, the genuine, and the spontaneous, until reality itself has been converted into stagecraft. Americans, he [Boorstin] writes, increasingly live in a 'world where fantasy is more real than reality.'"[33] Furthermore, Boorstin himself asserts, "We are the most illusioned people on earth. Yet we dare not become disillusioned, because our illusions are the very house in which we live; they are our news, our heroes, our adventure, our forms of art, our very experience."[34]

According to Hedges, we live in a world dominated by illusions. Those who manipulate our lives "are the agents, publicists, marketing departments, promoters, script writers, television and movie producers, advertisers, video technicians, photographers, bodyguards, wardrobe consultants, fitness trainers, pollsters, public announcers, and television news personalities who create the vast stage for illusion. They are the puppet masters."[35] Peoples' careers and lives are controlled by these cultural facilitators and intermediaries. No one attains celebrity status, no cultural illusion becomes "reality," without this legion of social enablers whose singular purpose is to hold attention and satisfy the spectators. As Hedges suggests, "The techniques of theater . . . have leached into politics, religion, education, literature, news, commerce, welfare, and crime."[36]

It is not surprising that all these conceptual changes have caused actual shifts within both secular and sacred communities. Both groups have felt the influence of the sundering of nature and culture and that of the human from one's given identity. The changing and interchangeable roles that both leaders and followers—celebrities and fans; ministers and congregants—must now navigate has brought tremendous confusion and angst to nearly everyone living in these communities. In a society where almost everyone has lost their sense of place, identities are no longer understood as gift but as something one creates and recreates seemingly overnight. We all suffer from an incredible lightness of being. We

32. Boorstin, *Image*, 240.
33. Hedges, *Empire of Illusion*, 15.
34. Boorstin, *Image*, 240.
35. Hedges, *Empire of Illusion*, 15–16.
36. Hedges, *Empire of Illusion*, 15–16.

have no fixed or permanent natures by which to establish our place in the world. Although no time in history has escaped change, the enormity and speed of the changes now taking place bewilder us. And nowhere has this change been felt more deeply or been more pervasive than in our religious communities and institutions.

Technology and the Church

In our self-created world, religious figures no longer have the sway they once had, therefore, we create new icons or idols to take their place, religious or otherwise. Chris Hedges suggests that celebrity role models have taken the place of religious role models, except that "celebrities are portrayed as idealized forms of ourselves. It is we, in perverse irony, who are never fully actualized, never fully real in a celebrity culture."[37] If we no longer ascribe to requisite religious beliefs, we reinvent them while making them more easily acceptable and more suited to our wants—perhaps even while still calling ourselves Christian.

The communities and religious institutions we have grown to depend upon and trust over the past several decades no longer seem equipped to address the needs and desires of our current generation. Our culture, with its so-called "cathedrals of consumption"—everyday venues such as shopping malls, superstores, and airports—have for many become the new religious sites.[38] More troubling, however, is that so few people of faith seem to give much thought to this roiling condition. The church and our culture are experiencing unparalleled transformation—and yet many seem barely aware of the enormity of the total makeover now underway. Nor have we figured out how to faithfully communicate Christian faith under such perpetually mutable conditions.

Robert Inchausti tells us that in the modern world, the church continues to exist as social practice, "but that it now lacks imaginative and intellectual substance. Modern 'Christendom' had become a civil order, given over to various hypocrisies and biblical pieties, but lacking any authentic relationship to the Absolute."[39] As we saw earlier, Kierkegaard used the term "Christendom" to refer to the church apart from a true, passionate relationship with Christ. Christendom refers to the church as

37. Hedges, *Empire of Illusion*, 19–20.

38. See Cavanaugh, "Consumption."

39. Inchausti, *Subversive Orthodoxy*, 33.

primarily a social entity and institutional organization, rather than a living body of men and women engaging in a vibrant faith in participation with a loving God. Christendom was the lie facing the Christian communicator in Kierkegaard's day. And, as Craddock suggests, this is eerily like the condition facing anyone trying to communicate the Christian faith in our own time. Kierkegaard understood "as well as anyone the difficulty of breaking an illusion in order to communicate the Christian faith."[40]

The myth perpetuated by what Kierkegaard called "Christendom" is a stain absorbed into the fabric of our "Christian Culture." It has become so pervasive and entrenched in the church that one scarcely even notices its stubborn hold on our attention and how subtly it shapes our lives. Not only the church, but the larger culture also is party to this illusion. Our culture's images and stories, holidays, rituals, economy, and politics all conspire to support a comfortable form of Christendom void of the cost of faith.

Our society, while still claiming to be Christian, no longer believes as it once did or in the truths it once so vigorously professed. Many in our culture do not live in a way consistent with a clear biblical faith. Knowledge abounds, but true Christian faith is vanishing. Christianity may be experiencing what Stuart Ewen called "images without bottoms."[41] By this he meant that styles or illusions become about surface meanings, which assumes a value or image within a culture; yet underneath the surface bubbles an array of antagonistic beliefs and values. As Ewen states, "Style makes a statement, yet has no convictions," just as today one may appear to be a Christian—that is, have the style of a Christian—and yet fail to embrace true Christian virtues or to maintain a passionate relationship with Christ.[42]

The early church did not have social or political power. Christians were outsiders who lived on the margins of the larger, more "credible" culture. Early Christians were not a significant part of the larger and privileged social structure and, as such, were often ostracized or persecuted for their beliefs. Today, it is a different story. Many of those in power are part of the church, or at least claim to be. In the United States the church is made up of people from all economic and social classes, and most of its members have at least some degree of social capital—if not economic

40. Craddock, *Overhearing the Gospel*, 31.

41. Ewen, *All Consuming Images*.

42. Ewen, *All Consuming Images*, 16.

capital. Among its members are the politically, economically, and socially influential. To be a Christian is not only acceptable but expected in many parts of our society. In some circles people still believe that they will get ahead if they support and at least occasionally attend a church.

It may surprise some, but a great number of people in the United States today are still familiar with the fashion and habits of faith. Although they may not be quick to recite the stories of Scripture, they have a general idea of the major Christian ideas and rituals. As a society, we still wrap our major cultural rituals in the language of faith and frame many of our most important social, political, and cultural events in the symbols of faith. Images of faith are still scattered throughout many of our most popular social and entertainment events. Consider, for example, the number of prayers present in Hollywood films or the large number of athletes advancing their religious faith, both on and off the field. Most of us feel comfortable with this low-cost, theatrical kind of faith; but too often real faith has not found its way into the deeper regions of our existence, where the true choices of life are made and sustained.

Even among those who still call themselves Christian, we see in the embrace of the new ontology of technology a withering of genuine religious faith, a disparaging and sneering that often leaves just the husk of a weary religion, a social façade we still call Christianity. Furthermore, many people of faith believe that Christianity—like almost everything else in our culture—comes with "choices." We consumers are "free to choose" from among many options, grabbing exactly what we want and jettisoning what we do not want at the altar of our own ego.

Os Guinness captured the effect this new culture of technology and endless transmission of information has had on the church. He states,

> We are all apologists now, and we stand at the dawn of the grand age of human apologetics, or so some are saying because our wired world and our global era are a time when expressing, presenting, sharing, defending, and selling ourselves have become a staple of everyday life for countless millions of people around the world, both Christians and others. The age of the Internet, it is said, is the age of the self and the selfie. The world is full of people full of themselves. In such an age, "I post, therefore I am."[43]

---

43. Guinness, *Fool's Talk*, 15.

Without question, information is disseminated farther and more quickly today than ever before. The mistake often made, however, is the belief that dissemination of information equals communication. In the church, the same myth sounds something like this: truth is its own evangelist. The challenge facing the church is that communication is not easy and straightforward.[44] Coupled with this are the technological advancements that have shaped the communicative and communal structure of the church.

Certainly, religious beliefs and institutions have changed significantly since the Enlightenment. In fact, massive changes have occurred since the early 1940s. At the end of World War II, religious messages were passed on mainly through the family; but as Lippy and Tranby point out, the family itself has undergone considerable change in that time.[45] In this modern or postmodern age, both the institutions of family and religion have weakened. The church has changed in many ways, with larger congregations attracted to the new media, hoping that it might support their communication efforts. This coupled with the growth of megachurches or multi-site churches changed the face of the church in the United States.

Foremost among those changes is a transformation in the forms of media used by both the church and its members. Today we have electronic sound equipment in the sanctuary, media displays in the church, power point sermons, video enhancements, text-to-the-pastor-as-he-preaches, weekly tweets from the church, and other technological innovations. For many churches, all these forms of communication have changed the nature of religious worship and the shape of the church body.

Now add to these extraordinary changes the profound diffusion of religious information and the commercialization of religious media products: apps, podcasts, tweets, video and audio streaming, social media, email, websites, blogs, audiobooks, e-books, printed books, television, film, radio, and so forth. It is easy to recognize that religion is being diffused in more and in profoundly different ways than ever before. Finally, relatively new technology—such as the Internet, social media, and various other instruments of the information age—has greatly expanded the opportunities for people to become aware of and learn about religion.[46]

44. Schultze, *Habits*.
45. Lippy and Tranby, *Religion in Contemporary America*.
46. Lippy and Tranby, *Religion in Contemporary America*.

Much of this reorganization of churches and their use of technology has resulted in the church trying to catch up to other organizations in learning how best to use the latest technology. Furthermore, the spectacular growth of nondenominational churches, the relatively small number of young people now attending church, and the large number of people who switch churches, make it obvious that tremendous change is taking place in religious behaviors and belief. In part, these massive changes are due to the role of media and technology in our culture.[47]

Daniel A. Stout reminds us that many rituals of the church "revolve around media of some kind, such as altars, statuary, or sacred writings."[48] With the phenomenal growth of the Internet and the "do-it-yourself" nondenominational churches, media once associated with sacred rituals of the past are changing or being repurposed to "better fit" new styles of worship. While change is inevitable, we need to remain vigilant in how we embrace those changes. We need to think through their place in the church as well as in our homes.

The dichotomy between religious and secular media has grown much less useful and applicable today. On the one hand, we find that "media rituals bring us a mythic quality, preserving moral beliefs through narratives."[49] Television programs, films, and even video games viewed in our homes or in community theaters present mythic heroes and villains that often confront us with moral dilemmas. The church can use these "secular" characters to challenge us and to help us rethink our morals and faith. Thus, family or personal "media rituals provide opportunities for moral engagement."[50] Modern religious practices, educational materials, and worship services need to take account of both our face to face and our mediated means of communication. On the other hand, Quentin Schultz warns that in using information technologies such as the Internet, social media, and so forth, we are sharpening our informational practices while dulling the habits of our hearts. In so doing, we privilege technique over relationship and promote raucous individualism while devaluing moral order and civilized behavior. The very speed and ephemeral quality of the Internet often precludes careful thought, even as it undervalues past events. These qualities do not serve the church in a suitable manner,

47. See Lippy and Tranby, *Religion in Contemporary America*, 98–110; and Webber, *Younger Evangelicals*, 61–70.

48. Stout, *Media and Religion*, 10.

49. Stout, *Media and Religion*, 10.

50. Stout, *Media and Religion*, 10.

which in part requires that we remember past events as well as present relationships. Schultz states that "our overreliance on informational ways of knowing deflates the meaning of intrinsically moral language."[51]

Schultz also cautions us to be wary of those who believe that the latest technological innovations will give us greater control over our destinies as men and women of God. The very technologies that seem to give us greater control over our lives are, in fact, "harder and harder to control."[52] We need to take full account of what it means to be human. Craig Detweiler offers a balanced approach to technology in the church recognizing the need for the church to be content with significant cultural changes brought by the new information technology and to be a force of fresh creativity, while at the same time the church should "identify the prevailing assumptions that undergird a technocracy and that compete for our loyalty."[53] He further warns that "technology's rise as an alternative faith system (the power of progress, the need for speed, the efficacy of efficiency) may reveal plenty about our own blind spots and shortcomings."[54]

As much as we might like to believe otherwise, there is no such thing as incontestable and unhindered human progress. If we consider the quality of our high-tech lives, we may well find "that we are growing increasingly hurried and anxious."[55] Schultz suggests that if we want "to regain our moral footing in contemporary life, we must dig deeper than information and knowledge."[56] In fact, we must look to the traditions that carry virtue and truth from one generation to the next. "We will have to invest as much time and energy in the habits of our hearts as we do in our high-tech practices."[57]

In one form or another, information technology is here to stay. Nevertheless, for people of faith our embrace of the new technology comes as a mixed blessing. Furthermore, the church is still struggling to find a way to appropriately use these new technologies. We need, of course, to consider our choices carefully.

51. Schultze, *Habits*, 56.
52. Schultze, *Habits*, 208.
53. Detweiler, *IGods*, 203.
54. Detweiler, *IGods*, 202.
55. Schultze, *Habits*, 209.
56. Schultze, *Habits*, 209.
57. Schultze, *Habits*, 209.

An Indirect Approach to the Art of Communication

The incarnation teaches us a great deal about the nature of our identity as people of God and how to communicate truth. Furthermore, it tells us something about the nature of our ways of seeing, knowing, and being. The incarnation is God's hidden message to us. If we pay careful attention to the meaning and mode of the incarnation, it will heighten our understanding of God and how he uses the flesh as a bearer and window in order to experience his presence and grace. Just as Christ is a stumbling block and a scandal to our modern, objective ways of seeing and knowing, so too art and indirect communication are often disturbing and adversarial yet crucial to our life of faith. All serious art has a transcendent quality that conflicts with the temporality of our lives. If individuals take the time to see and if they give careful attention to the stories and artistic artifacts presented to their senses, they may discover deep and beautiful truths not grasped by other means of communication. Thus, a work of art can, like indirect communication, fly "under the radar of people's critical filters and point them to God."[58]

God made us embodied beings and not simple cognitive entities. When he gives us life, he intends that we should live in a loving relationship with him and with one another. As Kierkegaard suggests, indirect communication is primarily about being, or existence, and not simply about knowing. Indirect communication and art does not necessarily present any new information but provokes inwardness, or realization, and self-reflection about such issues as human identity, social relationships, and God's divine purpose. For the person of faith, the indirect communication approach to communicating truth frequently presents enticing opportunities for individual reflection on the Divine life and one's participation in it. This approach to communication does not privilege didactic methods or rational arguments; rather it offers imaginative, thoughtful, even upsetting stories, as well as a variety of other narratives and provocations.

According to Kierkegaard, the incarnation—embodying God in the person of Jesus Christ who lived at a specific time and space—is clearly a form of indirect communication; one does not expect God to be a man. For him, indirect communication may be used to initiate self-reflection. In so doing an individual may be seduced into considering a larger view of human nature than he has previously possessed. Thus, a person is

58. Cron, *Chasing Francis*, 110.

empowered to imagine himself entering a new relationship with God and following his example. The Lord himself is not necessarily encountered through abstract ideas or technological enchantments but by passionately embracing the gift of life made available through Christ. It is the personal engagement with Christ and obedience to him that is determinative and not simply human knowledge. All life is essentially a gift from God and "the entire world is shot through with the Spirit of God, who moves in and through the things of this world."[59] God's grace cannot be separated from nature itself—and nature is his gift to us. He came in the flesh not merely to teach but to shed his blood, and it is his blood stream that becomes our own blood stream as we follow him.

Technology often disconnects us from nature by privileging material things and directing our attention away from the spiritual or eternal. Technology and its influence foster attitudes and beliefs in the material and temporal. Consequently, modernity and technology have a propensity to favor abstract and disembodied knowledge, which can disconnect us from nature. If we are serious about helping people live a meaningful life, we need to employ communication strategies that draw attention away from our constant devotion to technological innovations that devour time and attention and keep men and women from acknowledging the primacy of the Spirit in their lives. To be clear, technology is useful, but its use within the church community involves a certain degree of understanding about its limitations and deficiencies. As citizens of two worlds, the supernatural and the natural, we need to work vigilantly to keep our minds centered on the spiritual and inward life as well as the material world.

It is through our natural gifts as artists and storytellers that we can renew this world's interest in the inward life. Our work as artists, storytellers, and communicators takes on a variety of forms, all of which may potentially deepen and develop the inward life. One way to understand art and indirect communication is to see it as a mirror enabling people to examine their own lives, to bring them back to reality. Furthermore, redirecting our communication efforts to include the use of strategies of indirect communication—with their emphasis on the arts—may help revive interest in the church, in the Christian faith, and in Christ himself. Art can help move us from the superficial or surface knowledge of things to consider the depth of reality and a fuller understanding of the natural

59. Bruner, *Subversive Gospel*, 7.

world replete with vestiges of God, those things that are beyond man's ability to prove empirically yet are just as real.

We were made to create not just consume. Andy Crouch challenges people of faith to consider their priorities when it comes to their use of technology and the place they give to technology in their lives. Crouch differentiates between technology as tool and technology as device. A tool is used to create something, and it requires work and skills in order to use this tool to make something. A device, he suggests, takes no work or skill at all and is used by simply pressing a button—it is almost as if embodiment is unnecessary to use a device. If we are made to create, we need to be intentional in our use of technology in order to help us fulfill our natural and God-given purpose to create. Crouch's argument is that technology is not neutral. It comes with values and we must be intentional in our use of technology and vigilant in our efforts to not let technology control our mind-set.

We have created a society that for the most part is fixed on the illusions of modernity. Nevertheless, as humans we still have spiritual longings; we cannot retreat so far into our abstract spheres of existence that we can completely escape our natural inclinations for the supernatural. Vestiges of the sacred still prevail even in our secular age. James K. A. Smith remarks upon the classical Christian aesthetic which suggests that people are first and foremost made to love or desire (what he calls *homo liturgical*). From this, two ideas emerge. First, whatever else we are, we are affective, desiring, and liturgical animals. Second, "Whatever the degree of man's religious or secular beliefs, man, remains an essentially 'worshiping being.'"[60]

Perhaps Smith is right, and we *are* made to love and worship. In that case, if we do not worship God, we will find something else to worship, even if we do not believe in God and we do not identify what we are doing as "worship." It seems that the one who refuses to believe in God still participates in some sort of *formative* ritual. Smith suggests that a religious nature pertains to many so-called "secular" institutions that command our allegiance. He does not mean that they are necessarily concerned with God or spiritual things, but rather that a person's view of the good life is shaped by these institutions or individuals that have their own set of beliefs, practices, and artifacts. The point is that

---

60. Smith, *Desiring the Kingdom*, 90.

we are naturally religious, and as such, our cultures and technological advancements should be an extension of this natural propensity and not antagonistic to it.

We have seen that religious communities and celebrity culture share many characteristics; there seems to be a strong convergence between these two significant social structures.[61] Celebrities like Elvis, Michael Jackson, Lady Gaga, Oprah, etc. are honored and often serve as a role model for people to emulate. They tell us what to wear, how to live, and what to buy. In short, they show us what the good life is like. Smith argues that this very liturgy constitutes a pedagogy that teaches us to be a certain kind of person.

Craddock feels that preaching and other forms of communication by both clergy and laity has become too much of an intellectual exercise and formulaic experience. In short, and following the modernist penchant for reason and information, communicating faith today is too often direct, cerebral, and informative rather than conveying a passionate authenticity and narrative power which is so essential to our decision-making behavior and to the influence we have on others. If artists with Christian concerns cease to be prophetic, if they cease to awaken the hearer, and if their art and messages become overly predictable and stereotypical, they risk becoming irrelevant to the culture and to the church—no matter how well intentioned the artist is or how sentimental the story. To put it candidly, a work of art or a message must grab the hearers' or viewers' attention in order to communicate in any understandable or useful way.

If this is so, how can we effectively create culture and affect change? Twenty years ago, Michael Warren suggested that images and stories are central to shaping the life of the church and to influencing the identity of individual Christians. His concern was "not so much the images we see as those by which we see, that is, images serving as cultural lenses through which we perceive reality."[62] The stories we live and tell shape our shared life in many ways.

Most Christians believe the key stories in the Bible can be taken at face value, which in this modern age is surprising. In a fascinating study the Barna Group conducted a nationwide survey of about six stories of the Bible. The study found that two out of three adults accepted these

61. Fraser and Brown, "Media, Celebrities, and Social Influence."

62. Warren, *Seeing Through the Media*, 31.

stories as literal truth.[63] And while this may seem encouraging, it is important to note that the Barna Group noticed a significant disconnect between faith and practice.[64]

The basic presuppositions and values that have historically undergirded much of western art and culture are unmistakably Christian. Furthermore, those to whom we tell stories are, as a rule, individuals who often hear something of the gospel stories, possibly attend worship, and "generally find themselves at home in the language, rituals, and teachings of the Christian faith."[65] Although they are, for the most part, aware of the gospel stories and Christian theology, they do not necessarily apply the stories or the theology to their lives. Although biblical literacy is quickly fading from the United States, Europe, and the western countries in general, remnants of the biblical stories and rituals can still be found in many of our cultures' symbols, holidays, practices, and literature.

Warren suggests that "part of the problem of the church of our time is that of offering a compelling religious imagination of life in the face of other agencies offering attractive alternative imaginations."[66] In other words, considering the sheer number of images and stories presented to us through the media and other cultural conduits, the church has not provided images nearly as compelling or as readily available as these other institutions. "Yet," as Warren suggests, "the deeper problem is not that we look at images ceaselessly. It is that we look at reality through images."[67]

It is simply not true that knowledge of the truth is sufficient for one to live a Christian life. Knowledge of truth may be necessary, but

---

63. Barna Group, "Most Americans."

64. Barna Group, "Most Americans," 2. The Barna Group observed, "while the level of literal acceptance of these Bible stories is nothing short of astonishing given our cultural context, the widespread embrace of these accounts raises questions about the unmistakable gap between belief and behavior. On the one hand we have tens of millions of people who view these narratives as reflections of the reality, the authority, and the involvement of God in our lives. On the other hand, a majority of these same people harbor a stubborn indifference toward God and His desire to have intimacy with them. In fact, a minority of the people who believe these stories to be true consistently apply the principles imbedded in these stories within their own lives. It seems that millions of Americans believe the Bible content to be true but are not willing to translate those stories into action. Sadly, for many people, the Bible has become a respected but impersonal religious history lesson that stays removed from their life."

65. Craddock, Overhearing the Gospel, 17.

66. Warren, Seeing Through the Media, 10.

67. Warren, Seeing Through the Media, 152.

knowledge alone (even knowledge of the truth) is not enough to cause one to live according to the truth he or she knows. Craddock is surely right in identifying the gap between knowledge and behavior. Just because information is available does not mean it will be appropriated. In fact, "how" the truth is told is part of the message. How the truth is told cannot be divorced from the "content" of the truth. Truth does not exist apart from Christ, and for the Christian, truth is not merely an objective fact to be examined like all other facts. Rather, it is a personal encounter with God, resulting in personal knowledge.

Oets Kolk Bouwsma asserts, "one man's illusion gives support to another's," so much so that much of the church is deceived into the illusion that knowing or knowledge is all that is needed in order to live a godly life.[68] Bouwsma suggests that many "people are living out their lives under an illusion that prevents them from ever hearing the words of life."[69] "The illusion that one is a Christian arises out of a misunderstanding of the language," states Bouwsma.[70] In his view, the illusions come in part through "misconceptions concerning the workings of our language, misconceptions which may operate either consciously or unconsciously."[71] Here language is limited to the communication of thoughts. Regarding our understanding of Scripture and language, Bouwsma states,

> Men have treated the Scriptures as God's way of giving us certain information which God no doubt did his best to communicate but which he obviously had to do as though he were talking to children, which he was. To others he communicated in clearer, and one might say, scientific, *wissenschaft*, language. Here there is an illusion. And how does it arise? Through a misconception of the role of language, and, I guess of God. Here we meet the same idea, "Language is used in only one way." This is a prejudice, a recent one. The idea, however, is also present in, that god who is almost highest would be concerned only about what is highest and what is highest is that man should know. So, the original prejudice is fortified by the idea that knowledge is best.[72]

68. Bouwsma, "Notes on Kierkegaard's," 76.

69. Bouwsma, "Notes on Kierkegaard's," 76.

70. Bouwsma, "Notes on Kierkegaard's," 79.

71. Bouwsma, "Notes on Kierkegaard's," 84.

72. Bouwsma, "Notes on Kierkegaard's," 84.

In this understanding, the church focuses on what we know and not how we ought to live. This limited understanding of language places greater emphasis on our cognitive abilities than on our existence or how we live. This error underestimates the distance between knowing and doing. Placing the emphasis on knowledge fails not only to understand the role of language but ignores the importance of embodiment. We are emotional as well as thinking beings. Often it is not that we do not know the truth, but that we choose to ignore it. We do not act out of ignorance but out of selfishness, pride, or willful disobedience.

I know, for example, that I need to exercise every day; but often I do not do what I know I should do. In the same way, I know that to forgive someone who has offended me is the right thing to do, but again and again I fail to follow through with what I know to be the right thing to do. To place the emphasis on *knowing* at the expense of *doing* undervalues the truth we are called to live.

Bouwsma explains, "'What is Christianity?' is the wrong question. It evokes such answers as that it is a view, which leads to the idea that a Christian is someone who holds that view . . . A Christian is someone who looks" a specific way or holds a specific opinion rather than acts in a certain way.[73] Kierkegaard explains, "The basic flaw of this age is this teaching which leaves a person's inwardness completely secure."[74] It is here that the church can turn to indirect communication to help it establish a new way of seeing and a new way of living.

In summary, we have covered several elements that should be considered when thinking about our communication behavior. We have noted how the technological age and indirect communication take different approaches to communication. These differences can be found below in Table 1.

73. Bouwsma, "Notes on Kierkegaard's," 85.

74. Kierkegaard, *Søren Kierkegaard's Journals and Papers*, 1:265.

Table 1

A Comparison Between Technological and Indirect Communication

Each method focuses on or privileges the following:

Technological	Indirect
1. Outward appearance	Inward being
2. What one knows (knowledge)	How one lives (capability)
3. Facts	Knowing within a thick context (narrative)
4. Reason	Faith and reason
5. Nature as a human construct	Nature as gift
6. Identity as a human construct	Identity as gift
7. Clear and reasoned truth	Hidden or veiled truth
8. Objective knowledge	Subjective knowledge

Let us examine these two methods found in the table above more fully. First, as we have previously stated, indirect communication privileges capability over information; although some information is necessary it is not enough for navigating the changes that life presents. As such, indirect communication focuses on inwardness, seeing a person as more than just a material being and instead as both a material and spiritual being. The focus is on a person as a created and an embodied being whose nature is given. The focus is not on information but on a realization (capability), the realization of one's unique given nature.

Second, the difference between technological ways of knowing and the indirect communication approaches to knowing is that the technological is focused on what is known, while the indirect is focused on how one lives (this is an embodied knowledge, not simply a cognitive awareness). Artists or indirect communicators with Christian concerns are not simply transferring information as is often the case of those communicating from a technological sensibility, but they are creating and constructing provocations or stories that cause the reader, viewer, or hearer to wonder, imagine, and ultimately live life in a new way. The artist in this situation intends to help the reader or viewer to reflect on their own life in light of the story told or the dilemma presented to one's senses. Thus, the listener or viewer is also a creative being and must create meaning out of the story or provocation. The intent of the artist using an indirect communication approach is not to simply inform but to create a space for the reader or viewer to create new knowledge that is to be lived.

A third contrast between the technological and indirect deals with the part played by information. In a technological age information comes with little context, but the artist or indirect communicator requires that the viewer or listener be aware of the culture and context of the communicative act. Indeed, the meaning of the art, story, or provocation must be reflected upon so that it can be understood and acted upon. Thus, the context and culture are essential to indirect forms of communication.

Fourth, reason plays a role in both types of communication. On the one hand, reason is the major influence when communicating from a technological position; on the other hand, the indirect communication approach must give place to revelation, mystery, and faith—as well as reason—when creating art or when communicating indirectly. Obviously, we are in an age of reason, but the stories or communication that most often moves people to act are found in more passionate and emotional forms of communication such as art, story, or provocation.

In the comparison of the technological approach to the indirect approach to knowing, a fifth element, dealing with the different understandings of nature, is present. Nature, from the technological perspective, is often seen as something to be controlled, dominated, or determined, while the indirect approach, which sees nature as a gift from God, views one as needing to work with nature in order to express the truth and the presence of God as he determines.

Sixth, artists and communicators drawing primarily from the technological sensibility of this age see a person's identity as self-made, something they create themselves. They see individuals as having the right to determine the purpose and meaning of their own existence. Artists with Christian concerns see life as a gift from God and this extends to their identity. Humankind was made in God's image and we, in following him, must recognize that his will has authority over our lives and our bodies.

The seventh comparison understands that the technological age privileges clear and reasoned arguments as their primary style of communication—this is certainly true with Christians who are influenced by the technological age. However, like the incarnation, the indirect communication approach hides or veils meaning in order to reveal the actual nature and depth of the truth. We will discuss this more fully in the following chapter.

Finally, the technological age favors objective knowledge while indirect communication emphasizes the subjective approach. The subjective approach embraces truth in a passionate way. In fact, how can one not be passionate about the gift of life or in living in union with Christ?

Conclusion

This chapter considered the illusions that hinder and seduce our culture and the church. Illusions distract us from living as we should. In a culture obsessed with outward appearances and new technologies that promise visions of happiness they cannot possibly fulfill, these images and technologies, while often useful, may distract us from finding our real nature and purpose in life.

For us to better understand the place and value of art in communicating faith within the church and within the larger culture, we must first examine the role of revelation and reason within our culture and the church, after which we will examine the use of imagination in communicating truth. Clearly our understanding of revelation and reason is profoundly influenced by the modernist assumptions existent within our world today, just as modernism has diminished or dismissed the use of imagination as a legitimate way of knowing. In the next chapter we turn to examine the proper role of reason, revelation, and imagination in helping us understand and address the illusions that so entice us and how they may help us in communicating truth.

3

Reason, Revelation, and Imagination

We are well supplied with interesting writers, but Owen Barfield is not content to be merely interesting. His ambition is to set us free. Free from what? From the prison we have made for ourselves by our ways of knowing, our limited and false habits of thought, and our "common sense."

—SAUL BELLOW, EDITORIAL REVIEW
OF *HISTORY, GUILT, AND HABIT*

Introduction

THE PREMISE OF THIS work suggests that many within the church have good intentions but nevertheless have been swayed by the cultural shift towards objectivity and the concomitant direct approach to communication as being all determining. Christians have chosen to meet their rationalist detractors on their own turf by forging arguments that appeal primarily to reason, science, and history. As Robert E. Webber suggests, "Modern evangelicalism has identified with the Cartesian emphasis on reason and empirical method. These culturally defined evangelicals have used the modern paradigm of thought to develop a particular kind of evangelicalism encased in a culture that elevates reason and the attainment of propositional truth."[1] In this chapter we suggest how an indirect approach that draws upon the imagination might mitigate against this rationalistic tendency.

The Church's Embrace of Reason and Proposition

Kyle A. Roberts declares, "the age of reason had forgotten the necessity of divine revelation."[2] Those involved in the intellectual arena who are most influenced by modernity have marginalized the role of divine revelation and replaced it with objective reason and proposition. Roberts argues that during this period, many theologians and church leaders started to "emphasize the objectivity of theology, the power of propositional doctrine, and the authority of the Bible" to gain credibility, in response to those within the church or those outside communities of faith who questioned religious authority.[3] "In effect, they attempted to secure the Bible as an apologetic support for Christian faith and turned it into a sourcebook for the compilation of objective doctrines."[4] Myron Bradley Penner goes so far as to assert that for some modern apologists, "both knowing and showing . . . are ways of describing how Christian belief is rational (in the modern sense)."[5]

Faith, for Penner, is not "rationally justifying all our beliefs before we accept them," because human reason is not necessarily the grounds or source of Christian truth.[6] While "philosophical modernism and the Enlightenment is marked by an attempt to free human thought from its dependence on external sources—such as traditions [the church], assumptions [Scripture], or other authorities [Christ]—for the grounds of belief," human reason, unaided by revelation, will *never* uncover or discover the truth of the divine revelation of Christ.[7] Neither research projects nor any other effort by man's reasoning can replace revelation given by God. To assume so is to create an egregious categorical error, if nothing else, as in the Christian tradition. Unlike our present paradigm,

---

1. Webber, *Younger Evangelicals*, 14.
2. Roberts, *Emerging Prophet*, 15.
3. Roberts, *Emerging Prophet*, 16.
4. Roberts, *Emerging Prophet*, 16.
5. Penner, *End of Apologetics*, 31.
6. Penner, *End of Apologetics*, 73.
7. Penner, *End of Apologetics*, 29.

revelation is understood not as opposed to reason, but rather the perfection of reason.

Roberts finds that "the most significant existential and religious truths (e.g., the issue of eternal salvation) lie outside the access of mere rationality and scientific method."[8] This, however, is not to say there is no evidence or reason for God's existence, but that neither science nor reason can in themselves prove or disprove the existence of God. Reason and scientific knowledge may be helpful but are not complete themselves. As Gregory E. Ganssle states, "Science cannot encompass the being of God directly because God is not an empirical object. Any connection between scientific investigation and God will have to be indirect."[9] Still, that one cannot prove through reason and science alone the reality of God does not mean that reason has no influence on "how religious people acquire or maintain their beliefs about God."[10] What concerns us here is the *kind* of reason we have in mind (indifferent, objective reasoning or passionate, subjective reasoning) as well as what counts as evidence. We need to understand the role of divine revelation as well as reason in our understanding of truth.

Revelation is the supernatural disclosure and encounter of the divine. Thus, in the very place where human rationality is lacking, divine revelation gathers up reason into her courts. As Christ's divine nature perfects, it does not do away with his human nature; so too does supernatural grace perfect nature. Hence revelation does not do away with natural reason, but perfects it. As Roberts says, "The apex of revelation is Christ—the paradoxical God-man—who has acted in history and still meets us in the present; revelation is the disclosure in time and history of the person of Jesus Christ to individuals."[11] Further, "While Christ's historical existence is crucial, what matters most (and what makes salvation possible) is a person's existential encounter with Christ."[12] Jesus is not simply a fact of history, although he did exist in time; he is also a present reality who gives life to humanity in the here and now.

---

8. Roberts, *Emerging Prophet*, 16.

9. Ganssle, *Reasonable God*, 25.

10. Ganssle, *Reasonable God*, 31.

11. Roberts, *Emerging Prophet*, 19.

12. Roberts, *Emerging Prophet*, 19.

As one encounters Christ, "one is presented with a choice to have faith or believe (and so accept the gift of forgiveness) or to 'be offended.'"[13] "Knowledge of the person of Christ is too often equated, in conservative Christianity, with conceptual belief in doctrines (or a set of doctrines) about Christ or, in liberal Christianity, with knowledge about the historical (and moral) Jesus. Both can result in an intellectualizing and objectivizing of Christian faith."[14]

To its detriment, Christianity has been affected by the autonomous rationality of modernity, so much so that at times it has reduced or dismissed beauty and the imaginative, non-rational elements of faith. Following this logic, facts and value are now sundered; facts are taken to be true and the arts or imagination are seen as subjective and less valid ways of knowing. What is suggested here is that both reason (properly defined) and imagination are required to show us the wonder and the depths of truth. As Holly Ordway suggests, "Faith can never be reduced to a single argument, or a single image, because it is a living thing."[15] Michael Ward suggests, "in Lewis's view, reason could only operate if it was first supplied with materials to reason about, and it was imagination's task to supply those materials. Therefore, apologetics was necessarily and foundationally imaginative."[16]

In following the enlightened penchant for rationality, the church has left the arts behind. However, as we examine the work and words of Jesus in ch. 6, we will notice that he tendered a great many of his teachings in the form of stories, parables, and other forms of indirect communication. It would seem obvious, then, that telling stories should be a primary form of communication for the church. In fact, both Old and New Testaments include a variety of literary forms—letters, genealogies, historical narratives, laws, parables, stories, poetry, songs, prophecy, proverbs, questions, riddles, wisdom literature, and so on.

Furthermore, one can find drama, images, and a variety of art forms used by people of faith throughout the centuries. Why, then, should this kind of imaginative communication not be used to communicate truth today? Unfortunately, more recent expressions of art and story created by

13. Roberts, *Emerging Prophet*, 20.

14. Roberts, *Emerging Prophet*, 21.

15. Ordway, *Apologetics*, 177.

16. Ward, "Good Serves the Better," 61.

artists with Christian concerns have, to a large extent, been stilted and limited.

Stories, paintings, films, theater, and websites—all the so-called "fine arts" and "popular arts"—communicate meaning and value to a society. Too often, however, the church's attempt to communicate faith has undervalued these expressions of truth. Over sixty years ago, Amos N. Wilder stated, "The church is learning that it cannot ignore such [artistic] expressions of the society in which it lives."[17] As we look back over this period, we might have to gauge Wilder's assessment as overly optimistic, as the church has not really taken his warning to heart but instead has generally demonstrated that it can indeed ignore the arts.

Wilder more accurately states, "the re-education of the emotions is no doubt more difficult than that of . . . reason."[18] As embodied beings, we are creatures of emotion *and* reason, and the modernist penchant for overemphasizing reason over revelation or imagination has come at a serious cost to the church. "Christians," states Wilder, "need to be awakened from their dogmatic slumbers; and this is still widely the case, for dogmatism destroys sensibility as the letter kills."[19] Malcolm Guite argues that we have "a church culture that starved the imagination, was suspicious of mystery, but was unaware that in deifying a logical and syllogistic method in theology, it was in fact creating its own idol."[20]

One example of the neglect of the arts by artists with Christian concerns can be found in literary fiction. In an article called "Has Fiction Lost its Faith," Paul Elie asks, "how do Christian beliefs figure into literary fiction today?" Elie concludes that they lie somewhere "between a dead language and a hangover." He suggests, "if any part of culture can be said to be post-Christian, it is literature." Elie maintains that present-day novelists with Christian concerns are "thin on the ground."[21] Whether from story, sound, or visual art, "a society lives by its images, but its life is often stagnant and moribund where the living images fail."[22] In privileging reason, the church has diminished the role of the arts and most certainly the imagination in presenting the gospel. In a postmodern culture that is

---

17. Wilder, "Church's New Concern."
18. Wilder, "Church's New Concern."
19. Wilder, "Church's New Concern."
20. Guite, *Faith, Hope and Poetry*, 11.
21. Elie, "Has Fiction Lost Its Faith?"
22. Wilder, "Church's New Concern."

story- and image-driven, this diminishment of imaginative resources and strategies of communication is incredibly disturbing.

Awakening the Imagination

"At the heart of modernism," writes Roberts, "lies a rejection of a positive role for the religious imagination."[23] Garrett Green also comments on the influence of modernity in our culture, explaining that for many people the difficulty modernity presents is its denial of the constructive meaning or use of imagination in religious thought.[24] Roberts explains, "the modernist project included the deconstruction of the religious imagination in order to arrive at pure, 'objective' truth."[25] He argues that instead of setting aside the imagination, we should "reclaim a vital place for the imagination in the Christian life."[26] Alison Milbank reminds us that "all Christians are called, as part of the priesthood of believers, to recognize and affirm form and meaning wherever it may be found and in their own lives to use their imagination to call the world into participation."[27]

Imagination is defined or understood in several ways. One constructive understanding of the term suggests that we see it as a "family of related terms like *fantasy, fanciful, image, imaginary.*"[28] The *fantastic* refers to "what is commonly known as fantasy and includes the various fanciful or imaginary activities of the human spirit—for example, in art, in play, or in daydreaming. What is common to these uses of imagination is that they are deliberately fanciful and knowledge departures from the real world, whether in science or in everyday experience."[29]

Green contends that imagination is generally defined as "an image or picture representing some object that is not directly accessible to the imagining subject."[30] The key thing is that the imagined object is not itself present, or at least not present in such a way that is accessible to the senses. Green asserts the "imagination re-presents what is absent; it

---

23. Roberts, *Emerging Prophet*, 65.

24. Green, *Imagining God.*

25. Roberts, *Emerging Prophet*, 65.

26. Roberts, *Emerging Prophet*, 64.

27. Milbank, "Apologetics and the Imagination," 42.

28. Green, *Imagining God*, 62.

29. Green, *Imagining God*, 63.

30. Green, *Imagining God*, 62.

makes present through images what is inaccessible to direct experience."[31] Green's definition is useful, but he himself warns us that his emphasis on representation should not be taken too literally.

The imagination, then, is a vessel of possibility and hope. As such, an imaginative image may work to destabilize previous ways of knowing, whether cognitive or affective, by providing a new way of understanding or providing a new possibility aimed primarily at the affective level of knowing. In this way, the imagination acts as a means of indirect communication. In a sense, the imagination presents us with an opportunity that asks, "What if?" M. Mamie Ferreira asserts, "it is only imagination that can enlarge the horizon of possibilities through presenting the ideal self as an 'image' of what is not yet actualized."[32] The ability to change or transition to another view presupposes that we can recognize the value of another situation for it to appeal to us. Paradoxically, this possibility "toward which we strive must be concrete—imagination presents us with possibilities and concretizes them."[33]

This understanding and use of imagination and imaginative resources (stories, questions, songs, images, etc.) can be a valuable and creative way of presenting truth not immediately present to the senses, the very kind of truth found in communicating transcendent reality. Imagination plays a key role in enabling the emotion, intellect, and will to see things differently and may allow a person to avoid the social, intellectual, emotional, and spiritual snares placed in his or her spiritual path.

The Purpose and Influence of the Imagination

Robert L. Short argues that unless faith has relevance to all of life, it is not really faith at all. He goes on to suggest, "a faith that can find no significant meaning in art and laughter, in the tragic as well as in the hilariously comic, is a faith that will find no joy in life itself."[34] Through a work of imagination, artists or storytellers, whether they know it or not, are trying to affect the whole person and not just his or her mind. Roberts declares, "to become contemporary with Christ is to have one's imagination awakened to the fullest degree, but without losing oneself

31. Green, *Imagining God*, 62.

32. Ferreira, *Kierkegaard*, 26.

33. Ferreira, *Kierkegaard*, 27.

34. Short, *Gospel According to Peanuts*, 27–28.

to the 'fantastical'; to put it bluntly, one gains one's 'soul' without losing one's mind?"[35]

"If the Church fails to use the divine imagination given to it, to see the unseen, to see 'sermons in stones and good in everything,' to see 'that all that passes to corruption is a parable,' as Karl Barth has put it, it will constantly be embarrassed by a world capable of far more imagination than the Church itself."[36] Modern ways of knowing privilege reason and often devalue imaginative insight by treating imagination as an illusion. But much to the contrary, it may be that the imagination provides us with the opportunity to see the profound, transcendent truth of our existence in a way that reason alone cannot attain. Furthermore, the in-direct approach of the imagination may be useful in helping to dispel the aforementioned illusions. It is not until we steal past these illusions—falsehoods that so often charm us into a false existence—that we can honestly face God, one another, and ourselves. A person cannot come to God if he or she is not aware of one's self or, as Lewis asserts in *Till We Have Faces*, the veil is lifted.

James K. A. Smith argues for the importance of the imagination in helping us to know ourselves and our worldview. He writes, "We feel our way around the world more than we think our way through it. Our worldview is more a matter of the imagination than the intellect, and the imagination runs off the fuel of images that are channeled by the senses."[37] He then argues that images or pictures of the good life may in-fluence our behavior and thought. These aesthetic articulations, he sug-gests, are "found in images, stories, and films (as well as advertisements, commercials, and sitcoms). Such pictures appeal to our adaptive uncon-scious because they traffic in the stuff of embodiment and affectivity. Stories seep into us—and stay there and hunt us—more than a report on the facts."[38] Similarly, Taylor uses the term "social imaginary" to indicate ways in which people "imagine their social existence."[39] By "imaginary" he means "the way ordinary people 'imagine' their social surroundings,

35. Roberts, *Emerging Prophet*, 69.

36. Short, *Gospel According to Peanuts*, 28.

37. Smith, *Desiring the Kingdom*, 57.

38. Smith, *Desiring the Kingdom*, 58.

39. Taylor, *Secular Age*, 171.

and this is often not expressed in theoretical terms, it is carried in images, stories, legends, etc."[40]

Clearly, the imagination is a powerful force in constructing and reconstructing how we experience the world and our place in it. Despite the modernist penchant for rationalism and objectivity, it is imagination and images that really influence our vision of the social and spiritual life. It may well be that the images we feed upon and the rituals in which we engage present to our imagination concrete ways of ordering our lives that, in fact, truly inform our existence and move our hearts toward God.

Out of Illusion and Into Reality

Perhaps imitating Christ is a useful place to begin to understand the work of the imagination in bringing about faithful Christian existence. Christian faith *requires* the imagination in order to move us from potential to actual. As Brian Gregor explains, "Although possibility is not a sufficient condition for actuality, it is a necessary condition."[41]

So contrary to the imagination as an escape from reality into the fanciful, the imagination has the capacity to draw us out of our illusions and into reality—into decision, obedience, and engagement. It does so by tempting and luring a person to think differently. In a way it "deceives," and as Frances Maughan-Brown states, "It can deceive into the truth."[42] In fact, "the deceptive work of the imagination may be exactly what [i]s needed."[43]

For example, imagination can extend the range of possibilities through depiction; that is, through an "image" of what has not yet been actualized. As Ferreira suggests, "The ability to make a free transition to another perspective assumes that we can sufficiently appreciate another context for it to attract us before we actually accept its categories or values. This paradoxical possibility toward which we strive must be concrete—imagination presents us with possibilities and concretizes them."[44]

Today one might ask how a young man from a good home can conspire to leave the United States with the intent to join ISIS or some other

---

40. Taylor, *Secular Age*, 171–72.

41. Gregor, "Thinking Through Kierkegaard's," 450.

42. Brown, *Discipleship and Imagination*, 201.

43. Brown, *Discipleship and Imagination*, 201.

44. Ferreira, *Kierkegaard*, 27.

terrorist group and fight against people he knows nothing or very little about. What motivates him to behave in this way? Smith suggests that such a young man is "not merely *convinced*. He does not enlist for an idea, though he certainly signs up for an ideal—but the ideal to which he is devoted (the nation, freedom, a god) is not something he *knows*; it is something he *loves*. It is not a matter of having acquired some new bit of knowledge that tips the scale and makes it seem 'rational' to become a soldier."[45] Smith explains that perhaps the young man "has been conscripted into a mythology: he identifies himself within a story that has seeped into his bones at levels not even he is aware of. His being 'persuaded,' is not so much a conclusion he has reached as a sensibility he has imbibed."[46] It is an allure of the imagination rather than simply the work of the intellect and reason. This anecdote reminds us that the imagination, as with all human faculties, can be used for good or ill.

Imagination and the Self

Ferreira argues that one's imagination is essential to becoming a self. She maintains that "with no appreciation of possibility, one can have no conception of what the self can become."[47] It should be evident that for those of us who are both artists and Christians, we are to love our neighbor— and our neighbor is the one we address in our art, whether through writing, film, social media, literature, or other artistic endeavors. To love our neighbor, we need to see our neighbors for who they really are and who they can become in Christ. Thus, loving is a kind of seeing; just as the writer or artist must be able to see the "other" in order to create relevant art, including works of fiction. Ferreira states, "If our duty is to love the people we see, then we have to see them."[48] The one who loves only the person he imagines does not love the person he sees, but only "his own idea" of the person. Often "we are prone to love the self-generated image of the other person, but this is not loving the actual other person at all."[49]

Flannery O'Connor warns that the imaginative and creative process of the writer with Christian concerns sometimes hinders honesty and

45. Smith, *Imagining the Kingdom*, 16.
46. Smith, *Imagining the Kingdom*, 16.
47. Ferreira, "Surrender and Paradox," 155.
48. Ferreira, *Kierkegaard*, 134.
49. Ferreira, *Kierkegaard*, 134.

one's ability to see with integrity. That is, the writer or artist will inevitably see only what he or she believes, instead of seeing what is. While this is completely possible, it happens at the cost of truth and good fiction. O'Connor states, "The sorry religious novel comes about when the writer supposes that because of his belief, he is somehow dispensed from the obligation to penetrate concrete reality."[50] It is simply not true that writers or artists "can close our own eyes and that the eyes of the Church will do the seeing. They will not. We forget that what is to us an extension of sight is to the rest of the world a peculiar and arrogant blindness, and that no one today is prepared to recognize the truth of what we show unless our purely individual vision is in full operation."[51]

Thus, imagining is an inspired and creative work that helps finite humans comprehend all of reality, including the infinite God. Amos Wilder asserts that "the dialogue of the Gospels is directed to the heart rather than to some faculty in us of higher knowledge."[52] Ward echoes this sentiment by suggesting "that all narratives structure emotions, desires and hopes that impact upon what we believe and how we come to value certain acts."[53] Furthermore, Ward argues, "this structuring continually opens up a transcendent horizon."[54] God reveals himself to us through the reality of the imagination.

The Integral Imagination

Just as humans are symbol-using and symbol-creating beings, so are they imaginative creatures. Further, the work of the imagination is a human and therefore a social activity. As Green suggests, "All our language— whether biblical or secular; philosophical, poetic, or theological—is social and cultural."[55] Humans are thus imaginative and storytelling creatures at their core.

As we have seen, part of the challenge in understanding the role of imagination in revealing truth is that modern humans, even those within the church, have tried to understand religion in a purely rational

---

50. O'Connor, *Mystery and Manners*, 163.

51. O'Connor, *Mystery and Manner*, 180.

52. Wilder, *Early Christian Rhetoric*, 49.

53. Ward, "Narrative and Ethics," 439.

54. Ward, "Narrative and Ethics," 438.

55. Green, *Imagining God*, 2.

way. This explains why so many people wrongly believe that "religion as imagination is religion inadequately expressed. As imagination it is indistinguishable from illusion . . ."[56] In other words, imagination is seen as an inferior form of communicating and knowing truth, and therefore needs to be confirmed by philosophy, science, or journalistic evidence. For many moderns, as we have seen, reason has usurped a dominant or privileged role over imagination. The contention between reason and imagination is ubiquitous in our present era. O'Connor comments, "As grace and nature have been separated, so imagination and reason have been separated, and this always means an end to art."[57]

We seem to forget that none of our conscious contact with the world is free from the imagination's point of view. Green believes that imagination plays an integral role in our existence. He states,

> Imagination, properly understood as the name of the basic human ability—one of the things that people do in the course of living in, acting on, and thinking about the world—identifies the specific point where, according to Christian belief and experience, the Word of God becomes effective in human lives. More formally: imagination is the anthropological point of contact for divine revelation. It is not the "foundation," the "ground," the "pre-understanding," or the "ontological basis" for revelation; it is simply the place where it happens—better, the way in which it happens.[58]

Green adds, "Our language is full of implicit acknowledgments that imagination is related to truth and discovery."[59] Conceived in this way, imagination is present from the most basic acts of knowing to the encounter with revelation. As with reason, it must also be acknowledged that the imagination can just as easily be false and illusionary.

C. S. Lewis, in his article "An Experiment in Criticism," wrote that "literary [or imaginative] experience heals the wound, without undermining the privilege, of individuality."[60] For example, Lewis states, "in reading great literature I become a thousand men and remain myself. Like the night sky in the Greek poem, I see with a myriad eye, but still it

---

56. Green, *Imagining God*, 15.

57. O'Connor, *Mystery and Manners*, 83.

58. Green, *Imagining God*, 40.

59. Green, *Imagining God*, 64.

60. Lewis, *Experiment in Criticism*, 161.

is I who see. Here, as in worship, in love, in moral action, and in knowing, I transcend myself; and am never more myself than when I do."[61]

With regard to the operation or aesthetic of the imagination, Green indicates that in general, "there are two chief modes of physical nonpresence, *temporal* and *spatial*."[62] The objects of the imagination are either temporally absent (e.g., memory) or are not directly accessible to the person because they are spatially distant (out of the observer's view, like microcosmic reality). These objects are not present and, therefore, not directly observed; however, they could be directly apprehended if they were in some way made present to our senses.

Green mentions a third category of "real objects—including religiously significant ones—whose inaccessibility is not due simply to physical nonpresence."[63] This kind of inaccessibility is referred to as *logical* use of the imagination and, as Green asserts, this category includes such examples as souls, Satan, and gods.[64] It is assumed by some that these objects are real and that they cannot be made directly available to our senses—they are not subject to direct observation. Reality, in this case, is not something verifiable to the physical senses, so empirical verification is not possible. The imagination is therefore our best means of knowing or understanding certain kinds of truth. Furthermore, our imagination can affect a new way of seeing ourselves and the world around us. For example, the sacraments are objectively "real" in the sense that they are physically present to our senses in the Eucharist, yet for a Christian believer their spiritual meaning is a sign of something beyond what is materially manifest. The imagination apprehends that which transcends the sensible object, that which gives it meaning. A picture of a friend is not merely the material of paper and ink, but an image that points to or signifies one's friend. Senses alone do not signify, nor do the senses indicate why it is that we should be appalled should someone tear up the picture of our friend. Such is the transcendent meaning given to the imagination through the symbol.

What seems apparent is that both reason and imagination are useful in communicating truth and fostering faith. Therefore, it is an error to suggest that we can impart truth only by limiting ourselves to one method

---

61. Lewis, *Experiment in Criticism*, 161.

62. Green, *Imagining God*, 64.

63. Green, *Imagining God*, 64.

64. Green, *Imagining God*, 65.

of communication, either by the exclusive use of reason or imagination, and thereby diminishing the effectiveness of our knowing.

I do not mean to suggest that telling the truth will be easy or without cost. The truth is never simple. It is demanding. We must remain vigilant to continually stay open to God to direct and correct us in our efforts. Truth telling is a creative and challenging activity! Both the imagination and reason have been influenced by God *and* by the fall. Both our mind and our body (originally from God) have been wounded due to the lingering influence of the fall on us and on God's world. Therefore, both reason and imagination can be distorted and can bear a false truth—of embracing a lie and perpetuating an illusion. Just as we live in an imperfect world, so the methods at our disposal by which we communicate the redemptive messages are also imperfect. Fortunately, we are not left alone in this task. We have resources to provide a faithful witness, if not a perfect one. We may not have complete or perfect knowledge, but we have sufficient knowledge for our communicative task, and we have the guidance of the Holy Spirit.

So how ought we to use our imagination in our communicative endeavors? Janine Langan identifies four qualities for framing what he calls a proper use of the imagination.[65] She contends the Christian imagination is 1) anti-gnostic (i.e., humans are not divine souls trapped in a material world created by an imperfect god/demiurge, frequently identified with some perversion of the Abrahamic God); 2) typological (i.e., classifies/characterizes reality); 3) sacramental (i.e., material objects or things set apart for/by God); and 4) eschatological in scope, because it carries an end-time orientated (*telos*) view of the world.

Langan suggests several ideas for educating the imagination. First, the imagination is not a flight from physical reality. It does not see the world as a prison from which the soul must escape; rather, it is the stage of humanity's interaction with God. The imagination gratefully anchors itself in the gift of reality, seeking to decipher God's message—not become drunk on it.

Second, the imagination is a storytelling imagination that recognizes the creation-death-resurrection pattern in every era and in each life. Every life event is interpreted as an essential moment in the movement of time toward eternity. Imagination does not thrive in the disconnected moment, carnal thrill, or instant gratification of society; rather, it works

65. Langan, "Christian Imagination."

to insert the lived moments of our lives into the whole of human history under God. Flannery O'Connor often practiced a similar technique in her writing:

> The writer whose point of view is catholic in the widest sense of the term reads nature the same way medieval commentators read Scripture. They found three levels of meaning in the literal level of the sacred text—the allegorical, in which one thing stands for another; the moral, which has to do with what should be done; and the anagogical, which has to do with the Divine life and our participation in it, the level of Grace.[66]

Third, a Judeo-Christian use of the imagination is priestly and sacramental. The idea here is that nothing in the world is silent. Everything speaks, everything is a sign, and it is our priestly role to educate the imagination in this way. As Gerard Manley Hopkins once wrote, "Christ plays in ten thousand places, lovely in limbs and lovely in eyes not his."[67]

Finally, making use of imagination means grasping the paradox that lies at the heart of creation. We must learn to find fulfillment in another, new, and incommensurable world. According to Ryken, such an imagination is at home everywhere and nowhere.[68] Eschatological "logic" is both seductive and explosive, leaving common sense behind. It yearns for grace's necessary earthquakes and is haunted by Christ's sentence: "I have come to bring fire on earth, and how I wish it were already kindled!" (Luke 12:49). In other words, the Christian imagination is born of conversion. As Flannery O'Connor put it in a letter to a friend, "I don't know if anybody can be converted without seeing themselves in a kind of blasting annihilating light, a blast that will last a lifetime."[69] O'Connor's work demonstrates that a contemporary eschatological imagination sounds terrible, passionate, and comic all at once.

It seems that imagination plays an important role in the perception of transcendent truth. As Green states, "It is not the case that the physical event (called 'seeing') must first occur, after which a mental event (called 'interpretation') takes place. Rather, there is only one event, and it cannot be adequately analyzed into dichotomous 'physical' and 'mental' stages."[70]

---

66. O'Connor, *Mystery and Manners*, 72.

67. Quoted in Langan, "Christian Imagination," 70.

68. Ryken, *How to Read the Bible*.

69. O'Connor, *Habit of Being*, 427.

70. Green, *Imagining God*, 72.

To see is to interpret, for it is not your eyes that see but people as embodied beings who see. This experience of simultaneously seeing and interpreting is an important imaginative function, for it can tell us what the
world is like in its truest and deepest sense. O'Connor explains the role
of the fiction writer in creating truthful art when she states that the artist
is "looking for one image that will connect or combine or embody two
points; one is a point in the concrete, and the other is a point not visible
to the naked eye, but believed in by him firmly, just as real to him, really,
as the one that everybody sees."[71] Green reflects on this ability by stating,
"If imagination is the human ability to perceive and represent likenesses
(the paradigmatic facility), religions employ that ability in the service of
cosmic orientation, rendering the world accessible to the imagination of
their adherents in such a way that its ultimate nature, value, and destiny
are made manifest."[72]

Unfortunately, many do not embrace this view of imagination, as
both those within religious communities and those outside of them reject a spiritual view of the world. Green addresses this issue and argues
that the dramatic progress in modern science had lured leading western
intellectuals into a positivism that simply identifies truth with scientific
knowledge and rejects all other truth claims—including those of religion—as illusory.

> [Even thinkers] sympathetic to religion, defensive and apologet-
> ic, implicitly accept versions of this dichotomy while insisting
> that religion possessed its own kind of truth. As the positivistic
> view of science that produced and supported this dualism of
> "real" versus "imaginary" has been replaced by a more adequate
> and complex philosophy of science, the appeal of the dualism in
> its various guises has weakened accordingly.[73]

For Green, the imagination is not the opposite of reality but rather
"how manifold forms of both reality and illusion are mediated to us.
Religions characteristically employ this power of imagination in order
to make accessible the ultimate 'shape,' the organizing pattern, of reality
itself, thereby illumining the meaning and value of human life."[74] God created humans in his own image (Gen 1:26–27), and that image is essential

---

71. O'Connor, *Mystery and Manners*, 42.

72. Green, *Imagining God*, 79–80.

73. Green, *Imagining God*, 83.

74. Green, *Imagining God*, 83.

to human nature and vital to the connection between a person and God; yet it takes the imagination to grasp this level of reality.

The Imagination and the Image of God

Green asserts that the prevailing historical stance of "the ancient and medieval church identifies the *imago* with the reason or rational soul."[75] The *imago Dei* was often associated with the mind and intellectual powers. Wilder suggests that people are created in the image of God in that they, like God, speak, name, and communicate.[76]

Green's emphasis on the *imago Dei* moves us in a slightly different direction. He suggests that a more useful understanding of the *imago Dei* is viewing it relationally rather than rationally—it is a relationship between God and humanity. "Interpreting the *imago* relationally avoids the long-disputed issue of its content. Whatever its 'nature' may be, the text is telling us, the *imago* represents the original relationship between divine and human: man is like God in some basic and definitive way. There is a 'family resemblance' between God and human beings."[77]

In the creation narrative of Genesis 2, the writer illustrates graphically a Creator modeling the human figure out of the mud and empowering his creation with life. Here we can easily imagine "man as receiving his form—his actual shape—from God, while his material substance is taken from the earth."[78]

As Green points out, the temptation for man was to be "like God" (Gen 3:5), but the irony in the serpent's message was that "the very creature who was just formed 'in the image of God' is now lured into destruction by the promise of becoming 'like God'! The story thus captures at the outset the essentially irrational and self-destructive nature of sin."[79] Though man lost his original standing in the fall, it can now be restored by God's grace. "The *imago*, on the other hand, because it was understood to be the *sine qua non* of human nature as such, could not be lost through

---

75. Green, *Imagining God*, 86.

76. Wilder, *Early Christian Rhetoric*.

77. Green, *Imagining God*, 86–87.

78. Green, *Imagining God*, 86.

79. Green, *Imagining God*, 88.

sin—though it was 'wounded.'"[80] It is this "image," this likeness of God, that sin disrupts or mars.

One consequence of sin is man's loss of his ability, or diminished ability, to imagine what God is like, "since there is no longer a positive analogy between himself and God."[81] "Human possibilities are limited by human imagination. Sinners are unfree, and at the mercy of the *servum arbitrium*, because (quite literally) they cannot imagine what it would be like to live in conformity to the will of God."[82] Madeleine L'Engle says essentially the same thing when she states, "One of the great sorrows which came to human beings when Adam and Eve left the Garden was the loss of memory, memory of all that God's children are meant to be."[83]

Human beings, then, are limited in their ability to imagine. Dorothy Sayers advances the Russian religious philosopher Nikolai Alexandrovich Berdyaev's view of imagination: "God created the world by imagination."[84] For the creature, however, this ability is limited by space and time as well as by the truth that humans are created and therefore, not God. The consequence of the fall extends to persons' imaginative capacities. Imaginative gifts must be guarded and scrutinized as with any human activity, as sin may take what was intended for good and twist or distort it to diminish or damage the good and God's purposes.

Green asserts, "the religious imagination does not 'image' God (i.e., construct picture of God) but imagines God (i.e., thinks of God according to a paradigm). The paradigmatic imagination is not mimetic but analogical; it shows us not who God is but what God is like. Practices of idolatry, reduced to an epigram, confuse the 'is' with the 'as.'"[85] "The key lies in the use or function: a picture reproduces; an image exemplifies."[86] "The picture shows us something; and image seeks to show us what that something really is."[87]

Green uses the metaphor of impressing or imprinting for describing God's work in renewing our imagination: "The human likeness to God,

---

80. Green, *Imagining God*, 88.

81. Green, *Imagining God*, 89.

82. Green, *Imagining God*, 89.

83. L'Engle, *Walking on Water*, 10.

84. Quoted in Sayers, *Mind of the Maker*, 29.

85. Green, *Imagining God*, 93.

86. Green, *Imagining God*, 93.

87. Green, *Imagining God*, 94.

worn away by sin, has been newly 'minted' in the humanity of Christ. Through faith in him, according to the New Testament, the *imago Dei*, the *eikon* of God in Christ, is impressed upon the imagination of believers, conforming them to God (cf. Rom. 12:2)."[88] The *imago Dei* is the impression that God made upon us. As we can now see, the act of revelation is an imaginative activity.

Images affect our vision of the good life and become entrenched in our attitudes and dispositions. Smith suggests that these images influence our "adaptive unconscious" by being pictured in concrete, alluring ways that attract us at a noncognitive level:

> By "pictures" of the good life I mean aesthetic articulations of human flourishing as found in images, stories, and films (as well as advertisements, commercials, and sitcoms). Such pictures appeal to our adaptive unconscious because they traffic in the stuff of embodiment of affectivity. Stories seep into us—and stay there and haunt us—more than a report on the facts. A film like *Crash* gets hold of our hearts and minds and moves us in ways that textbooks on racism never could. This is because it is a medium that traffics in affective images, and such affective articulations are received by us on a wavelength, as it were, that is closer to the core of our being. Such compelling visions, over time, seep into and shape our desire and then fuel dispositions toward them.[89]

We are thus made to imagine and to communicate our imaginative lives with one another. Indeed, the metaphorical quality of language which renders our communication so rich and vital is meant to foster the stories we build through words and images (the visual arts).

An Alternative Strategy Which Uses and Speaks to the Imagination

In the introduction to *Imaginative Apologetics: Theology, Philosophy and the Catholic Tradition*, Andrew Davison argues that literature and the visual arts can play an important role in apologetics. He states, "these might be works that illustrate the Christian faith, or argue for it, or they might be works further from the Christian fold, and here especially novels, that

---

88. Green, *Imagining God*, 105.

89. Smith, *Desiring the Kingdom*, 58.

disclose something important about the cultural context within which we present the gospel."[90] Apologetics, he contends, concerns faith's appeal to reason; but he suggests that we need "to take a step back and consider the nature of reason."[91] For him and for several other scholars, "Christian apologetics requires a Christian understanding of reason . . . The Christian faith does not simply, or even mainly, propose a few additional facts about the world. Rather, belief in the Christian God invites a new way to understand everything."[92]

C. S. Lewis understood that reasoned apologetics has its limits, and in his later years he focused increasingly on writing novels and stories designed to edify and appeal to the imagination. Perhaps a more useful approach today to fostering true discipleship and new or renewed belief is through what several scholars have called "imaginative apologetics."[93]

Art, music, and story address primarily imaginative ways of knowing and so can renew our vision by transforming "the ordinary, to reveal in 'utter visibility' that things are 'alive with what's invisible.'"[94] This, of course, is why so many ghost stories and supernatural tales have become so popular. This generation, as every generation, has a desire to worship *something*, and if it chooses not to worship the God of Scripture, it will look for another deity to worship.

As Malcolm Guite states, "The wisdom of the ancient world, both Judeo-Christian and Classical, was embodied in myth, story, and song"[95]—so why not use these imaginative arts today? Certainly, we have artists with Christian concerns working in this area, laboring hard to create images that speak to the imaginative part of man; but there are far too few of them. One might argue that some situations and times almost demand imaginative apologetics over other types of apologetics. Without question, theology and reason have their place within the contemporary church; but as we have argued before, the reasoned, logical, and propositional approach is overused today and not always the most helpful approach in presenting truth to this generation. Guite explains:

90. Davison, *Imaginative Apologetics*, xxv.

91. Davison, *Imaginative Apologetics*, xxv.

92. Davison, *Imaginative Apologetics*, xxv.

93. Davison, *Imaginative Apologetics*.

94. Guite, *Faith, Hope and Poetry*, 2.

95. Guite, *Faith, Hope and Poetry*, 3.

In some quarters, particularly in classical Calvinism, the imagination is seen as somehow more degraded and overthrown than the reason. Theology is therefore pursued and presented in highly syllogistic and logical form, as pared of imagery as possible. The problem with this approach is that it privileges one faculty over against another, as though reason were itself somehow less "fallen" than imagination. This goes together with a misreading of Augustine's doctrine of illumination, which assumes that the Logos, as the 'light which lightens everyone who comes into the world,' is to be identified with the light of pure reason rather than a direct intellectual apprehension or grasp of the truth the involves imagination as well. The consequence of this has been a church culture that starved the imagination, was suspicious of mystery, but was unaware that, in deifying a logical and syllogistic method of theology, it was in fact creating its own idol. This kind of theology refuses the full consequence and meaning of the incarnation, of believing that the word was made flesh.[96]

Regarding faith and the poetic imagination, Guite argues, "truth-bearing language does not have to be purged of ambiguity to be truthful."[97]

Perhaps, with the late John Hughes, it is time to acknowledge the limits of scientific reason and admit that "the rationalist attempt to establish consensus through an appeal to universal reason has been deconstructed and unmasked as in fact just one way of looking at the world (Western, scientific, male, dominating, and so on)."[98] Hughes writes, the "modern approach to apologetics [which] is complicit with an ahistorical, uncritical, and anti-Christian account of reason" has been soundly discredited; but that just because faith may not be able to provide "proof" in the restricted sense of the term, it does not mean that it is any less rational.[99]

Davison argues that human beings "discern meaning."[100] Furthermore, he asserts that to discern meaning, a person must start with some basic assumptions, axioms, or convictions that all people, both non-religious and religious, possess. Faith may be a good word for these basic convictions, because as Davison states, "They are so basic that we cannot

96. Guite, *Faith, Hope and Poetry*, 11.
97. Guite, *Faith, Hope and Poetry*, 5.
98. Hughes, "Proofs and Arguments," 7.
99. Hughes, "Proofs and Arguments," 3.
100. Davison, *Imaginative Apologetics*, 13.

argue our way to them from something more fundamental. This does not mean that faith is irrational, just that it is where reason begins rather than where it ends."[101] For Davison, "To present the Christian faith is to present a new way to understand life and the world in which we live. Put another way, Christian faith is a new way to understand what is real."[102] He explains, "Christian reason thinks about truth in close proximity to goodness and beauty. This sets Christian reason in sharp contrast, for instance, with the desiccated vision of reason typically upheld in British philosophy departments. There we find reason reduced to logic, severed from beauty and goodness as guides to truth."[103] "No longer can any perspective claim to be neutral, supposing that all the others are biased . . . there are always preconceptions."[104]

Of course, different understandings of reason exist. For our purposes, two deserve attention. The first understands reason as "abstract and ahistorical," which is in strong contrast to the second view that understands reason as involving "history and story, imagination and desire."[105] The fault line between these two views may well be seen be examining where one stands with regard to reason and imagination.

In joining imagination not only to reason but also to beauty and goodness, we can see the world in a different way. As Davison states, "People, things and events are seen as accepted as a gift; they are recognized as possessing a depth that gestures to God."[106] Milbank calls the apologist to uncover a nearly liturgical potency in literature and the visual arts that can arouse a new sensitivity to the wonder and strangeness of the world. What is needed is "a religious imagination to give us access to the divine and to the reality of otherness of the world beyond the self."[107]

Milbank further articulates the church's calling about communicating faith. She states, "Our primary task as the Church is surely to awaken people to their own creative capacity, for in so doing we shall quite naturally awaken also the religious sense. Part of our problem in presenting the Faith is that our world deadens desire, and many people do not know

---

101. Davison, *Imaginative Apologetics*, 14.

102. Davison, *Imaginative Apologetics*, 15.

103. Davison, *Imaginative Apologetics*, 16.

104. Davison, *Imaginative Apologetics*, 17.

105. Davison, *Imaginative Apologetics*, 16.

106. Davison, *Imaginative Apologetics*, 31.

107. Milbank, "Apologetics and the Imagination," 32.

that they are missing anything."[108] We ought to learn how to encourage individuals to embrace existence as a gift from God passionately and subjectively.

Much of this concern over revelation and reason came to the fore with what Robert Webber calls the "new evangelicals" and what Kyle Roberts calls the "postmodern people of God."[109] Today, many young believers have grown dissatisfied with the rational apologetic of the modernists. In fact, Webber points out that the twenty-first century has seen a cultural shift away from the use of objective reason and the young no longer default to reason and science to prove or disprove a fact. This situation does not mean they embrace irrationalism, but as Webber argues, "it points rather to the postmoderns' conclusion that we deal with 'interpreted facts.' Thus, in the postmodern world, both believers and nonbelievers are people of faith."[110] They either have faith in the story of the Bible or they have faith in the story of science, reason, or some other story of their own making. The point here is that in the postmodern world, story is seen as crucial, and telling our story well is important to the hearing of the gospel.

We are all embodied. A person can never step out and transcendentally survey the whole from an objective or eternal point of view. Roberts argues that this does not mean "knowledge about faith is impossible or that we never come to know anything related to religious faith with personal conviction. Rather, it means—for one thing—that knowledge is never complete because existence is never complete. It also means that objectively speaking, despite the passion of one's religious convictions, one could always be 'mistaken.'"[111] This is a humble but perhaps no less effective approach than the constant attempts to use cold, objective facts to provide arguments that may not move people. Are we really convinced that old (or new!) arguments focused on the mind are the best way to present truth? Is not humanity more than a thinking animal?

Webber may help us here.[112] He suggests that the early Christian church—or what he calls "Classic Christians"—interpreted the faith more as a story. If he is right, then we can use narrative or story to communicate

108. Milbank, "Apologetics and the Imagination," 35.

109. Webber, *Younger Evangelicals*; Roberts, *Emerging Prophet*.

110. Webber, *Younger Evangelicals*.

111. Roberts, *Emerging Prophet*, 40.

112. Webber, *Ancient-Future Faith*.

Christian faith. This is not to say that reason plays no part in our story-telling, but it does mean we take seriously not only the content of the story, but *how* meaning is constructed. It may be that the church, in its effort to make the Christian faith respectable to the modern mind, has neglected the art of storymaking and storytelling. Furthermore, we may have spent so much time and energy trying to create a "reasonable faith" and develop scientifically informed arguments for communicating our faith that we have forgotten how to see the book we so love for what it really is—a collection of stories, poetry, proverbs, narrative, apocalyptic and other forms of *literature*—rather than a historical and scientific text. All good stories have a narrative logic. They do not merely illustrate. The structure of storymaking and storytelling can awaken the heart and offer new meaning to a listener or viewer. The story carries its own logic and meaning, and if it is changed to any other form (for example, a proposi-tion), the meaning changes and may lose its power.

Our best words, and those of Scripture, should lead one to the Living Word. Even good words believed are never enough to convey the whole truth as we seek to bring people to Christ. We try to make others aware of the importance of life and then take them to Christ, where we must leave them. He must do his work in their life. We are only the midwives; he alone is the life-giver. Our words are not complete in themselves, but serve as pointers to something greater, living, and eternal: Christ himself.

Augustine taught us that we love what we see as beautiful, and love aspires upward toward eternal beauty.[113] Lewis teaches us that beauty awakens a sense of wonder, not at the object, but at the transcendent power to which the beauty or story directs our attention. Cron suggests that "we approach every painting, novel, film, symphony, or ballet un-consciously hoping that it will move us one step further on the journey toward answering the question, 'Why I am here?'" He suggests that "we turned to the arts and aesthetics to satisfy our thirst for the Absolute. But if we want to find our true meaning in life, our search cannot end there. Art or beauty is not the destination; it is a signpost pointing toward our desired destination."[114]

Most of us feel dazzled by the temporal and surface appearance or structure of beautiful things. But too often we fail to look deeply enough or long enough to see the real beauty in an object or person, especially

113. Augustine, *Confessions.*

114. Cron, *Chasing Francis*, 106.

those that do not conform to our culturally-constructed ideas of beauty. Few of us are patient enough to take the time to meditate on a work of art or to read the great novels. If art does not quickly "speak" to us, we abandon it and move on to something else. But knowing, understanding, or seeing the beauty in something can take time and a great deal of effort. Good art—worthwhile art—demands something of us. It requires our undivided attention. But it also offers something magnificent in return. Great art and other works of beauty have the power to reveal a hidden glory. The church has historically called these "icons," but today it does not need to be limited to icons.

For the Christian, communication is a subversive force, a thing not to be feared but instead highly respected; by it we come to an awareness of selfhood and begin to look critically at the social situation in which we find ourselves.[115] To participate in the transformation of our society, we must be free to imagine both within the religious community, and just as importantly, outside the community. This may be done best as we emulate our Maker by imagining and creating images that live and come alive outside the church. Perhaps this is done best in stories that address the heart and the mind to enable humans to see anew the world and their place in it. However, this action makes us capable of participating with the Maker in His making.

Conclusion

Artists or professionals, through the imagination, see the world in new ways and express themselves through word or image to communicate something out of their own lived experience. The purpose is to gain the attention of the audience, listener or viewer, in order to help them discover a new world within the story or art. This is what O'Connor suggests when she said, "All novelists are fundamentally seekers and describers of the real, but the realism of each novelist will depend on this view of the ultimate reaches of reality."[116]

115. Freire, *Pedagogy of the Oppressed.*
116. O'Connor, *Mystery and Manners*, 40.

Section Two

Strategies and Use
of Indirect Communication

Chapters 4–6

4

Strategies of Indirect Storytelling

Every religious writer, or speaker, or teacher who absents himself from danger and is not present where it is, and where the Evil has its stronghold, is a deceiver, and that will eventually become apparent.

—SØREN KIERKEGAARD, *THE POINT OF VIEW OF MY WORK AS AN AUTHOR*

Introduction

A FEW YEARS AGO, I had lunch with a friend. As we sat and chatted, we both knew that he had been profoundly changed by the sudden death of his thirty-year-old son just a few days before. We talked about recent events, but what he really wanted to know was why his son was killed in an avalanche while skiing. The one thing I felt sure of was that I could not give him a satisfying answer.

All our lives can unalterably change in an instant by forces beyond our control, be it a hurricane, tsunami, an avalanche, a visit to the doctor, the sudden end of a relationship, or an abrupt change in the stock market. At such times we are thrown from the throne of our comfortable and seemingly invincible ways of understanding and are forced to flounder and grapple with the cold winds of a bitter reality. In these moments, we are changed. We are forced to reconstruct our lives to accommodate the new and the unspeakable.

My friend, now changed, had become a stranger to me. We attempted to make sense of this incomprehensible reality, and yet we did not want to make sense of it, or even think about it for an instant. But of course, we could not help ourselves; so there we sat, my friend and I, strangers.

Sometimes words fail. They prove inadequate for the task, just as times come when we have no answers. Moments arrive when no quotation, no argument, no scriptural passage, and no prayer can bring instant help or healing. And so, we must sit in naked silence. It may be that during these times of seeming abandonment, when we are struck dumb and mute, we become aware of the other sitting at the table with us. Our silence awakens us to another way of knowing. Eliot writes,

> Silence! and preserve respectful distance.
> For I perceive approaching
> The Rock. Who will perhaps answer our doublings.
> The Rock. The Watcher. The Stranger.
> He who has seen what has happened
> And who sees what is to happen.
> The Witness. The Critic. The Stranger.
> The God-shaken, in whom is the truth inborn.[1]

At times, we all become strangers, both to others and to ourselves. Perhaps we need to sit more and listen to the stranger, to the Rock who can speak without words into the human soul. He will answer our questions without resorting to our usual notions of reason or common understanding. He sends the Spirit to rebuild our lives without our knowing how or even when it happens. It seems to me that this is what Bonhoeffer means when he suggests that spiritual love proves itself such that "everything it says and does commends Christ."[2] Spiritual love does not strive to sway "others by all too personal, direct influence, by impure interference in the life of another. It will not take pleasure in pious, human fervor and excitement. It will rather meet the other person with the clear Word of God and be ready to leave him alone with this word for a long time, willing to release him again in order that Christ may deal with him."[3]

---

1. Eliot, "Choruses From 'The Rock'-1934," 148.

2. Bonhoeffer, Life Together, 26.

3. Bonhoeffer, Life Together, 26.

This, too, is what Kierkegaard meant when he said, "I certainly do not deny that I still recognize an imperative of understanding and that through it one can work upon men, but *it must be taken up into my life . . .* and that is what I now recognize as the most important thing."[4]

In a strange way, this is how Flannery O'Connor's stories work on us as they confront us again and again with the grotesque (death, sickness, pain, and struggle), the strange, the unusual, and the comic. But I see from the exaggerated characters in her stories that they speak about something real that matters to me, just like the challenge facing my friend in trying to make sense out of the unthinkable. O'Connor, through her stories, forces us to look at ultimate, transcendent concerns. She does so in characters like the Misfit, a serial killer; Shepherd, a young recreational director who has lost his wife and who as a single parent is neglecting his own son; or Parker, a newly married farmhand covered from head to foot in a disarray of tattoos, which mirror his undisciplined life, so that the only place left for the image of God to appear is on his back. These figures invite us to reconsider our place in life in light of the grace offered to each of them in unusual, even extreme ways. In them grace is hidden and offered to us. In this way literature, and especially stories, can facilitate or at least initiate self-change.

This chapter explains the purpose and use of indirect communication. Particularly we will examine several key strategies of indirect communication: hidden grace, overhearing, taking away, without authority, double reflection, and awareness and invitation. These indirect approaches should serve to illustrate the conveyance of capability by the indirect approach.

Strategies of Indirect Communication in Storytelling

Indirect communication is veiled or hidden communication used for conveying capability. As we have discussed, knowledge is a necessary but not a determinative prerequisite to personal change and transformation. Information alone is not enough to enable a person to change. We are often freed from our flawed perspectives and cognitive limitations as we imagine ourselves in the shoes of another. Often it is through story and artistic literature that we find the emotional fortitude to change our beliefs and behavior.

4. Kierkegaard, *Journals of Kierkegaard*, 44.

In fact, knowledge can sometimes contribute to our inability to change. It does so in several ways. First, familiarity stifles the imagination, as sometimes people tell themselves that they know the old stories or propositions and therefore do not consider—or reconsider—the issue or subject presented to their senses. They need to see from a new slant or from a new perspective. Second, some individuals already have an emotional resistance or an emotional investment in a particular way of thinking. A direct approach to "correct" their way of knowing serves only to strengthen their resolve to maintain their current beliefs. Third, people may truly think that by consuming information, they are engaging with the issue. From this perspective, people can mistake media consumption or acquisition of knowledge with action. The narcotizing effect of the media (information or knowledge) gets substituted for actual behavior. In this way, people can learn more but still not act upon the truth they know—like the person who has read four books, seven articles, watched five films, and taken a class on forgiveness, yet still does not forgive his neighbor. This man or woman substitutes knowledge for capability. He or she allows the mind to grow as the heart and spirit wither.

We are *homo narrans* (human storytellers), male and female artists and storytellers. The stories we tell are important to the vitality of the community. The art in a fictional story is a social influence with the power to help "people understand and feel, and even change their selfhoods."[5]

Stories help people change through a variety of indirect communication strategies. In this chapter we identify and address some of the most useful strategies. Two common threads run through these strategies. First, they don't start out with the message they desire to convey. Rather, they veil or hide the truth in order that the listener or viewer may discover it and act upon it. Second, these indirect communication strategies center on capability, not information.

With this in mind, we will examine several useful indirect communication strategies. What follows is not a complete list, of course, and many important literary devices are given little or no attention. The devices presented are intended to provide examples of how to use various forms of indirect communication strategically.

5. Djikie and Oatley, "Art of Fiction," 498.

The Hidden Grace

While writing a paper on the use of media in conversion experiences, I came upon an unusual story. At that time, most of the academic literature on my subject took the view that media played only a small or no role in the conversion process. Generally, it is thought that what helps most people convert to the Christian faith is interpersonal interaction at times of great change in a person's life. I wanted to see what role media might play in the conversion process.

To my surprise, I found that if one takes a longer look and asks converts to tell the full story of their conversion, most will reveal that both media *and* interpersonal interactions played a part. I did not expect that many people would mention films or stories that initiated their conversion process. Even more to my surprise, it was not necessarily films made by people of faith that played the key role, but films like *Amadeus* or *The Breakfast Club*. These individuals explained that in the quiet and dark of a theater, they were confronted with moral and spiritual questions that disturbed them and provoked them into asking serious questions about the meaning of their own lives and reasons for living. They went to the theater expecting nothing more than to be entertained. They certainly did not imagine the movie would have such a profound impact on their lives. Nevertheless, as they watched the film, elements and characters in the story confronted them in unexpected ways, prompting questions that haunted them as they left the theater.

When I asked one man why the film *Amadeus* sparked his search for God, he replied that as he sat in the theater watching the movie, he began to wonder, "Am I as jealous, scheming, and evil as Salieri?" Films and stories can raise profound moral and spiritual questions of faith that disturb and trouble us, and in so doing provoke us to look for answers.

Stories and art engage our emotions but often do not immediately or directly confront us with the gospel. In hearing or following someone else's story, we often are led into examining our own life in light of the issues presented. Nevertheless, the experiences in these stories trigger our emotions and allow us to reflect upon them. In this way, hidden within a provocative story, lies the potential for change. As Loevlie states, "Belief relates to that which cannot be ontologically fixed or verified, be it God, angels, or spirits. Literature, because it releases and sustains this ontological quivering, can transmit the ineffable, the repressed and transcendent."[6]

Although God is hidden, he is not absent. He continues to reveal himself, although often in unusual ways. Ferreira points out that "God's hiddenness is not absolute."[7] He shows himself to us in limited ways. God hides that he may be found, and of all the places God has chosen to "hide" and so let himself be known—the chief place is the cross: "For there is nothing hidden, except to be disclosed; nor is anything secret, except to come to light" (Mark 4:21–22). The Christian faith finds God hidden most significantly in a first-century Jew hanging on a cross. God hides within the anguish, shame, and humiliation that Christ endured on the cross. God also dwells within in the secret lives of the saints and in the parables and odd stories of sacred Scripture. When Christ is misunderstood and has so much cultural baggage attached to him, we would do well to hide him in our stories. Readers and viewers need to develop a deep interest in the stranger who is ultimately revealed as Christ.

Christ and his truth can be concealed in fictional stories that haunt us, as in Lewis's novel, *The Great Divorce*. Or perhaps hints of him can be found in MacDonald's fantasy, *The Princess and the Goblin*. We need to smuggle transcendent truth into our stories, so they can challenge or enchant us, as in the works of Chesterton or Sayers. Possibly we can see him through the eyes of the drunken priest in Green's *The Power and the Glory*. Truth, hidden in the stories of Tolkien and O'Connor, may become for many the seeds of transcendence, whispering the offer of grace. These stories can awaken in men or women a longing for something they have not yet grasped.

Bonhoeffer suggests that God hides in the humble means of grace that is first the gospel itself—"that God was reconciling the world to himself in Christ" (2 Cor 5:19)—but also the gospel is made visible in bread and wine and in the water of baptism. These earthly words and signs, like the life of humiliation itself that our Lord lived, can seem to human sight like nothing at all—but faith knows better. Through his word he conveys more than information; he conveys the very person of Christ himself.[8]

We cannot look on God's face the way we look at the face of a neighbor or friend, but like Moses, we must look only at his "back side." For

6. Loevlie, "Faith in the Ghosts," 336.

7. Ferreira, *Kierkegaard*, 178.

8. Paustian, "Beauty with the Veil."

us, God remains hidden in many ways. Nick Trakakis asserts that, "God's nature, intentions, will, even his very existence and love or concern for us do not present themselves in an entirely clear manner to everyone, not even to every sane, well-balanced, honest adult."[9] God *intends* to hide. Could that be more obvious? Schellenberg argues that God could reveal himself more clearly if He wanted to, but He chooses not to. For Schellenberg, divine hiddenness accomplishes a positive service in that faith intensifies subjectivity. Centuries ago, Thomas Aquinas lent his voice to the notion of God's hiddenness concerning our accurate but not adequate language about God.[10] He states, "The created intellect cannot see the essence of God, unless God by His grace unites Himself to the created intellect, as an object made intelligible to it."[11]

Artists or communicators with Christian concerns often move too quickly to reveal or unveil Christ; and in so doing, they unwittingly diminish His identity. Dressing up the incarnation with the clear light of human reason often diminishes the mighty mystery inherent in the incarnation—mystery that should be reflected in our writing. What is at issue here is not whether Christ is the "Logos" of God as he is in the truest sense the "reason" or "Logos" of God. Rather what is at stake is what is meant by reason. And our current definition of reason becomes unreasonable about the mystery of Christ by reducing Christ to the wrong sort of reason. As we saw in the previous chapter, by limiting the definition of reason to acceptable modernist sensibilities we exclude or diminish both mystery and faith; in so doing we turn a vast sea of divine depths into a little saucer. Our stories need not appeal to reason alone; rather, they must provoke honest thought and contemplation. Walter Jost suggests,

> one teaches, not so much by giving direct doctrines—although it is significant to note that indirect communication does not *preclude* such direct giving or teaching . . . but by providing a meaningful space, a gap or absence into which the hearer can step, that is, by adding his own appropriate context of thought and feeling and behavior to make the communication meaningful, by completing it.[12]

9. Trakakis, "Epistemically Distant God," 214.

10. Schellenberg, *Divine Hiddenness and Human Reason.*

11. Aquinas, *ST*, Ia.12.4.

12. Jost, "On Concealment and Deception," 69–70.

Even worse, efforts to communicate Christ apart from the Spirit's revelatory work may well be idolatrous. By reducing his deity to understandable terms, or by using overly simplified, blatantly sentimental visual references so as not to offend anyone with the enigmatic and sometimes difficult truth of the incarnation, we severely distort truth. In fact, the type of mind that can "understand" the incarnation is not necessarily the educated mind, but the same kind of mind that understands good fiction: "it is the kind of mind that is willing to have its sense of mystery deepened by contact with reality, and its sense of reality deepened by contact with mystery."[13]

As artists with Christian concerns, we feel pressure to unload the whole dump truck every time we prepare to "speak for God." We forget that the God of the Bible frequently "hides" himself, as the prophet Isaiah reminds us (Isa 54:8; also see Deut 31:17). Jesus Christ, as the "express image of God" (Heb 1:3), did the same thing. We would do well to remember that Jesus once told his preoccupied disciples, "I still have many things to say to you, but you cannot bear them now" (John 16:12)—and so he saved much of what he had to say for a later time.

The judicious use of deception as a form of hiddenness can benefit readers and viewers of our stories in that it may provide the distance or space needed for an individual to consider or reflect on their lives while reflecting on another's story. It may prove useful to the author as well. Hiddenness, Malesic argues, "offers a Christian ethic of responsibility for the other, in which concealing one's faith and love becomes not only permissible but imperative for maintaining ethics' integrity, for the discipline of intentionally concealing one's charity stands as a safeguard against allowing one's works of love to become works of reciprocity."[14]

Christ was not always clear or quick to reveal himself to others. He gave each person the time and space to discover or realize for themselves just who he was and is. His parables, for example, were intended to conceal immediate understanding in order to allow hearers to seek the truth which often seemed hidden from them. As he piqued their interest and provoked individuals to honest thought and reflection, he allowed each one to have a part in discovering just who he was, and in so doing, he provoked them to consider just what it might mean for them to truly follow him. As artists with Christian concerns, we are often too eager to

13. O'Connor, *Mystery and Manners*, 78.

14. Malesic, "Secret Both Sinister and Salvific," 464–65.

create stories designed to seem affable and easily grasped. In order "to be relevant" and reveal Christ, we often mislead those seeking to understand Christ by not fully explaining the cost of following him. Neither a single work of visual art nor a single story can present the whole of the Christian narrative. In fact, the whole story of Christ and the church cannot yet be completely understood. In our haste to achieve our own desired ends, sometimes we fail to leave sufficient time for God to work. Men and women interested in following Christ need time to earnestly consider the consequences and implications of the decisions he or she is considering. In our zeal to make God known, sometimes we truncate the decision-making process that does not allow an individual to fully consider the cost.

Some might object that the hiddenness employed by earnest communicators appears to be a form of deception. Herner Saeverot suggests that a deception, or indirect communication approach, is necessary to communicate "existential concerns"—concerns that influence the person's whole existence and shape one's behavior "not only to think differently, but to start acting differently as well."[15] In this sense, deception is a form of hiddenness and is often necessary because the deception initiates the seeking after truth. One may ask, "But why not simply present the truth directly so the other can grasp the truth in a straightforward way?" Saeverot would respond that the direct communication approach often does not help change one's behavior because it does not require dwelling, thinking, or reflection. To overcome a psychological predisposition or *illusion* that one knows something when in fact one does not, requires a provocation to help the individual to think for oneself or to reflect on one's life in a new way. Old thoughts deep in our psyche are hard to unhinge!

The artist with Christian concerns attempts to unsettle and make others aware of the gap that exists between knowing and willing. Saeverot argues that "by giving aesthetic devices a prominent place, for example in the form of pictures, literature, or music, one speaks to a large degree to the sensual and the emotional."[16] In so doing these aesthetic devices affect the whole existence of a person. As Kevin Gary contends, religious truth is "not a theoretical enterprise but fundamentally a way of life."[17]

---

15. Saeverot, *Indirect Pedagogy*, 1.

16. Saeverot, *Indirect Pedagogy*, 7.

17. Gary, "Kierkegaard and Liberal Education," 152.

Christianity is not simply a way of thinking but a way of living. God in his hiddenness is found indirectly, not in new knowledge, but in a realization of capability or in "being known" (1 Cor 8: 2–3). Therefore, we need stories that provoke a new hearing and an awareness of the eternal in the temporal dimensions of life.

Overhearing

One day, as Kierkegaard sat quietly in a cemetery, he gained insight into a powerful indirect approach to communicate spiritual truth. Late one afternoon as he rested on a bench, minding his own business, he became aware of a conversation taking place close by, yet hidden behind a hedge, just out of sight. An old gentleman with white hair conversed tenderly but passionately to his ten-year-old grandson.

As they stood together talking over the new grave of the grandson's father and the grandfather's son, the grandfather in his sorrow spoke so sincerely yet so tenderly with his grandson that Kierkegaard could not help but feel moved. The passionate and revealing conversation tempted Kierkegaard to leave, but he didn't want to disturb the two visitors. And so he sat silently, gripped by the intensity of the truth he overheard.

Kierkegaard never forgot this solemn moment, precisely because the conversation *was not meant for him*. He only "overheard" the conversation of the grandfather pleading with his grandson to follow Christ. Kierkegaard felt deeply moved by this conversation, even though the message was addressed to someone else. Later he reflected that it had such power *because* the message was not directed at him. Nothing in it aroused his resistance or caused him to argue against the message that cast such a powerful influence over him.

Overhearing a narrative or story presented in this manner sidesteps any emotional resistance to the message and creates a distance between the communicator or message and the audience. In so doing it makes space for an individual or audience to reflect on the message presented.[18]

Although no one was trying to coerce him, nor was anyone even aware of him, still Kierkegaard found himself deeply moved. And what moved him? No intellectual argument penetrated his heart, for it was but a simple declaration of love from a grandfather to his grandson. And because no one was trying to persuade him, he could lower his defenses,

---

18. Kierkegaard, *Concluding Unscientific Postscript*, 1:237–41.

listen, and judge for himself the truth of the statements. Overhearing this conversation gave Kierkegaard the freedom to consider the veracity of this somber exchange and then to decide if he would truly believe and act upon what he had heard. The importance of this event on Kierkegaard cannot be overstated. It continued to influence him and his writings for the rest of his life.

Michael Brothers argues, as does Craddock, that "'overhearing' begins and ends with a concern for the hearer."[19] Just as both Brothers and Craddock assert that the experience of hearing or listening is "the governing consideration" in the communicative event of preaching, so too is the experience of the hearer, reader, or viewer the governing consideration for the artist or communicator with Christian concerns. They should harness all "the imaginative, emotive, and cognitive powers" they have at their disposal to contribute to their art. The "posture" of hearing or listening is called "overhearing," and is constructed out of two elements: distance and participation.[20]

Brothers sees two advantages of distance for the listener. While the first benefit of distance is the protection of the message, the second is a concern for the listener. The first element, distance, provides the listener room in which to contemplate, accept, reject, or work out his or her thoughts. For change to take place, the listener must have freedom to choose or decide how to act, and more so if the matter concerns ultimate consequence.[21] Regarding the second element, participation, Brothers states, "Participation means the listener overcomes the distance, not because the speaker 'applied' everything, but because the listener identified with experiences and thoughts related in the message that were analogous to his own."[22] By creating a story or a message that allows an individual to overhear, distance will be preserved, but the language, imagery, and expressive detail will allow moments in this process when the listener can "enter" the experience, identify, and participate. This participation or transportation may be involvement with the story or with characters in the story. This ultimately leads the hearer to free participation and involvement (such as transportation or identification with the characters) in the story or with characters in the narratives.

19. Brothers, *Distance in Preaching*, 7.

20. Brothers, *Distance in Preaching*, 7–8.

21. Brothers, *Distance in Preaching*.

22. Brothers, *Distance in Preaching*, 14.

Kierkegaard's retelling of the story of Abraham and Isaac, entitled *Fear and Trembling*, is one such story. It allows readers the distance to reflect and make up their own minds, precisely because he does not tell his readers what to believe but creates artistic provocations that allow readers the distance to reflect and decide for themselves.

Brothers references several definitions and uses of *distance* in the arts. He argues, for example, that Bertolt Brecht's "signature use of distancing through 'alienation devices' pushed audience members away from emotional identifications with characters in order to see the play's greater significance for social change."[23] Furthermore, he asserts that *Our Town* by Thornton Wilder (1879–1975) used a bare theater stage to reflect "a vision of providing 'room for the audience's imagination' through the removal of 'obtrusive bric-a-brac.'"[24] Brothers points out that "Although Craddock's proposal of distance may have been new to his homiletical audience, writers in philosophy, the performing arts, and literature were well acquainted with its use."[25] He explains that

> As a form of aesthetic experience, "aesthetic distance" is a particular kind of recurring response to performance involving the artwork and the perceiver. As part of an aesthetic attitude, aesthetic distance can be described as responses that occur when people distance themselves from an object they perceive, suspend their desires and other feelings, and are left with the mere experience of contemplating it.[26]

Distance is achieved by separating the object and its allure from one's own self to allow space for reflection. Perhaps another way to look at it is that this change of outlook is due to the distance "between our 'own self' and the self's 'affections'" that allows us to experience art or story in a new way.[27]

Overhearing is just one form of creating distance. There are others. The important thing is to create awareness of the subject matter and still allow individuals to reflect on its importance for their own lives.

---

23. Brothers, *Distance in Preaching*, 9.

24. Brothers, *Distance in Preaching*, 9.

25. Brothers, *Distance in Preaching*, 10.

26. Brothers, *Distance in Preaching*, 12.

27. Brothers, *Distance in Preaching*, 16.

Taking Away

Another indirect communication strategy is the art of "taking away." Kierkegaard told a story of a man who was starving to death, even though he had a mouth full of food—so full that the man could neither chew nor swallow. How could another person help this person? By providing more food? By laying mounds of additional food at his feet . . . or by taking a little away so he could chew, swallow, and so nourish his body?

With regard to "taking away," or what Alison Milbank calls "making strange," Muench suggests two aspects must be taken into consideration.[28] First, like Socrates, the principal objective is a kind of blameworthy *ignorance,* where the reader or viewer thinks he or she knows something but does not; in such a case the artist strives to make readers *aware,* or to *remind* them of "something they have *forgotten.*"[29] The second aspect of taking away resembles the first but in this case the artist, as a midwife, attempts to help readers or viewers gain greater self-awareness. Taken together, the artist helps readers or viewers become aware of or remember what is possible and then assists them in acquiring insight into their own lives.

Sometimes we need to communicate in an indirect form in order for our readers or listeners to take notice, for they think they know something and yet do not actually know or practice it. As Craddock states, "Most communicators speak to those who know in order to be approved or to those who do not know in order to teach."[30] Some messages are heard so often that they are no longer taken seriously, understood, or acted upon. It is as if one has been inoculated against truth and needs a fresh understanding. The old perception needs to be rejected and a new realization should be embraced.

Because many individuals do not fully realize what it means to call oneself a Christian, a straightforward approach is often misguided, as it may only reify old and impotent understandings and emotions that frequently accompany the symbols and stories of faith without containing the true essence or fervor of faith. In such a case, the direct approach would not bring about a deeper, more passionate understanding of the truth. It might only create the misconception that knowing *about* is knowing. For example, I remember a woman who was leading a women's Bible

28. Milbank, "Apologetics and the Imagination."
29. Muench, "Socratic Method," 139.
30. Craddock, *Overhearing the Gospel,* 77.

study that was going very well as far as the number of people attending. She explained to me just how many hours of time she was putting into her study of the Bible and the growth of her knowledge of Scripture that was taking place as a result of her class. Unfortunately, all her study was not able to carry over into her own personal life and marriage. For all her knowledge of Scripture she was not able to love her husband faithfully.

Craddock doubts that the illusions formed through a story's or a doctrine's repeated telling are easily disregarded.[31] Rather than providing more information to break the illusion, one must stir up and bring forth new deliberation, provoking thought or reflection in order that what has been so often heard or seen can be grasped in new ways. *Taking away* is like stripping a piece of furniture that has been painted several times in many colors. By removing the paint, the beauty of the wood beneath the paint reappears. So too we need to help people reflect on their own life, so they can remove any inadequate and erroneous understandings of themselves they may have. This inward reflection is needed before an individual can begin to reflect upon the truth presented to them. Robert Short explains it this way, "In order for a man to understand with his heart the truth, which is by nature completely foreign to his heart, something first must 'be taken away' from his heart—namely, that hardness which surrounds his heart and prevents his 'seeing,' 'hearing,' 'understanding.'"[32]

I know it seems strange to suggest that knowledge may be a liability, but it may well be, particularly if it prevents a person from reexamining his or her life. Muench points out that this approach can work with "someone who knows too much; here a person's knowledge seems to be interfering with her ability to live well."[33] If one wishes to communicate with someone who has effectively forgotten, or perhaps never really understood what it means to exist, or who has finished trying to understand the Christian faith, then indirect communication may be needed. Stories of this sort can shatter encrusted shallow meanings long held by those who some time ago lost their true passion for Christ.

An artist or communicator with Christian concerns takes away some of what a person knows or thinks they know about Christianity or God by disguising it so that readers or viewers do not immediately recognize it. In this way the communicator defamiliarizes the object

---

31. Craddock, *Overhearing the Gospel.*

32. Short, *Gospel According to Peanuts*, 21.

33. Muench, "Socratic Method," 142.

under consideration so that a person will recover an awareness of what human life is all about, of what it means to exist as a Christian. The communicator's aim is to bring the individual to the awareness that they have "forgotten what it is to exist as a Christian together with the difficulties associated with such an existence."[34] The purpose is therefore not merely to lead someone to affirm a doctrine, but to prompt the person to live for Christ through a lived encounter.

Without Authority *(let God be authority)*

Fred Craddock suggests that to communicate the truth of God, one must first learn to hear him. He argues that one does not communicate from a privileged place, but from a concrete situation grounded in place and time.[35] In this way, artists or communicators are never isolated from the events around them but listen to the community or culture from which they speak, write, or otherwise create. Thus, our art and all our communicative activity belong to time and space. In other words, our art and stories must be concrete and fit into our understanding of the world we inhabit. They are specific, not abstract.

Perhaps the most difficult challenge is that our egos often prevent us from giving the necessary time and attention we need to listen within our communities in order to form an entertaining and provocative story. The indirect artist must give up claims, authority, public esteem, appearance, and notions of advancement. Kierkegaard, for example, claims,

> [I have] nothing new to proclaim; I am without authority, being myself hidden in a deceit; I do not go to work straightforwardly but with indirect cunning; I am not a holy man; in short, I am a spy who in his spying, in learning to know all about questionable conduct and illusion and suspicious characters, all the while he is making inspection is himself under the closest inspection.[36]

Elrod reminds us that "the decision to speak [or create] without authority set Kierkegaard in opposition to the religious and philosophical establishment of his day and to the authority of its representatives—pastors, theologians, and philosophers."[37] Both pastors and theologians drew

34. Muench, "Socratic Method," 144.
35. Craddock, *As One Without Authority*.
36. Kierkegaard, *Point of View*, 87.
37. Elrod, *Kierkegaard and Christendom*, 257.

their authority from ecclesiastical and biblical sources, while philosophers benefit from the authority of reason. Elrod states,

> to accept a proposition as true on the authority of either the
> church or philosophical idealism requires no other activity than
> mental assent on the part of the receiver. The individual is com-
> pelled neither to analyze the claim for himself nor to attempt to
> reduplicate the truth in his own life. Thus, to speak with author-
> ity merely reinforces the subjective neutrality encouraged by the
> direct communication of truth in the propositional form.[38]

If the artist is more concerned with authority, appearance, or advancement than he is with the message, what results is a frantic search
for the popular or the exotic, which ultimately sacrifices truth itself. The
question for artists is this: Will they be a creative force in the world, committed to communicating the truth, or will they be the handmaidens of
the whims of a hurried and distracted culture? A culture that worships
at the altar of the current celebrity superstar or media icon will have no
more time for a Messiah than the sons of Abraham did in Palestine about
two thousand years ago. Truth does not come without cost, and it most
certainly does not come quickly. As Craddock states, "this glib haste sig-
nals a distance between the inquirer and the message, but a distance hidden in the illusion of enthusiastic participation and 'really knowing the
Bible.'"[39] Time—a most valuable commodity—is required to really know
and communicate the truth.

All this presupposes two truths about the listener. First, listening
is a quality of character and a loving act crucial for presenting the truth.
Second, merely presenting information does not equal communicating
truth. Access to or availability of information is not enough to guarantee
a proper hearing.

Our communicative activity is not lifeless or merely a record of past
events, but an action that awakens dialogue. As artists and communicators, we must defer authority to Christ and not arrogate it to ourselves.
We must remember that we do not come from a privileged place or
occupy a special station in life. In fact, artists and communicators with
Christian concerns stand "in need of betterment," as they contend with
this modern and postmodern age.[40] As Kierkegaard declares, one must be

---

38. Elrod, *Kierkegaard and Christendom*, 257.

39. Craddock, *Overhearing the Gospel*, 26.

40. Kierkegaard, *Point of View*, 88.

prepared to "express the thought that the world, if not bad, is mediocre, that 'what the age demands' is foolishness and frippery, that in the eyes of the world the truth is a ludicrous exaggeration; and that the good must suffer."[41] In other words, one must be prepared to communicate a difficult message without the benefit of status or authority. While still struggling to become what God has called us to be, we strive to dialogue with those very different from us and who most likely hold us in contempt. This was certainly true of Christ.

The point is that the listener should respond to Christ and not feel preoccupied by the posture of the one communicating. If one must humble himself to be heard, so be it (1 Pet 5:6 and Jas 4:10). As artists we must make ourselves small, so Christ can be seen. We do not focus authority on ourselves but defer authority to another, Christ. Ultimately, he is the one who must interfere and reveal himself as the offence and paradox of God. In this way, the illusion may be replaced by a deep, transcendent reality—far deeper than the shallow counterfeit we quite likely have been playing with for years.

Successful indirect communication requires careful listening, observing, and interacting with individuals of one's community, not as a person of God but as a fellow human being. Instead of challenging them about their behavior or beliefs, an artist desires first to get to know the other and take their beliefs at face value, without judgment. Eugene Peterson asserts that his "metaphor of choice for grasping what is involved in listening and meditating on God's word is 'eat this book.' It occurs first in Jeremiah (15:16) and Ezekiel (3:3) in their role as prophets during the devastating Babylonian exile."[42] The phrase "eat this book" is very close to a phrase used by the Maasai in Tanzania and Kenya. When meeting a friend whom they have not seen for a long time or when someone new is visiting their community, before they can be properly introduced and explain why they are visiting, the two parties must sit and "chew the news." That is, they must sit, talk, listen, and meditate on what has happened since their last meeting or what is currently happening. This custom compels each party to listen to each other and think about what has happened or is happening from the other's point of view. This is a very strategic listening ritual woven into the very fabric of this oral culture.

41. Kierkegaard, *Point of View*, 88.
42. Peterson, "Foreword," xi.

"Art," Craddock writes, "implicates and involves the reader, listener, or observer in ways more complex than agreeing or disagreeing. One's world, one's values, one's lifestyle can be confirmed or called into question by art."[43] The artist, storyteller, or communicator does not create from an esteemed place or position, but they are involved in the struggles that characterize the life of the reader, listener, or viewer. He or she is first of all a listener and must have a firm understanding of the challenges and struggles of the life of the reader, listener, or viewer. They must have a sense of place, either real or imagined, and need to communicate in concrete ways. Therefore, we need to get in touch with the culture and know the audience we intend to address.

Double-Reflection

It is fair to assume that most people living in the West, especially in the United States, have heard of, have some sort of impression of, or have at least a limited knowledge of Christianity. Therefore, it is a reasonably sure bet that readers or viewers have an emotional investment in the impression or knowledge they already possess of Christ and the church. Although this view of the Christian faith may not be negative, more than likely it is inaccurate and culturally conditioned by larger social influences. These inaccurate or inadequate understandings of the Christian faith challenge any artists who desire to help their audience see the truth of their existence. The challenge is not simply to inform, but to help the reader or viewer address the illusion, an illusion that they may not know they have, before the audience can consider the truth and challenge of the Christian faith. In short, an emotional attachment to the false understanding or emotion must be addressed and considered. Direct communication tends to reify the reader or viewer's illusion.

A storyteller needs to assist readers or viewers to reflect deeply about their current beliefs before they become open to considering the new meaning found in the Christian faith. This process includes first reflecting on the meaning currently held, and then on the new meaning. A person's reexamination of their current knowledge can be aided by the artist's use of defamiliarization. Ferreira helps us understand this process as she notes that "the Danish word for repetition (*Gjentagelse*) is

43. Craddock, *Overhearing the Gospel*, 83.

translatable as 'take again,' 'take back,' or 'retake,' as in a retake of a film scene."[44] This is how the artist assists the audience in seeing the familiar in a new way or within a different context, so that the initial or flawed view no longer has the same meaning or emotional hold on the individual. The original meaning is defamiliarized. Then, and only then, is the individual free to devise a new understanding.

Double-reflection is a reflection on something that then gets reflected back into one's self. Words or images "are an inevitable necessary 'first reflection'—an expression or externalization of a thought in public language—but the concern of becoming a human being, an existing subject, requires a 'second reflection,' namely, the 'second reflection' . . . [that] renders the existing communicator's own relation to the idea."[45]

Ferreira asserts, "the 'first reflection' will directly communicate something (since it is in the form of a language we understand), but not what is most crucial to the communicator."[46] Of course, for Kierkegaard, what is most crucial is appropriation. Johannes Climacus suggests that indirect communication conveys what is "essentially a secret."[47] "Where the 'essential content' of a message is a 'secret,' the secret may seem to be directly communicated but is only understood by one who is in a certain state," that is, emotionally, intellectually, or spiritually ready to receive what is communicated.[48] "That the knowledge cannot be said directly, because the essential in this knowledge is the appropriation itself, means that it remains a secret for everyone who is not through himself doubly reflected in the same way, but that this is the essential form of truth means that this cannot be said in any other way."[49]

At this point we find indirect communication necessarily serves two functions. First, one is always in the process of becoming; and second, the essence of truth (and our stories) lies not in providing information but in the appropriation of truth—the conveyance of capability. This requires self-reflection or inwardness.

Ferreira suggests that the necessity of indirect communication is a response to two difficulties. "First, the agent is always in a process of

44. Ferreira, *Kierkegaard*, 43.

45. Ferreira, *Kierkegaard*, 103.

46. Ferreira, *Kierkegaard*, 103.

47. Kierkegaard, *Concluding Unscientific Postscript*, 1:79.

48. Ferreira, *Kierkegaard*, 103.

49. Kierkegaard, *Concluding Unscientific Postscript*, 1:79.

becoming . . . so, how can one communicate what one does not have completely or is not yet fully? Second, the essence of truth lies in the appropriation of truth—so, how can one communicate what one is inwardly?"[50] The answer to these two questions can be found in the use of indirect communication, which requires double-reflection. This allows us to appropriate the truth for ourselves and to develop the inward life. Therefore, an artist who wants to provoke inwardness and reflection may want to begin with an imaginative leap in order to help the reader or viewer see "the world in a new way and express that 'seeing' in a visual [and challenging] form."[51] Furthermore, an artist should seek out and deal with themes "relevant to our spiritual journeys."[52] Artists who are serious about helping their readers or viewers reexamine their lives need not simply express "things as they are"; rather, their art can stir new and imaginative feelings by creating a mood, subject, or story that points beyond itself, "from the material to a deeper immaterial reality."[53]

Now I want to turn to a current strategy that, if properly understood, may offer a useful approach to developing a method of communication and storytelling. Invitational rhetoric, in its current form, may provide us with a useful model to support the objectives of indirect communication. Together, indirect communication and invitational rhetoric may help us find a better way to respectfully communicate transcendent truth. As artists and imaginative apologists, this approach may help us develop a useful strategy of communicating faith.

Awareness and Invitation

One problem for artists and communicators with Christian concerns, particularly in the past few years, is the incautious creation of stories or art that uses coercion or intimidation to produce change in another. Following suit, Christian apologists—often with good intentions—create stories or arguments frequently seen as heavy-handed and favoring reason to the detriment of imagination. Sonja Foss and Cindy Griffin argue rhetorical scholars often use discursive strategies that "infringe on others' rights to believe as they choose and to act in ways they believe

50. Ferreira, *Kierkegaard*, 103.

51. Kidd and Sparkes, *God and the Art of Seeing*, ii.

52. Kidd and Sparkes, *God and the Art of Seeing*, ii.

53. Kidd and Sparkes, *God and the Art of Seeing*, 3.

are best for them."[54] Instead, they suggest that "invitational rhetoric" addresses this concern by inviting "the other" to enter a discussion absent of domination, competition, and intimidation. Jennifer Bone, Cindy L. Griffin, and Linda T. Scholz maintain that an exchange of "ideas from positions of mutual respect and equality," is a more useful approach to communication and the creation of art.[55] Foss and Griffin have identified equality, immanent value, and self-determination as three assumptions that serve as the basis for invitational rhetoric.[56]

First, Foss and Griffin are committed to building relationships of equality so as to dismiss any dominance or elitism that characterizes some rhetorical approaches. As Jason A. Sharier states, "As humans, we must first recognize that we exist within a realm of equality; we share the same Image."[57] This, of course, accords well with the Scripture's understanding that all men and women are created in the image and likeness of God.

Second, they recognize the immanent value of all living beings and so disdain any hierarchy, as a person is valued not for what they do but just because they are—that is, they exist. From the invitational rhetoric perspective, the value or worth of an individual cannot be earned or acquired, as it is already a right based on his or her existence. Furthermore, Foss and Griffin assert, "concomitant with a recognition of the immanent value of another individual is the eschewal of forms of communication that seek to change that individual's unique perspective to that held by the rhetor."[58] This last statement might seem strange; one may ask if a person should believe because they have been argued into belief, or because of the authority of the one speaking to them. Coming to faith does not mean coming to a doctrine or to a bit of knowledge; it means we come to Christ and to him alone. This, of course, does not mean we cannot make a person aware of the reasons for the faith within us; but faith should never be based upon the ability of one person to out argue another or upon the authority of one person over another.

This leads to the third principle: self-determination. Foss and Griffin state, "Grounded in a respect for others, self-determination allows individuals to make their own decisions about how they wish to live their

54. Foss and Griffin, "Beyond Persuasion," 3.

55. Bone et al., "Beyond Traditional Conceptualizations," 437.

56. Foss and Griffin, "Beyond Persuasion."

57. Sharier, "Redefining Interfaith Discourse," 91.

58. Foss and Griffin, "Beyond Persuasion," 4.

lives. Self-determination involves the recognition that audience members are the authorities of their own lives and accords respect to other's capacity and right to constitute their worlds as they choose."[59] The language is not helpful here, as our place before God is never self-determined; instead, we come to Christ through his self-revelation. Nevertheless, we are given a choice and those choices are real. God has granted us a part to play in choosing to embrace his gift and we do well to respect the choice of each person as he or she chooses to embrace God's freely given work of grace in us. Quite simply, this freedom of choice is the respect we should show *every* person made in God's image.

Perhaps one major difference between invitational rhetoric and indirect communication is the focus on *understanding* for invitational rhetoric and the focus on *appropriation* found in our understanding of indirect communication. Simply knowing something does not, in and of itself, change one's behavior. But the two approaches may not be as far apart as it seems, for as Foss and Griffin suggest, the invitation to understanding is a means to create a relationship between the two parties entering the dialogue. The "result of invitational rhetoric is not just an understanding of an issue."[60] The invitational rhetorical theory is intended to be a nonhierarchical, nonjudgmental, nonadversarial framework which promotes interaction and an understanding of the participants themselves—"an understanding that engenders appreciation, value, and a sense of equality."[61] Essentially, one is invited to enter the rhetor's world and to see it as the rhetor does.

The key here is that one does not judge or denigrate the other's position or beliefs, but is open and tries to appreciate the other's position. Sonja Modesti succinctly captures the spirit of invitational rhetoric by stating that "its essence . . . must stem from individual communicators' choice to abandon their tendencies toward hierarchy, defensiveness, and/ or argument in lieu of the desire to listen, learn, and understand others' perspectives."[62]

Much like indirect communication, the artist does not impose his or her view on the other, nor is the artist required to surrender his or her own view. Rather, one does open up himself or herself to learn from

59. Foss and Griffin, "Beyond Persuasion," 4.
60. Foss and Griffin, "Beyond Persuasion," 5.
61. Foss and Griffin, "Beyond Persuasion," 5.
62. Modesti, "Invitation Accepted," 4.

the other. We walk the narrow ridge in order that others will examine their views as well. Rhetors, using invitational rhetoric, approach their audience in a relationship of equality, respect, and appreciation. This changes the communicative environment so as to allow both parties in the dialogue to more honestly embrace the communicative event. "In invitational rhetoric . . . resistance is not anticipated, and rhetors do not adapt their communication to expected resistance in the audience. Instead, they identify possible impediments to the creation of the understanding and seek to minimize or neutralize them, so they do not remain impediments."[63]

Because of the invitation or the offering, change may happen; but change to the rhetor's position is not the goal of invitational rhetoric. According to Foss and Griffin's understanding of the traditional rhetorical model, "change is defined as a shift in the audience in the direction requested by the rhetor, who then has gained some measure of power and control over the audience."[64] Invitational rhetoric, however, sees change occurring as the result of insight gained in the exchange of ideas. This, of course, differs somewhat from indirect communication, in that change is ultimately the result of a process of two steps. The first step is the individual becoming aware of an issue; the second step is the reflection of this new knowledge when considering their relationship to God. Kierkegaard's understanding of indirect communication highlights that what is needed is an emphasis on the heart of a person. So, in indirect communication the rhetor must draw back and not use his authority or influence to coerce change but must trust God to deal with the other person. There should be no thought of superiority or authority of one person or perspective over another, but choices are made as God alone deals with the individual. Such a change as this is brought about by a supernatural work of God—not by human intervention—no matter how powerful the arguments or images made by a person.

Foss and Griffin argue,

> [I]n traditional rhetoric, the change process often is accompanied by feelings of inadequacy, insecurity, pain, humiliation, guilt, embarrassment, or angry submission on the part of the audience as rhetors communicate the superiority of their positions and the deficiencies of those of the audience. In invitational rhetoric, on the other hand, rhetors recognize the valuable

63. Foss and Griffin, "Beyond Persuasion," 6.
64. Foss and Griffin, "Beyond Persuasion," 6.

contribution audience members can make to the rhetors' own thinking and understanding, and they do not engage in strategies that may damage or sever the connection between them and their audiences. This does not mean that invitational rhetoric always is free of pain. In invitational rhetoric, there may be a wrenching loose of ideas as assumptions and positions are questioned as a result of an interaction, a process that may be uncomfortable.[65]

Likewise, with the indirect communication approach, the absence of pain is not guaranteed, and the decisions made are often difficult and painful.

Whether one agrees with the beliefs of the other or not, it is important to recognize and affirm the beliefs of the other. To affirm another's beliefs does not mean we agree with him or her, but that we acknowledge the other—even in our disagreement with them—and in so doing we demonstrate respect for the other as someone who is made in the image of God.

Indirect communication, much like invitational rhetoric, is marked by civility and respect in *offering* rather than *imposing* one's beliefs. Approaching another in this way does not dismiss disagreements, nor does it rid "the atmosphere of awkward tensions, but it allows us to empathize with another human being."[66] Both approaches to engaging the "other" focus on how we show deference. Will we approach them with an attitude of regard, civility, and openness in order that we might truly understand and listen to them, and in so doing affirm their humanness as one made in the image of God? Or are we interested only in advancing our own perspective and affirming our point of view?

To be sure, some differences exist between indirect communication and invitational rhetoric. Just as indirect communication is not the best fit for every occasion, so invitational rhetoric may be a useful, but not the only, rhetorical strategy one should have available in one's communication toolbox.

While both approaches to communicating come out of a posture of respect and self-determination, there seems a clear divergence in the purpose or goal of these two approaches. Foss and Griffin identify the goal of invitational rhetoric as "sharing what they know, extending one another's ideas, thinking critically about all the ideas offered," while indirect communication is most concerned about freeing people from old concepts

---

65. Foss and Griffin, "Beyond Persuasion," 6.
66. Sharier, "Redefining Interfaith Discourse," 92.

that keep them from really living and helping them to consider the meaning of their own existence.[67] As Benjamin Daise states, "The object of [indirect] communication is therefore not knowledge but a realization."[68] Here the realization touches the heart of the person.

Whatever the case, it may be useful to take seriously the advice of Bone, Griffin, and Scholz when they assert that it is unfair to argue, "scholarship must support a preexisting theory in its entirety, if it is to use any aspect of that theory."[69] It may well be that we can find much to appreciate and use from invitational rhetoric when employing indirect communication. We do not, however, need to embrace the entire theory.

Furthermore, as artists with Christian concerns who believe each person is made in the image of God, we need to treat every person with love and respect even if we disagree or abhor their behavior. We are to love and respect our enemies, as they too are made in God's image. In her short story, "A Good Man is Hard to Find," Flannery O'Connor makes this clear for anyone with eyes to see. The story recounts the last moments of the grandmother's life as she reaches out to touch the serial killer responsible for murdering her children, just seconds before he takes her life. In creating the most extremely difficult situation for one person to love another, O'Connor was trying to say that we are all made in the image of God and no one falls so far that grace cannot reach them. In her last minute on earth while facing a serial killer called the Misfit who just ordered her son's and grandchildren's deaths, "the grandmother's head cleared for an instant. She saw the man's face twisted close to her own as if he were going to cry and she murmured, 'Why, you're one of my babies. You're one of my own children!' She reached out and touched him on the shoulder."[70] The grandmother made the offer of grace regardless of the cost to herself and to her family, and regardless of the evil deeds that proceeded from the interaction between her and the Misfit.

Both invitational rhetoric and indirect communication share a criticism of direct attacks on another's beliefs, convinced that they serve only to create opposition and entrench defensiveness in the individual or audience addressed. When speaking to another about their belief in God, it seems most prudent to know *how* we present the offer of grace.

67. Foss and Griffin, "Beyond Persuasion," 8.

68. Daise, *Kierkegaard's Socratic Art*, 19.

69. Bone, Griffin, and Scholz, "Beyond Traditional Conceptualizations," 438.

70. O'Connor, *Flannery O'Connor*, 132.

Listening is probably more important than speaking. Trust and respect for the other is a foundation necessary for anyone engaging in serious dialogue, as people seek out those who truly love and respect them. In the indirect approach, vulnerability and openness is valued more than power and authority.

Finally, the indirect approach lacks effectiveness when the listener lacks information about the issue. In these cases, the direct approach as articulated by invitational rhetoric may be a better choice. Kierkegaard realized, as did Jesus before him, that "he could not, nor could anyone else, negotiate life always by indirection."[71] Jesus used parables as his chosen form of communication, but at times he spoke and acted directly. Often, he had to explain his parables to those closest to him in order for them to understand his point. He told his stories honestly and faithfully.

A story has power when told truthfully and honestly. When telling a story, we should not clean it up or make it sound doctrinally correct, but rather speak as closely as we can to the reality we experienced. It is *these* stories, which ring true with a fidelity and coherence, that gain a hearing. *They* are the stories that lend a note of confidence and authenticity that will convey truth to the listener.

Both invitational rhetoric and indirect communication are essentially narrative modes of communication. The narrative style of communication is filled with humor, irony, wit, and artistry. This method parallels the approach of Jesus when He told stories, which so compellingly broke "up the encrusted soil of the religious community's assumptions, illusions, and calculations about the kingdom."[72]

Our calling as artists and professionals with Christian concerns is to tell the truth. But we need to give serious thought to *how* we tell the truth. Through parables, myth, and various other literary devices we enter a dialogue with our audience so that we may capture their attention and perhaps their hearts. The life of dialogue begins where humanity begins—in our common, everyday life. We are all storytellers and we can all enter dialogue with our fellow human beings. Martin Buber argues that in dialogue we can choose to treat the other person as a "Thou," one made in the image of God and one with whom we enter into a relationship. Or we can see the other person in a perfunctory way, as a means to an end,

71. Craddock, *Overhearing the Gospel*, 73.
72. Craddock, *Overhearing the Gospel*, 72.

an impersonal "It."[73] That is, someone to be targeted or manipulated to fit our own ends rather than an individual made in the likeness or image of God. In dialogue and story, we open ourselves to the other and become vulnerable to them.

For the Christian, this approach to life and faith can invite "a quest toward authenticity of self, genuine religious passion, a constructive exercise of imagination, and the unconditional love of neighbor. It is a quest that is not driven by the need to be right, the desire to win arguments, or by an exclusive or superior attitude. Rather, it is driven by a sense of gratitude for God's persuasive grace and the priority of divine forgiveness."[74]

Our Message and Our Meanings

A proper grasp of the direct and indirect approach to communication does not in every case firmly divide these two concepts from one another. They may be better understood as opposite ends of a continuum. Each end of the spectrum is certainly separate from the other, but between these two poles, there are overlapping gradations of the concepts.

Just as there is a metaphorical element of all language and therefore variations of meaning to all words, so all communication has an element of meaning supplied by the context, by the individual trying to make sense of the message, and by the storyteller, artist, or communicator. The storyteller and the context both bring constraints and possibilities for the participant to construct meaning from the message. It is possible that two individuals can construct completely different messages from the same set of works or words.

Consider an example from the Old Testament. Jonathan, the son of Saul the king of Israel and the friend of David, the future king, called out to a small boy who had accompanied him to retrieve his arrows, "Isn't the arrow beyond you?" Then he said, "Hurry! Go quickly! Don't stop!" The child understood the words as directed to him, and he most likely understood them as encouraging him to quickly collect the arrows. But David, who hid close by, recognized the words as a secret message from Jonathan, telling him that it wasn't safe for him to return to the house of King Saul. In fact, David had to flee. The message made one kind of sense to the small boy collecting the arrows, but a very different kind of sense

73. Buber, *I and Thou*.
74. Roberts, *Emerging Prophet*, 62–63.

to David. The message to the boy carried a disguised or hidden message to David, one that only David would understand. In this way, the true meaning of the words was veiled; only the one listening for the secret meaning understood.

In Flannery O'Connor's story "The Lamb Shall Enter First" she tells of a single dad whose wife has recently died; he must deal with his own grief while trying to raise his young son. The meaning of the story can be understood from many vantage points: a tragic story of anguish and an attempt to rebuild one's life; a psychological study of grief within a family; a stinging critique of modernity; or finally, a religious journey of tragedy and the offer of grace. The short story can be read at any of these levels without consciously understanding the meaning of any of the other levels.

The same veiled message can be seen (though not as deeply hidden as in O'Connor's work) in the children's story by C. S. Lewis, *The Lion, the Witch and the Wardrobe*. I know of many readers who have read the story without recognizing the Christian symbolism woven into the narrative. These stories are meant artistically to awaken the reader through reflection on both the story and on one's own life. If readers are not aware of the deeper meaning of the symbols in the story, it still can prepare them for a later time when such understanding may occur. As John Elrod states, "The ethical [and religious] writer must deflect the reader's attention away from the world of objects and toward subjective inwardness. The goal can be accomplished only by luring the reader into a world of discourse that both mirrors and provides the means for cultivating his own subjective inwardness."[75] In this way, the communicator does not simply provide propositional knowledge, but stimulates the individual reader's subjective activity in coming to know and accept oneself as having an "obligation to accept and to affirm as good one's own historical identity and the identity and freedom of one's neighbor as well."[76] In all of this reflection, self-reflection in particular is required—something our society, to its detriment, seems to have little interest in or use for.

Dietrich Bonhoeffer in his book *Life Together* rejects the direct approach to communication of transcendent truths, by recognizing that there is an essential part God has in our communication interaction. He states,

75. Elrod, *Kierkegaard and Christendom*, 265.
76. Elrod, *Kierkegaard and Christendom*, 265.

Christ stands between me and others, I dare not desire direct
fellowship with them. As only Christ can speak to me in such
a way that I may be saved, so others, too, can be saved only by
Christ himself. This means that I must release the other person
from every attempt of mine to regulate, coerce, and dominate
him with my love. The other person needs to retain his indepen-
dence of me; to be loved for what he is, as one for whom Christ
became man, died, and rose again for whom Christ brought
forgiveness of sins and eternal love.[77]

For Bonhoeffer, we do not have direct or immediate access or communication to the other person. In Bonhoeffer's understanding of how
to communicate Christ to another, one does not desire the other's love
or approval but chooses instead to serve the other without thought of
compensation, for Christ has already done all that is needed for us. Our
communication and stories should reflect this truth. Bonhoeffer argues
that Christ is not only the mediator between God and humanity, but as
Christians we can approach the other through Christ—our communication and stories can do this indirectly. In this way Christ is the mediator
between human and human. Therefore, as people of faith we can communicate to the other through Christ; we see him or her best as Christ
sees the other. As Bonhoeffer states, "We can meet others only through
the mediation of Christ."[78] In this way too, we "recognize the true image
of the other person which he has received in Jesus Christ."[79] Communication that springs from spiritual love does "not seek to move others
by all too personal, direct influence, by impure interference in the life
of another."[80] Likewise, if our communication behavior emanates from
spiritual love, it will not use direct emotional influence to persuade another, but it will release the other from any claim we may have on him
to allow God to deal with him. This, of course, speaks to storytellers that
are trying to walk a narrow ridge of telling powerful stories on one side,
yet seeking to guard against being overly sentimental on the other side.

Bonhoeffer's writings fit well with what Kierkegaard has to say
about not trying to persuade another person to believe in Christ by direct
means; rather one may be able to make the other aware of Christ—that
is, to awaken the other to the possibility of belief. Bonhoeffer's counsel is

77. Bonhoeffer, *Life Together*, 25–26.
78. Bonhoeffer, *Life Together*, 26.
79. Bonhoeffer, *Life Together*, 26.
80. Bonhoeffer, *Life Together*, 26.

analogous to the advice found in the parable of the sower (Matt 13:3–9). In this parable the farmer is called to scatter the seed. The seed falls on various kinds of soil and finds different degrees of reception. Some of the seed landed on good soil, which nourishes growth, while other seeds fell on land that was not receptive to the seeds, nor did it foster growth. But when growth does occur, it is God who produces the harvest. What seems clear is that we have a part to play in awaking others to the possibility of the work of God in their life, but God must do the crucial work in the conversion process. Conversion is not just changing a worldview or believing in a fact or a doctrine, but Christ must meet and deal with everyone in a personal and subjective way. This is a divine act that Christ alone must do, and no amount of knowledge, good intentions, or right thinking can bring about the spiritual transformation. Our stories and communication need to provoke the other to become aware of his own existence (self) and the existence of the other (Christ).

Conclusion

As suggested earlier, an indirect approach to the communication of truth is often best done in the form of a narrative or story, but it can take form of several different literary models. Indirect communication is a veiled or hidden approach to communication that intends to impart capability rather than information. This chapter identified several strategies of indirect communication such as: a hidden grace, overhearing, taking away, without authority, and double-reflection. These strategies assume that something of the message being communicated is already known and that the individual is likely to not fully understand the implications of the message being communicated or resist the message in some way. The indirect approach to communication focuses on emotion rather than simply the cognitive life of the listener or viewer. In the next chapter we will examine the power and use of narrative for communicating faith and provoking earnest reflection.

5

Narrative Truth

What then is the good of—what is even the defense for—occupying our hearts with stories of what never happened and entering vicariously into the feelings which we should try to avoid having in our own person?. . . The nearest I have yet got to an answer is that we seek an enlargement of our being. We want to be more than ourselves. Each of us by nature sees the whole world from one point of view with a perspective and a selectiveness peculiar to himself . . . We want to see with other eyes, to imagine with other imaginations, to feel with other hearts, as well as with our own . . . We demand windows . . . Here, as in worship, in love, in moral action, and in knowing, I transcend myself; and am never more myself than when I do.

—C.S. LEWIS, *AN EXPERIMENT IN CRITICISM*

Introduction

Almost all indirect communication comes to us through story or narrative. The short story "Car Crash While Hitchhiking" by Denis Johnson is both disturbing and violent. It clearly illustrates, in a twisted and unforgettable way, how stories can unexpectedly provoke one to question one's culture, one's view of reality, one's place in the universe, and surprisingly, one's beliefs about God.

The story concerns a drug-addicted, or at least a drug-influenced, hitchhiker who gets picked up by many people over a several state excursion. Throughout the journey, the reader follows this young man, who narrates the story through a series of conscious or unconscious episodes. With the narrator, the reader jumps back and forth in the story, following his hazy adventures from one state to another, and from one car to another. Finally, at an exit just beyond the city limits, the driver of a Volkswagen lets him off just as rain begins to fall. The hitchhiker falls asleep at the exit, only to wake up completely drenched by the rain. In his wet and drug-influenced state, he gets picked up by a young, middle-class couple with an infant and a small child. Driving in the downpour, the family from Marshalltown has a head-on collision, killing the man driving the car.

The remainder of the story chronicles the young hitchhiker's memories of the aftermath of the event. At one point, the hitchhiker recalls a moment after the crash and describes the husband's last moments, "His blood bubbled out of his mouth with every breath. He wouldn't be taking many more. I know that, but he didn't, and therefore I looked down into the great pity of a person's life on this earth. I don't mean that we all end up dead, that's not the great pity. I mean that he couldn't tell me what he was dreaming, and I couldn't tell him what was real."[1]

How quickly narrative brings us into the presence of powerful questions and situations! As the story ends, the hitchhiker mentions that later on in his life he spent time in detox. At one point he says he had hallucinations. The last line of the story reads, "And you, you ridiculous people, you expect me to help you."[2] We may ask, Where does this last line come from, and what does it signify? Lorin Stein, the editor of *The Paris Review*, commented on this line in the story:

> It raises a bunch of questions about the story as a whole. Like, who exactly are these people? Maybe they're us readers. (But did we expect him to help us?) Who knows—maybe they're a hallucination. Or people in an AA meeting, possibly. Or: I can't help hearing a possibility that the narrator thinks he's Jesus Christ. That this is a story about someone who has (or thinks he

1. Johnson, "Car Crash while Hitchhiking."
2. Johnson, "Car Crash while Hitchhiking."

has) the power to play God—but doesn't save the people around him.[3]

In a later article in *The Atlantic*, Stein adds,

> Whoever he is, whoever he's talking to, it's hard for me to read the story without feeling that God is the problem here. To me this is a story about faith, about the idea that there is an omniscient being who may be working in us, and making demands of us, demands we're really not allowed to shirk. And whether you live up to those demands in the way Jesus is supposed to have done, or don't, may not be under your control.
>
> So much is happening in that last line, and yet I still have a hard time nailing down one single meaning of it. Much of the payoff here is emotional, not intellectual—I can feel it even if I can't articulate it. There's a certain kind of beauty that comes from precision, deep literacy, sense of rhythm, and awareness of the musical possibilities of plain language, that evades logical understanding but hits us in the heart.
>
> Instead of pointing you toward a definitive interpretation, the story opens up a limited ambiguous space. That seems more realistic to me than they lived happily ever after, or then I figured this or that thing out.[4]

Lorin Stein declared that this story illustrates three qualities of good stories that "not only interest people but move them to act."[5] This is a serious story and it seems apparent that Stein is using it to help identify three important qualities he feels every strong story should have. First, he looks for the voice of a narrator "who urgently needs to speak." Second, the narrator needs to "persuade you that he or she is telling the truth." And third, he is excited by "a kind of moral authority, or at least the effort to settle a troubled conscience."[6] This seems to be the kind of story that awakens and causes the reader to question his or her existence, the sort of story that conveys capability. It is art that questions us the readers, not we who question the art. This story is an example of how we can communicate truth through narrative more effectively and powerfully than through proposition. It displays the capacity of narrative to convey transcendent truth, that which lies beyond mere logical proposition.

3. Fassler, "Lorin Stein."

4. Fassler, "Lorin Stein."

5. Fassler, "Lorin Stein."

6. Fassler. "Lorin Stein."

Indirect communication is more than a tool, it is an artform. As an artform it privileges narrative and story. In this chapter we will look more closely at the narrative form of indirect communication. We first consider the need for three qualities in the creation and communication of a strong narrative: passion or urgency, truth, and moral authority. Second, we emphasize the need for good stories to confront the reader, hearer, or viewer. That is, good stories invite the listener to question one's self and one's place in the world. Third, we explore the role of indirect communication in constructing stories and evaluate the degree of indirectness required in creating a story. Finally, we assess the need for a variety of methods in indirect storytelling today in order to convey capability.

The Need for Narrative Truth

Fred B. Craddock suggests that the study of communicating the gospel is, in a real sense, worship. He illustrates this by recalling a saying that rabbis have taught their congregations: "An hour of study is, in the sight of the holy one, blessed be he, as an hour of prayer."[7] If a person wants to present an offering to God, a sacrifice of service, then the posture appropriate to this creative and artistic service is gratitude. In this spirit, the artist, composer, or writer with Christian concerns is involved in an incarnational activity. That is, the artist is speaking for Christ and through his power. Christ is the creator and we reflect his work in us and through us. As Madeleine L'Engle explains, "There is nothing so secular that it cannot be sacred, and that is one of the deepest messages of the Incarnation."[8] In so doing this incarnational activity of creation transcends culture, reflecting the eternal.

We begin to understand L'Engle's vision of the artist as "a servant who is willing to be a birth giver."[9] By now it should be clear that the stories one creates do not need to be religious or have religious themes. They need to be stories on any topic that confront us with the transcendent, or they must require that we question our place in the world—stories of joy or sorrow that bring us to wonder at the nature of our existence.

7. Craddock, *Overhearing the Gospel*, 35.

8. L'Engle, *Walking on Water*, 50.

9. L'Engle, *Walking on Water*, 8.

Story can give birth to truth. Stanley Hauerwas and L. Gregory Jones argue that we need to "rediscover narrative's significance."[10] Flannery O'Connor explains that "the basis of art is [imaginative] truth, both in matter and in mode. The person who aims after art in his [or her] work aims after truth, in an imaginative sense, no more and no less."[11] Unfortunately, the truth is often messy. Not only is it difficult, but at times it can be painful and ugly. This applies both to the culture and to the church. Too many artists and storytellers with Christian concerns want to "clean up" the truth and make it more presentable for their audience. George Kilcourse references O'Connor's response to this issue:

> In a 1963 letter to a new correspondent, she [O'Connor] reminds Sister Mariella Gable that people who ask fiction writers "to make Christianity look desirable" distract a writer from "what you see" and seek a description of Christianity's "essence." But such an "Ideal Christianity," she reminds, doesn't exist because everything a human being touches ("even Christian truth") "he deforms slightly in his own image." Flannery considers this to be one of the effects of original sin.[12]

In *The Confessions*, Augustine offers a corrective to the temptation to present Christianity in an idealized way, all neat and tidy. The book is a clear and candid appraisal of the author's early life, both the good and the bad, and in writing in such an honest way, he not only gains our attention but our respect. We live in a culture that thirsts for truth, but too often we offer an idealized form of the truth that does not match the audience's actual experience. Take an honest look at the church in the West today and one can't help but see its imperfections. It is not perfect—nor even close to perfect—nor has it ever been. But why should this surprise us? Our own lives are no different. We all have grotesque imperfections that we try, perhaps, to cover up with a bit of rouge and perfume. As Christians we still struggle with our imperfections; we are all in process of becoming what God wants us to be. We therefore need to see ourselves as we really are—imperfect and flawed beings. Once we admit this truth, we don't have to be afraid to present characters that match our own reality. Far from being a detriment to communicating the truth, our vulnerability and candor can bring great strength to our stories.

10. Hauerwas and Jones, *Why Narrative*, 5.

11. O'Connor, *Mystery and Manners*, 65.

12. Kilcourse, *Flannery O'Connor's Religious Imagination*, 224.

When artists present an idealized view of faith, those who do not share our faith see the inconsistency between their experience with people of faith and the sentimentalized view frequently presented—and this causes them to doubt the veracity of the message. The place to begin seeing and speaking the truth is with ourselves and the church. When we communicate honestly, as Augustine does in *The Confessions*, we become more trustworthy and accessible to those who do not share our views. Augustine's honesty, truthfulness, and his willingness to speak openly about his sin and shortcomings gives the church hope as it struggles to live up to Christ's calling. Augustine's text reminds us that we share with all men a common heritage of sin and a need for transformation. Artists with Christian concerns don't need to hide the church's or the culture's failures; they just need to tell the truth, as unpleasant as it may be.

Honest and real stories, like other forms of art, have a way of by-passing intellectual and emotional predispositions in order to provoke thought. Robert Short argues that story and art have this ability to dodge many intellectual and emotional challenges because "art always speaks *indirectly*—whether in being the vehicle for delivering a new *answer* or in causing a new kind of *question* to be asked that must be asked before any new answer can make sense."[13] Due to its subtlety and elusiveness, story gets to the heart of a matter in imaginative and provocative ways that may help to dislodge deeply held beliefs, making even the most (apparently) immovable person capable of change.

George Kilcourse identifies the power of O'Connor's conversion stories in helping us to reflect and question our own deeply held convictions. He states:

> Near the end of "A Good Man Is Hard to Find," O'Connor's character, the escaped criminal who calls himself The Misfit, announces, "Jesus threw everything off balance." He comes to blame Jesus for upsetting things by raising the dead. "He shouldn't have done it," he protests. The great Christological mystery of the incarnate Jesus's life, death, and resurrection as the redemptive act of unconditional love pulses at the heart of Flannery O'Connor's art. I can think of no title more apt for a study that investigates how her Catholic imagination theologizes than to fathom the meaning of Jesus throwing everything (and everyone) off balance. Her stories of conversion summon us time and again to contemplate the mystery of the Christ who

---

13. Short, *Gospel According to Peanuts*, 7.

throws off balance every status quo that threatens to seduce and
paralyze us with its tempting illusion.[14]

Here we see the true nature of the gospel coming through a story that
forces us to deal with the terrible speed of mercy and the implications of
God's unrelenting grace.

The art of story and storytelling may aid in piercing a person's
emotional prejudices by showing the person who he or she really is. It
does this by setting before a person a story or an image that acts like a
mirror, allowing the person to see an image of himself or herself that accurately reflects his or her own pretentions, foibles, and anxieties. What
seems clear is that story, whether created by a person of faith or not, is
potentially transformative in that it points beyond the temporal to the
transcendent, and in so doing, conveys capability.

As we have seen, art or story can transport us into a confrontation
with ourselves, and the effective artist may sometimes disguise the truth
in order to get it through another's defenses. "This is why all . . . art,
though at first it may seem to be a most welcome escape from reality, will
inevitably lead one into a face to face encounter with reality—but always
with reality in a different light from which it was first seen."[15] Short reminds us,

> The language of faith uses the language of culture even when it
> must transmute the meaning of the language. Further, the lan-
> guage of faith will always find the language of art particularly
> appropriate. Both have a deeper, more passionate vision of real-
> ity than is commonly given; and both are bent on communicat-
> ing something of this vision to the heart of man through forms
> which will stop his attention. The Church will always need
> "fresh" parables—whatever their original "intent"—in which to
> pour the "new wine" of the New Testament.[16]

Flannery O'Connor clearly understood the power of stories to
transform an individual, and in her stories, she always made a fervent
effort to present the reader with concrete facts. For her writing begins
with the author's perceptive abilities because the beginning of human
knowledge comes through the senses. One's writing appeals to the audience "through the senses and you cannot appeal to the senses with

14. Kilcourse, *Flannery O'Connor's Religious Imagination*, 13.

15. Short, *Gospel According to Peanuts*, 10.

16. Short, *Gospel According to Peanuts*, 16–17.

abstractions."[17] In O'Connor's view the author creates movement in the story through concrete details that carry immediate meaning for the audience. However, she explains, "In good fiction, certain of the details will tend to accumulate meaning from the story itself, and when this happens, they become symbolic in their action."[18] For O'Connor, these details or symbols "while having their essential place in the literal level of the story, operate in depth as well as on the surface, increasing the story in every direction."[19] In this way the fiction writer can increase the meaning found in his or her story. O'Connor identifies this aspect of story writing as an anagogical vision. Furthermore, she states that this kind of vision "is able to see different levels of reality in one image or one situation."[20]

In her essay "The Nature and Aim of Fiction," O'Connor provides a compelling example of how a symbol can convey meaning at two levels at the same time. In this case she references a character, Hazel Motes, from her own book, *Wise Blood*. O'Connor describes Hazel Motes as the hero and his rat-colored automobile as his pulpit, his coffin, and a means of escape. She states,

> He is mistaken in thinking that it is a means of escape, of course, and does not really escape his predicament until the car is destroyed by the patrolman. The car is a kind of death-in-life symbol, and his blindness is a life-in-death symbol. The fact that these meanings are there makes the book significant. The reader may not see them, but they have their effect on him, nonetheless. This is the way the modern novelist sinks, or hides, his theme.[21]

For O'Connor stories are an important means of communicating the gospel and her artistic narratives are meant to have a scope and strength that ties them to the life of a larger community. Art and story have memory and hope, which binds them to the full range of human intellect and emotion. A story conveys a sense of movement from one place to another and progresses at a pace that most closely represents the pace of the narrated tale. Narrative art, by its structure, provides order and meaning, as well as shape and sequence. If, for example, one changes the shape of a narrative into a logical syllogism, the message of the story

17. O'Connor, *Mystery and Manners*, 67.
18. O'Connor, *Mystery and Manners*, 70.
19. O'Connor, *Mystery and Manners*, 71.
20. O'Connor, *Mystery and Manners*, 72.
21. O'Connor, *Mystery and Manners*, 72.

is profoundly altered, and in the process, loses the function of the message as a narrative. Craddock explains that "narratives do not summarize events and relationships with commentary and application following. No listener overhears that."[22]

In his book *Fear and Trembling*, Johannes de Silentio (Søren Kierkegaard's pseudonym) retells the story of Abraham offering up Isaac in four very different ways. Each of the four versions of the story are compelling and provocative. Often readers feel perplexed in trying to understand the meaning of the book and struggle to determine which version of the story is the "right" interpretation. But in writing this story, Kierkegaard did not intend to provide "right" information; instead of trying to help clarify the story or provide the correct interpretation for the reader, he purposely tried to provoke his readers to find out for themselves. In so doing he wanted them to appropriate the story into their own lives.

Kierkegaard created a deliberately ambiguous text—certainly he did not try to impart new information. The ambiguity of the four versions of his story serves to provoke the reader to reflect on the story and its original meaning found in the Hebrew text, and perhaps to help the reader see the tale in a different light. Readers are not made more knowledgeable or comforted, but rather they are empowered and provoked to find out for themselves the true meaning of the story.

The Abraham and Isaac story shows how readers, through repeated hearings and familiarity with the story, may forget or distort the meaning of the narrative. The reader knows how it ends, which means the story often is read or heard from a place of comfort and assurance. All will end well, so no reason to get uncomfortable. Craddock explains,

> but if the ending is allowed to scatter its smile back over the long and torturous path of Abraham, his faith is no longer seen as faith; it has been robbed of fear and trembling and is far removed from the pilgrimage of the hearer. A narrative that reproduces the painful journey up Mount Moriah reexperience all the churning chemistry of a faith that is absolute in its obedience.[23]

Consequently, Kierkegaard's retelling of the story allows readers to struggle to understand the difficulties and challenges inherent in the actual experience of Abraham, and so in some way perhaps see their own faith renewed.

22. Craddock, *Overhearing the Gospel*, 117.
23. Craddock, *Overhearing the Gospel*, 118.

If communicators with Christian concerns are trying to speak to a culture, "which," as O'Connor states, "doubts both fact and value," and if they want this culture to see and judge their stories, then they must sometimes create stories that make all of us uncomfortable.[24] For such artists the day of comfort lies in the past, and they need to present a prophetic voice within their artistic efforts. The communicative efforts must stir or awaken hearers to a message that, in all probability, they do not want to hear or—if they have heard it before—do not really understand. Too often stories from such artists drip with sentimentality, thus diminishing and distorting the truth. Such stories do not sound real, because they are not, and few outside the church give any actual credence to tales that lack coherence and fidelity with the reality they experience.

If our hearers are to listen with new ears, see with new eyes, and read with new minds, our stories must be honest and unaffected—or at least stories that surprise the audience with the mysterious action of grace on "territory held largely by the devil."[25] If one is serious about entering into a conversation with this present generation, then one might set their sights on telling stories that leave room for the hearer or viewer to reflect upon that which is communicated in order to make their own sense out of the story. In such a situation stories can be used to provoke thought and invite others to use their God-given imaginative gifts to reimage the world.

In the current cultural environment, with all manner of voices and media vying for our attention, little room exists to be heard. As almost every serious and successful writer states, "Show, don't tell." Yet much of the church continues to dismiss this approach, continuing to create stories with stereotypical, two-dimensional characters, and overly simplistic answers for people already distracted from the real questions of life.

The Art of Storytelling

All humans have a strong attraction to good stories. Good tales burst the sterile structures of our normal existence and awaken us to new understandings. "They are unpredictable things—which often change the teller as well as the listener. That's part of the risk and the delight

---

24. O'Connor, *Mystery and Manners*, 117.

25. O'Connor, *Mystery and Manners*, 118.

of storytelling."[26] Stories not only help in education, business, lectures, preaching, and psychotherapy, but they aid in personal contemplation regarding how each of us compose our world. In the broadest sense, they lead us into creating our own distinctive spirituality.[27]

Belden Lane asserts, "The consciousness that story produces is one that forces us to think differently about the world. It helps break down the limited structures that often have bound us in the past, especially since the Enlightenment."[28] That's why so many people feel suspicious of the storytelling venture. It seems so imprecise, so naïve. It subverts the world of hard realism and logic.

In a playful analogy about story, Lane argues convincingly, "we need to rethink the importance of the story teller as priestly fools. The fool, after all, may be one who lives by a different reality—who may deliberately break down the structures that are seen by others as most holy and most traditional. This is done so we can see a still higher conception of what is holy."[29] Through story we create a little folly in our lives in order to break down what is often seen as fixed or settled, and consequently we see anew. This is exactly what the Hebrew prophets did in the unusual and unexpected symbolic actions that often accompanied their message. Their zany antics and stories often made them (e.g., prophets such as Ezekiel, Jeremiah, and Hosea) look like divine fools. Lane continues, "This was the way God spoke—through imagination and freedom of absurd, eccentric action. The prophets altered those binding and artificial structures of consciousness, so as to make room for faith."[30]

The skill and art of storytelling is profoundly different from the more content-oriented approaches used in most religious organizations today. Walter Ong reminds us that stories were first given in oral settings. This continues to be true for many in our world today. For moderns, however, and to a large extent in the West, the task of storytelling has been taken over by various forms of media—media that privileges direct communication and *data*, as we have seen.[31] Wilder argues against this

---

26. Lane, *Story Telling*.

27. Lane, *Story Telling*.

28. Lane, *Story Telling*.

29. Lane, *Story Telling*.

30. Lane, *Story Telling*.

31. Ong, *Orality and Literacy*.

modernist tendency and calls for the church and artists to return to using stories when communicating truth. He states,

> The meaning of things, the coherence of the world, its continu-ities, values, and goals, all these are established for the multitudes and for societies of men by this or that word-picture or mythos, with its associated emblems, archetypes, paradigms, fables, he-roes, cults. Man's very being is affective and imaginative, and his power of survival and creation are nourished by dynamic im-pulses which mediate themselves to him through inherited and ever-renewed dramatizations which define his world. Reason is implicit and diffused in his *mythos,* and even when it orders itself as a conscious critical instrument it draws its vitality from the faith impulse associated with the myth-making faculty. If the Word of God must necessarily speak with the mythopoetic words of men, it is all the more inevitable that this should be so when the ultimate issues of existence are in question.[32]

Narratives and stories make up the bulk of both the Old Testa-ment and the New Testament. Not only is our culture constructed and maintained to a considerable extent by stories, but we as humans can be understood as worshiping storytellers (both *homo liturgicus* and *homo narrans*). That is, the kind of stories we tell speak forcefully, although sometimes indirectly, about the things we love. Our symbolic activities take on the form of stories. Over and over again, our meanings—when given time to develop—grow consciously or unconsciously into stories that form our identity. We are, as Walter Fisher calls us, *Homo narrans* (human storytellers), in that the shape of our words and symbol-making behavior takes on the form of story.[33] Although the story styles may vary and the details of a story may differ in every culture, Christopher Vogler suggests that the blueprint is universal. He states, "All stories consist of a few common structural elements found universally in myths, fairy tales, dreams, and movies."[34] The story pattern, Vogler argues, "is fundamen-tally the same in every culture, in every time."[35]

Story is a useful tool for Christian reflection in that it uses the imagination to engage the individual and allows for revelation. Story is the prime genre of Scripture and certainly the crucial form of Jesus's

32. Wilder, *Early Christian Rhetoric*, 121.

33. Fisher, *Human Communication as Narration*.

34. Vogler, *Writer's Journey*, 1.

35. Vogler, *Writer's Journey*, 10.

teaching. It can be argued that transcendent truth is best understood when communicated in appropriate story form. It often succeeds where reason, logic, and proposition fail. Robert Inchausti asserts,

> The incarnation, like the resurrection, and like the very notion of divinity itself, cannot be reduced to a precept, fact, or theory; nor is it even, strictly speaking, a doctrine. It is, rather, a revelation that must be experienced in order to be understood, a reality wrapped in mystery inside an enigma, miniaturized into a narrative that proves itself apodictically true by the realities it reveals. The false knowledge that blocks our capacity to experience this shift in awareness from the mundane to the sublime changes from epoch to epoch and from place to place, and this is why myth, rather than logic, is the only means through which the sublime can be expressed.[36]

Effective storytellers do not believe they can best address the present challenges facing Christianity by offering more religious information. Instead, they value an approach that has much in common with how Christ approached his Jewish audience, which is significantly different from the message-centered approach often employed by Paul on his missionary journeys in Greece and Rome. I do not mean that Jesus was right and Paul was wrong! In fact the backgrounds of their respective audiences—Jewish communities in Israel for Jesus; Greco-Roman and/or mixed gentile/Jewish communities in other Mediterranean regions for Paul—were very different, and these differences can account, at least in part, for the differing communicative approaches. Jesus usually employed the indirect method, while Paul usually chose the direct approach—especially when speaking to gentiles.

Jesus spoke to audiences steeped in Jewish history, religious law, and literature. His hearers knew well the stories of Abraham, Moses, David, and Elijah. They considered themselves heirs to a rich tradition many centuries old and spent large amounts of their time rehearsing that tradition to each other. They did not lack information! Paul, by contrast, spent most of his time with men and women who more than likely knew next to nothing about Jewish history, literature, law, or religion. If he mentioned "Abraham" or "Moses" to them, or even "Yahweh," almost certainly he would have to explain the significance of these characters and names. Therefore, Paul's conveyance of knowledge is entirely appropriate as his audience lacked a great deal of context and information!

36. Inchausti, *Subversive Orthodoxy*, 18.

Whereas the indirect approach that Jesus employed is primarily interested in provoking thought and initiating a dialogue among an audience rich in information.

In this way the indirect approach to storytelling is "the mode for eliciting capability and action from within the listener."[37] It does not work by means of providing additional information or a reasoned argument, especially when someone thinks they already know a story's intent. What do people need who think they already know? Kierkegaard answers that we "take away some of the knowledge by making the knowledge strange" and thus defamiliarize the knowledge so that "we can reintroduce the knowledge."[38] In this way, we overcome the audience's resistance to the truth. We need to see old truths through new eyes and at the same time see old and comfortable deceptions for what they are: lies.

At their best, stories—especially fantasy—ought to challenge persons' understandings of themselves and the world around them, as well as inspire their passion for adventure. Here we begin to see that stories and films can positively inspire an audience. The power of literary fiction resides in its refusal to "give us ready-made answers to our questions."[39] It does not intend to convey a specific effect as much as to make readers or viewers aware that they need to make a choice about the nature of their existence.

Johannes Climacus, one of Kierkegaard's pseudonyms, emphasizes passion in his book, *Philosophical Fragments*. In this work he argues that we can challenge a reader's understanding through paradox. He states that "one should not think slightingly of the paradoxical; for the paradox is the source of the thinker's passion, and the thinker without a paradox is like a lover without feeling: a paltry mediocrity."[40] Therefore, we are encouraged to contest a person's understanding and arouse passion through our stories.

The parable or story is one of the most obvious indirect forms of communication. In the New Testament Jesus used these brief narratives containing vivid and arresting metaphors, and with them "lured his followers into listening and then caught them in a new vision, a new

---

37. Kierkegaard, *Concluding Unscientific Postscript*, 1:275.

38. Kierkegaard, *Concluding Unscientific Postscript*, 1:275.

39. Djikie and Oatley, "Art of Fiction," 502.

40. Kierkegaard, *Philosophical Fragments*, 46.

perspective, an alternative way of seeing life in the kingdom."[41] Such stories are central to our identity and being. The stories we live and tell shape our lives in countless ways. Fantasy or fiction can often challenge our longings and call us into question.

Degrees of Indirectness

As we have seen, stories and other narrative techniques are almost always indirect in that they appeal primarily to the heart rather than to the head. They empower us to address issues that we cannot, for a variety of reasons, approach directly. Like the parables of Jesus that so energized the crowds that came to hear him, all stories are aimed at the imaginative side of humans and engage them in a conversation that compels them to look and reflect on the world and one's place within it. We have also seen how stories are especially useful in addressing an individual who labors under the illusion that he or she already knows or understands what is being communicated—when in fact he or she does not. They also prove useful with individuals emotionally predisposed against a message, but who do not understand its true meaning.

Narratives both veil and reveal. They enter our lives and engage our imaginations without announcing their purpose. Many stories address us quickly with the concerns of the author, while others mask their true purpose, leaving us to ponder their meaning. Each story has its own level of clarity, but most good stories hint at or hide their true purpose, which can be found only as one seeks to understand the story. In this way most good stories hide or bury the truth within the plot or characters and reveal the truth only to those who take the time to search out their true meaning. Jesus often told parables that the majority of his audiences—including his disciples—did not understand. Only those who took the time to carefully and faithfully listen and contemplate their meaning came to understand.

Several aspects of the communication event or situation contribute to determining how indirect, veiled, or hidden the communication strategy should be in shaping the narrative's plot or characters. How does one determine this? If the artist is confident the message is unknown, needed, and sought, and that the person for whom the communication is intended is not emotionally, ideologically, or intellectually predisposed against the message, then some degree of direct communication is most

41. Craddock, *Overhearing the Gospel*, 74.

likely to be preferred. If the artist anticipates resistance to the message, however—be it emotional, ideological, or intellectual—then some degree of indirect communication is called for. Because communication is an art and not a science, there is no one simple or definitive answer to this question. However, we can indicate the degree to which indirect communication might be required by answering the following questions:

1. How strong is the emotional, ideological, or intellectual resistance to the message?

2. What is the social or cultural context in which the message is encountered?

3. How motivated is the audience to attend to the message?

4. Is the communicative purpose cognitive or behavioral (information or appropriation)?

5. How trusting is the audience of the perceived source of the message?

6. What kind of images can awaken this audience?

While this series of questions does not constitute a complete list, they do provide a good place to begin and one would do well to take them into account. It is worth noting again that direct and indirect communication do not always form discrete concepts. Upon careful consideration the direct and indirect distinctions form a continuum, from direct to indirect. For example, one could say, "Close the window," which is a very direct statement. Others may achieve the same effect by saying, "It is cold in here. Is the window open?" This statement is a little more ambiguous, but the careful listener may hear a request to close the window. The approach here is less direct and takes greater attention and involvement by the listener to understand and act upon the intended meaning. Finally one may say, "It is cold in here." This is clearly indirect, if the purpose is to prompt the other person to close the window. The final example of indirect communication does not even mention the window. Here we can see different ways of asking the same thing with varied degrees of indirectness prompted by the language, context, culture, and social situation and with different possibilities of misunderstanding.

One of the challenges of using direct and indirect communication is determining just how direct or indirect a message should be. Obviously there are many factors that go into determining exactly how direct or indirect the message should be. The influences mentioned above, as well as other considerations, are relevant to every communication event and each individual needs to attend closely to these determinants.

Storytelling Today

The artist or communicator with Christian concerns must write for those whose lives are invested in the larger community. Artists do best if they attempt to engage the culture's intellectual, emotional, and volitional life, rather than limiting their story to a single aspect of the culture. An attempt must be made to be as real and as honest with the story as possible. Artists would do well to present truth as compellingly and as forcefully as they know how, as art in all its forms is truth telling.

For Craddock, narratives should be constructed to be overheard rather than presented directly. Several literary devices can assist in creating the indirect narrative structure. The artist or communicator may feel tempted to idealize or oversimplify, but one does so only by sacrificing the story's credibility. The strongest stories, in whatever form they take—fantasy, myth, parable, novel, etc.—work best if they authentically embrace life, with all its ambiguity and perplexities. The language of the artist must embrace the truth found in story.

Artists need not yield to the temptation of limiting their work to a narrow range of concepts and ideas or toward adjusting stories or their characters to make them more *acceptable*. We must also remember that rational argument has its place in that "it serves to keep the communication self-critical, athletically trim, and free of sloppy sentimentality that can take over in the absence of critical activity."[42] "In short, we are talking about being *appropriate*, appropriate in language, mood, and style to the message, the listener, the occasion," and the specific story.[43]

Portraying all of Reality:
The Good and the Evil in Story or Narrative

Lorin Stein, editor of *The Paris Review*, insists, "the best stories ask more questions than they answer."[44] This attention to asking provocative and morally important questions strikes me as sound advice for any storyteller,

---

42. Craddock, *Overhearing the Gospel*, 116.

43. Craddock, *Overhearing the Gospel*, 69.

44. Fassler, "Lorin Stein."

and perhaps even more so for storytellers with Christian concerns. Far too often, authors speak with urgency and high moral authority but are not taken seriously because their stories seem unreal.

Additionally, every story should leave something out for the reader to imagine and supply. Stories invite dialogue and incite readers to join the author in creating the story. The full story need not be told, as it is often too much for a person to take in all at once. We must leave room for the reader to imagine and create. Questions that confront readers invite them to reflect on their own lives and their place in the world. Strong stories ask profound questions and cause us to reflect deeply. In this reflective state we become open to the work of God within our lives, even if we are unaware that it is happening.

The kind of profound personal and social change the gospel calls for needs time and space to embed itself into one's life. Stories that really matter and disturb us can provoke and help move us along in finding out who we are and who we want to be. We cannot give what we do not have, and until we know ourselves, we cannot really give ourselves to anything. Stories help us know ourselves, and every important story we read, both secular and sacred, brings us closer to knowing ourselves. In a sense, the story challenges us to look at ourselves and examine our lives by asking probing questions.

Embedded or hidden within each story is a view of humanity, an understanding of who we are. In these sometimes somber and sometimes joyous images, humans are often wounded—if not corrupted—and this too can be found in almost every strong story. Artists or storytellers who want to face their world truthfully, who desire to probe the depth of their reality, must first have ground where they can begin. They must plunge that pick into the midst of humanity's weaknesses and vices, as well as its joys and laughter, and there reveal the universal in the narrow world where men and women have learned to love and suffer.

In the last few years of his life, C. S. Lewis lost his wife, Joy. He wrote a book about his struggle trying to make sense of her death. Part of the strength of *A Grief Observed* was his refusal to try to excuse or justify his battle with God over Joy's passing. Nor did he dismiss his depression and spiritual questioning. In *A Grief Observed*, we see a noteworthy Christian apologist struggling with issues of faith, and in the record of his struggles and weaknesses, we find strength to see that our doubting need not be the final statement of our lives. We see that God is patient with us and does not abandon us; rather he comes to us in our uncertainty, in our weakness, and in our despair. I have a friend who is decidedly not a Christian but who has read *A Grief Observed* and is clearly taken in by the honesty found in the pages of this work. My friend stated that Lewis is so honest when discussing the pain and anger he felt at the loss of his wife. He felt the same way when his wife died and so could not help but appreciate this book. Although not a Christian, he certainly became aware of the way one man faced such loss in his life and how he continued to live, even if imperfectly, by the faith he possessed.

François Mauriac reminds us that the mystery of evil is still active—even if denied or ignored by pious people—and fundamental to the reality of our world and to anyone creating or communicating within it.[45] The artist can either deny evil or accept it, as it appears both within and without each individual, as well as within and without the church. Mauriac warns that we cannot shy away from the real characters in our stories. Nor can we dismiss the mystery of evil in our world or in our stories. In his 1952 "Banquet Speech" at the Nobel Banquet given when he received the Nobel Prize, he stated,

> Do not for a moment imagine that as a believer I pretend not to see the objections raised to belief by the presence of evil on earth. For a Christian, evil remains the most anguishing of mysteries. The man who amidst the crimes of history perseveres in his faith will stumble over the permanent scandal: the apparent uselessness of the Redemption. The well-reasoned explanations of the theologians regarding the presence of evil have never convinced me, reasonable as they may be, and precisely because they are reasonable. The answer that eludes us presupposes an order not of reason but of charity. It is an answer that is fully found in the affirmation of St. John: God is Love. Nothing is impossible to the living love, not even drawing everything to itself; and that, too, is written.[46]

The mystery of evil that so vexed Mauriac—the "secret of my torment"— eventually led him to the secret of his peace.

For artists and authors with Christian concerns, human frailty is both a nurturing and a subversive force, a thing not to be feared but highly respected. By it we can come to an awareness of our own selfhood and begin to look critically at the social structures in which we find

45. Mauriac, "Banquet Speech."
46. Mauriac, "Banquet Speech."

ourselves.[47] To participate in the transformation of our society, we must be free to imagine both *within* and, more importantly, *outside* the religious community. This may be done best as we emulate our Maker by living and creating images that live and come alive outside and inside the church. Perhaps this is best accomplished through stories that address the heart and the mind so as to enable us to see anew the world and our place in it. Through an imaginative leap, the artist or professional communicator sees the world in a new way and expresses himself through word or image to communicate something out of his or her own lived experience—which is true even with fiction. If our stories are to be taken seriously and if they are true to our lived experience, we need to present characters who are forced out to meet evil and grace. We, as well as the characters in the stories, must learn to act on trust that is beyond ourselves—to engage in lives and situations that involve the whole of life—beauty, joy, and goodness as well as the unsightly, miserable, and evil.

Conclusion

Narratives or stories are crucial to indirect communication in that they show us truth rather than tell us the truth. A story slips under the radar of our cognitive capabilities and engages the heart and emotions before the mind can figure out the meaning of the story. Strong stories defamiliarize old meanings or they have an element of ambiguity about them that allows the reader or viewer to construct new meaning. Stories or narratives are not the only strategies available to those creating indirect communication messages. In the next chapter we will examine irony, humor, and other literary devices that can be used to convey capability both within stories and by themselves.

47. Freire, *Pedagogy of the Oppressed*.

6

Irony, Humor, and Various Literary Devices

If someone were to say, "Christianity is God's irony over us men,"
I would reply: No, my good man, but we men have the power to
transform Christianity into irony, into biting irony. The matter is
very simple. In his majesty God set the pitch so high that if a person
is unwilling to let go of this finite common sense, will not abandon
flat, self-indulgent mediocrity—then what God calls help, salvation,
grace, etc. is the most biting irony. Finite understanding is scarcely
to be blamed for saying: No, thanks, I would rather not have that
help, salvation, and grace.

—SØREN KIERKEGAARD, *JOURNALS AND PAPERS*

Introduction

As PEOPLE MADE IN God's image, we are uniquely
equipped to communicate Christ's presence creatively
and artistically. Many apologists and artists today use clear, reasoned
arguments to communicate eternal truths, which can be very useful.
However, all too often our postmodern audience is not moved by or even

concerned with rational arguments or religious information. In our image-oriented and technologically bewitched culture, doctrinal arguments and reasoned explanations do not generally move people to faith. This chapter builds upon the former by examining several literary devices that contribute to our supply of indirect communication strategies. Apart from story and narrative, irony and humor are some of the most effective forms of indirect communication. We will first examine the use of irony to stimulate the hearer to self-examination and then explore the use of humor to incite provoking and puzzling incongruities within the hearer. We draw upon Kierkegaard, a master of irony, to define, illustrate, and inform our understanding of both irony and humor. Kierkegaard's works are full of irony, humor, and sarcasm. He used a passionate polemic designed to provoke personal reflection and decisive action. We will conclude the chapter with a brief overview of other indirect literary devices such as riddles, hints, insinuations, and suggestions.

Literary Devices Used in Indirect Communication

In an age where the average person is confronted with thousands of advertisements each day, our minds are keen to defend any attempt to sell or argue us into another's viewpoint—let alone another's faith—no matter how reasonable the argument. As we have seen, our culture does not nourish trust in judicious arguments aimed at the mind, but rather adores images that titillate the mind. In this context, stories that entertain and aim at the heart or imagination have a way of drawing others into dialogue rather than debate. Furthermore, such stories feel less contentious. Even a subtle or ambiguous story can stir the imagination and haunt the heart, which can begin the process of contemplation and engagement.

Through the ages indirect communication has been explored using various theoretical lenses, including pseudonyms, poetic authorship, and the Socratic method of midwifery, each of which includes calling upon audiences to see their responsibility—with God's help—and to author their own lives from their existential situations. One may also use such literary tools as story, irony, paradox, humor, questioning, hinting, deception, and other indirect communication strategies that focus on man's imaginative and affective nature.

As we have repeatedly seen, the salient factor in indirect communication involves the communication of capability, rather than the communication of additional information. To accomplish this, indirect communication employs several literary tactics, such as irony, humor, riddle, satire, seduction, and similar devices. These devices typically obscure the actual communicative purpose and subvert the hearers' or viewers' inadequate understanding of truth. Using literary strategies and techniques to unsettle readers or viewers prompts them to rethink their situation in life. In this way the reader or viewer is confronted with provocative and unexpected questions as well as various interventions and comparisons, all of which make him or her uncomfortable and thus leads the individual to question his or her own notions of security. This strategy defamiliarizes the old meanings that inevitably limit our spiritual growth.

Just as the parables of Jesus challenge the cherished assumptions of his and our culture, so too can stories challenge us to reflect about the meaning and nature of our existence. They spur us to see things differently and encourage us to contemplate the story or communicative act and consider the challenge it presents to our usual way of seeing. Lewis used this strategy in *The Silver Chair* when he described how Puddleglum, the Marsh-wiggle, gathered all his courage to stamp on the fire with his bare feet—knowing it would hurt him badly—in order to break the enchantment of the witch through the awful smell of burning flesh. In a similar way, literary devices unsettle us and sometimes cause us pain, but in so doing awaken us from our treasured illusions and material enchantments.

As artists and people of faith, we can strive to make men and women aware of God's claim on all our lives through unusual and unfamiliar stories or other types of art in the hope that they will choose to question their life situation and begin to examine their lives. The mystery of God's presence in our world requires the use of various literary devices to evoke self-reflection and to help others focus on the transcendent qualities of life.

Stories with Christian concerns, no matter how vague or ambiguous, can challenge or encourage proper respect for reality and for the common difficulties that confront everyone. The indirect strategy that begins by focusing on the imaginative part of a person is especially effective with people who find the difficulties they face easy to explain even when they are not so easy to understand—if it is possible they can be understood at all—or, with those who have an emotional resistance to the presence of God in our world.

Literary devices such as irony, humor, riddle, hinting, insinuation, suggestion, intimation, sarcasm, allegory, and a host of other techniques can be woven into a strategy of indirect communication. It is not necessary to identify and discuss *all* the available literary devices one can use in implementing the indirect approach. A closer look at two prominent and useful literary tactics may allow us to better understand this strategy and to see how it can be used most effectively. Therefore, we will look more closely at irony and humor.

The Use of Irony

Although irony is a major tool used by indirect communication, it is not usually associated with communicating transcendent truth. In the following passage, found in the Old Testament book of 1 Kings, we find an obvious example of the use of irony:

> The messenger who had gone to summon Micaiah said to him, "Look, as one man the other prophets are predicting success for the king. Let your word agree with theirs and speak favorably." But Micaiah said, "As surely as the LORD lives, I can tell him only what the Lord tells me."
>
> When he arrived, the king asked him, "Micaiah, shall we go to war against Ramoth Gilead, or shall I refrain?" "Attack and be victorious," he answered, "for the LORD will give it into the King's hand." The king said to him, "How many times must I make you swear to tell me nothing but the truth in the name of the LORD?"
>
> Then Micaiah answered, "I saw all Israel scattered on the hills like sheep without a shepherd, and the LORD said, 'These people have no master. Let each one go home in peace.'" The king of Israel said to Jehoshaphat, "Didn't I tell you that he never prophesies anything good about me, but only bad?"
>
> Micaiah continued, "Therefore hear the word of the LORD: I saw the LORD sitting on his throne; with all the host of heaven standing around him on his right and on his left. And the LORD said, 'Who will entice Ahab into attacking Ramoth Gilead and going to his death there?' One suggested this, and another that. Finally, a spirit came forward, stood before the LORD and said, 'I will entice him.' 'By what means?' the LORD said. 'I will go out and be a lying spirit in the mouths of all his prophets,' he said. Then he said, 'You will succeed in enticing him,' said the Lord. 'Go and do it.' So now the LORD has put a lying spirit in the

mouths of all these prophets of yours. The LORD has decreed disaster for you.[1]

Micaiah's words to the king seem both difficult and puzzling. In his first speech, he pronounces the same palliative sentiments as the court prophets. The rankled king apparently recognized his ironic statements and reminded him to only tell the truth when speaking for God. This, of course, serves to intensify the cynically ironic tone of the whole narrative.

Micaiah then foretold the death of the king, using the familiar ancient metaphor of the shepherd. Certainly we see a degree of ambiguity in this passage, a lack of clarity that has caused many students of the Bible to reflect on the source and purpose of deception and how or when one can be misled by another. Our purpose here is not to enter that conversation but to begin to understand the nature of irony and how using its intrinsic deception to tell the truth is an important tool of indirect communication.

Why is it difficult today to awaken people to what Bonhoeffer called "costly grace?"[2] The difficulty arises from the dynamic that so few people understand the depth of love and the full measure of new life available through grace. Ancient peoples settled for false gods under the illusion that they would bring them happiness. Modern men and women worship the idols of the age without even realizing it or recognizing it as worship. They are under a spell and so distracted that they are barely even aware of the depth of love and attraction they have for these things, or idols, that so occupy their time.

One reason why *No Country for Old Men,* both the book (published in 2005) and the movie (released in 2007), had such a powerful effect on audiences worldwide was that it used a haunting and violent story to give a clear warning that something in our culture has gone desperately wrong. Even if a reader or viewer remained unaware of the warning, at the subconscious level the story had a note of authenticity about it. No serious reader or viewer could walk away from that book or movie without recognizing that something was terribly wrong with the culture portrayed in the story—and it is difficult indeed not to see the parallels between the culture portrayed on screen and our own.

When crafting stories that call people to account, it is often better to do so out of a posture of weakness and vulnerability than to rely on

1. 1 Kings 22:13–23.
2. Bonhoeffer, *Cost of Discipleship.*

the strong arm of status or authority. People often respond better to authentic and honest stories than they do to stories from authority figures and experts. While we must be careful not to veer into the error of rank populism, we must also be aware that our culture is inundated with "expert" advice that we all recognize as fraudulent.

In a culture that prides itself on its individualism and objectivity, it often feels easier to engage a person by using direct and straightforward speech than to carefully shape or craft a message to stir within them a desire to grow as a person. Confronting someone through direct speech, however, is usually viewed as combative, rude, and offensive—in other words, anything but loving. Being confronted in a direct way often only strengthens a person's resolve to resist a message and intensifies his or her resolve to continue unchanged. Irony can help to break through that resistance. Irony is clearly a major theme found in many forms of indirect communication. It is especially helpful in grabbing the reader's attention and provoking thought and can be employed in various ways.

Kierkegaard demonstrates an ironic style of writing in almost all his works.[3] M. Mamie Ferreira noticed that Kierkegaard's lively, facetious style of writing, particularly in his pseudonymous works, provides a clear example of the way irony can disturb the clarity of the message he strives to articulate. Regarding Kierkegaard's ironic style of writing, Brian Söderquist states, "While a reader might expect or demand a clear, conceptual argument, his irony hinders that approach. Moreover, the fact that his authorship offers a plurality of voices via pseudonyms—few of whom declare their intentions unambiguously—is often viewed as a form of ironic indirection."[4]

Irony ranked high among Kierkegaard's philosophical preoccupations and recurs often in his writings. Kierkegaard thought of irony not only or exclusively as a specific kind of speech act but viewed irony as "a particular way of engaging in public (interpersonal) activity in general; speech (or writing) is only one of the activities that may be so engaged in."[5] Further, "When Irony is not merely used in isolated comments here and there but is employed more methodically—as we see in Socratic dialogues, for example, or an entire book written in an ironic

3. Elrod, *Kierkegaard and Christendom*.

4. Söderquist, "Irony," 344.

5. Cross, "Neither Either Nor Or," 126.

tone—immediate comprehension is impeded. And decoding the irony is not a simple matter."[6]

In this situation, the intended meaning of the dialogue as a whole remains ambiguous and becomes difficult to discern. "Precisely how many, and which, of the utterances in Kierkegaard's texts should be taken as ironical (or in some way indirect) is a matter of considerable controversy."[7] We need not attempt to resolve this issue here, as others have discussed it more fully.[8] Without dismissing the larger context sometimes referred to in Kierkegaard's writing, we will continue to focus on his use of irony as a literary or rhetorical device.

A Definition of Irony

Nassim Bravo Jordan states that our word "irony" comes "from the Greek εἰρωνεία, dissimulation. According to its lexical meaning in Danish, it is the expression of something that the speaker does not mean or that is the opposite of what he means."[9] It can refer "to the freedom or arbitrariness of fantasy over its object" or it may refer "to the state of mind that puts the finite in contrast with the infinite, thus stripping the former of all its value. Finally, it also refers to the method used by Socrates."[10]

Jordan distinguishes two types of irony: irony as a rhetorical device, and irony as a life-view or existential position. C. Stephen Evans argues that in *The Concept of Irony*, Kierkegaard identifies two kinds of irony. The first form of irony is that which is said in earnest, which is not meant to be earnest; while the second form of irony is to say something in jest that is meant to be taken as earnest. In either case the meaning is circuitous and may not be immediately understood.[11]

Like all definitions of irony, Kierkegaard's is dubious, as it is not immediately apparent what it means, and it requires skill or care in handling and coping with its meaning. Andrew Cross states that "ironic speech

6. Cross, "Neither Either Nor Or," 126.

7. Cross, "Neither Either Nor Or," 125.

8. See again Cross, "Neither Either Nor Or"; Evans, "Role of Irony"; and Söderquist, "Irony."

9. Jordan, "Irony," 39.

10. Jordan, "Irony," 39.

11. Evans, "Role of Irony."

intends to convey the opposite of the literal meaning of what is said."[12] In his writings Kierkegaard uses many different forms of irony, and it is not immediately apparent how these different types of irony—such as Socratic interrogation, Romantic imagination, witty speech, literary indirection, and other such forms—are related. According to Söderquist, Kierkegaard's own understanding of irony asserts that "there is no positive 'something' these ironies aim to bring about. Rather, they all function 'negatively:' Indirectly, irony says 'that is not what I mean;' 'this is not who I am;' 'that is not true:' 'that is not authentic.' Irony is negativity, even 'infinite absolute negativity,' as he puts it in *On the Concept of Irony*."[13] With irony, therefore, it is specifically what has *not* been said that is so vital. This implies irony is not only a tactic that complicates direct communication, but also that one intends to communicate in an indirect or ambiguous manner. As Söderquist states, "Univocal meaning is disrupted, but intelligibility is not thereby eliminated."[14]

Irony Requires a Contradiction

Like humor, irony "always involves a contradiction (or opposition) between the external and the internal, between the ironist's inner state and his outward behavior."[15] For Kierkegaard, irony implies a particular way of engaging in public discourse—both through one's life and through various artistic expressions—whether speech, writing, film, etc. Instead of viewing irony as just another speech act, Kierkegaard wanted to articulate the distinctive structure of how one could live ironically. Cross argues that Kierkegaard "examines what it is to speak ironically, in short, in order to determine what is it to live ironically—to manifest in one's life, unqualifiedly, and attitudes and types of orientation toward the world that constitute irony."[16]

Therefore, Kierkegaard identifies irony as a way of living and communicating. Rhetorical irony focuses not on what we say or communicate, but on how we say it. Consequently, irony is an assertion that expresses the opposite of what one means. Söderquist gives several examples of

---

12. Cross, "Neither Either Nor Or," 127.

13. Söderquist, "Irony," 344.

14. Söderquist, "Irony," 346.

15. Cross, "Neither Either Nor Or," 127.

16. Cross, "Neither Either Nor Or," 126.

irony when he states that irony is "a seeming compliment that is really an acrimonious critique, a playful amorous innuendo that is meant in earnest, a triviality that is expressed in a deadly serious tone, or something painful spoken of as if it didn't matter at all. You say one thing but mean another. In all such cases, he says, what is uttered and what is meant are in tension."[17]

Climacus writes, "Irony is only a possibility," and by this he means that irony is not actualized communication but should be understood as a "consciously understood, possibility of ethical self-choice."[18] With this understanding of irony, Kierkegaard draws "attention to the disparity between the meaning the ironic speaker would like to convey indirectly—the essence—and the literal words he or she presents to the world outside—the phenomenon."[19] The phenomenon is not to be taken at face value and immediate comprehension is encumbered. What you see or hear is not what you are to grasp . . . at least not right away.

For Kierkegaard, irony cancels itself; it is like a riddle in which one is made aware and at the same time has within grasp the explanation. When one uses an ironic trope, he or she speaks in a kind of code. For example, one may say, "Lovely weather we're having," when one actually means, "What a crummy day!" Part of the intention for using this trope is to call to mind an incongruity between those who would unpretentiously take what a person says at face value and those who are sufficiently discerning what one really means.[20] Thus, ironic communication does not *wish* to be immediately understood, but wants the audience to pause and think about what is really being communicated. Therefore, only those who really attend to what is said or presented may understand. Irony requires much of the audience, who must remain alert to the true meaning of the interaction. It should be clear that not everyone will understand an ironic statement.

17. Söderquist, "Irony," 345.

18. Kierkegaard, *Concluding Unscientific Postscript*, 1:505; Cross, "Neither Either Nor Or," 150.

19. Söderquist, "Irony," 346.

20. Cross, "Neither Either Nor Or," 128.

Actor Oriented Irony
and the Construction of Meaning

When used by Christians, irony liberates only in the sense that the final decision or apprehension of truth occurs within the person hearing or viewing the art. We make people aware through ironic and provocative stories or art, and in so doing we can put God as a question before them—and we are called to love them no matter how they answer the question.

If one lives in a country or a culture with no perception of Christ and what he has done for us, then Kierkegaard might well encourage us to communicate directly (not ironically) when communicating the gospel. If one lives in a community that already has heard of and understands Christianity however—regardless of the accuracy of their "knowledge"—then a different approach to communicating faith is probably necessary. Kierkegaard's pseudonymous author Climacus states, "In a Christian country it is not information that is lacking; something else is lacking, and one human being cannot directly communicate this something else to another."[21] Notice the requirement for using this approach "in a Christian country."

A second qualifier also requires mention. Perhaps some information is known, but there exists an emotional or social resistance to the information. In this case, as in the case where an illusion exists, an indirect and possibly an ironic approach is generally preferred. The indirect approach and the use of irony is used primarily for those times when doubt is present or when a person is in some way not amenable to the message. When the individual has in some way been immunized against the message, the indirect approach is often favored.

In an article in the *New York Times* called "God Is a Question, Not an Answer," William Irwin reminds us that "Bertrand Russell was once asked what he would say to God if it turned out there was one and he met him at judgment. Russell's reply: 'You gave us insufficient evidence.'"[22] While this sounds like we need more information and better arguments, I doubt that's true. Irwin explains, "Even believers can appreciate Russell's response. God does not make it easy. God, if he exists, is *deus absconditus*, the hidden God. He does not show himself unambiguously to all people, and people disagree about his existence."[23] The article explains that we

---

21. Kierkegaard, *Concluding Unscientific Postscript*, 1:614.

22. Irwin, "God Is a Question."

23. Irwin, "God Is a Question."

should all possess and express humility in the face of the question of God's presence in our world, even if we think the odds are skewed heavily in favor of a specific answer.

Dark Glasses to Mask the Meaning

Ludo Anolli, Rita Ciceri, and Maria Giaele Infantino use the metaphor of the "dark glasses" to explain how one can hide or mask one's emotional or physical state by hiding the eyes. "Irony," they suggest, "can be likened to a pair of 'dark glasses,' uncovering" what it apparently hides. Moreover, just as dark glasses "conceal what they display," so irony is "a strategy for indirect speech."[24]

As a "meaning-full" mask, irony has the capacity to render flexible the borders of the field of meaning, allowing for a renegotiation with the situation. An ironic statement may be viewed as a violation of fidelity in that the words spoken or written do not accurately depict the literal meaning of what is said or written. For example, if a person gets fired from his or her job, a friend may come up and say, "How goes retirement?" This is both an ironic and humorous statement. But if the person fired does not, at least not at first, understand that it is an ironic statement, he or she may get defensive and say something like, "I am not retired," and completely miss the irony and the humor. Since both irony and humor are very contextual, they are both very easily misunderstood. Nevertheless, these words provide the possibility of seeing the *event*, the loss of one's job, in a different light and may even encourage or emotionally support the one who lost their job.

The Fencing Game

The metaphor of the dark glasses is the starting point of what Anolli, Ciceri, and Infantino consider "a model of irony seen as a 'fencing game.'"[25] According to this model, "irony is considered as a mask revealing, paradoxically, what it apparently hides."[26] They build their study on two theories: symbolic interactionism and planning communication.

24. Anolli et al., "Behind Dark Glasses," 76–77.
25. Anolli et al., "Behind Dark Glasses," 76.
26. Anolli et al., "Behind Dark Glasses," 76.

The authors analyze and identify three social functions of irony: 1) to evade censure in a socially correct way, 2) to safeguard private space, and 3) to renegotiate meanings. I will discuss these more fully later in this chapter, but now I want us to consider irony as a fencing game, "a script of actions that people use astutely in order to strike antagonists in a graceful but 'stinging' way, just like fencers in a competition."[27]

Within the fencing game model, irony takes on two characteristics: First, "irony has a mask aiming at indirectly calling into question both situations and events (from the Accadic etymology, irony is a 'covering,' from the Greek etymology, ironist is 'the one who asks a question pretending to be naïve or less known than he is')."[28] The second characteristic is that, "irony is strategy (because the ironic remark implies a plan and intentional process in order to subtly manage one's own face according to a cultural standard)."[29]

Some may question this tactic and regard it as too playful or even deceptive, worried that it will not be seen as a serious or earnest communication approach. Muench, however, argues that irony and earnestness can both be present at the same time, as they are not mutually exclusive. For Muench, irony is one way of handling difficult communication situations or helping others come to a new understanding of a long-held belief.[30]

An earnest charge from the Old Testament and repeated by Jesus himself makes sharp use of irony: "The secret of the kingdom of God has been given to you. But to those on the outside everything is said in parables [perhaps meant as riddles] so that, they may be ever seeing but never perceiving, and ever hearing but never understanding; otherwise they might turn and be forgiven!" (Mark 4:11–12) Harrington explains, "The irony contained in Isa 6:9–10 is continued in Mark 4:12 ('. . . because the last thing they want is to turn and have their sins forgiven!')."[31]

Irony is an important literary device or visual tactic available to artists and professional communicators. The strategy of indirect communication may use one or more visual tactics and literary devices in order to spark change or decision. Therefore, indirect communication is both

27. Anolli et al., "Behind Dark Glasses," 76.

28. Anolli et al., "Behind Dark Glasses," 77.

29. Anolli et al., "Behind Dark Glasses," 77.

30. Muench, "Socratic Method."

31. Harrington, "Gospel According to Mark," 605.

a planned and intentional process as well as an artistic strategy carefully designed and purposively implemented. Ironic art or communication should be carefully developed in order to subtly interact with cultural standards. Ultimately irony is not simply a single entity but is found in a family of forms: sarcastic irony (blame by praise); kind irony (praise by blame); and bantering irony (back and forth blame or praise).

Anolli et al. found three primary situations where irony is especially useful. First, irony may be a "pretense upon agreement: evading censure in a socially correct way."[32] Irony may be found useful when a direct and impetuous expression is unsuitable or inappropriate for the context. The ironic act should be presented in a subtle and diplomatic way. They state, "irony is an effective strategy for hitting the mark on an implicit and indirect way without violating the norms required by one's own cultural background."[33] In this way, irony attempts to show respect for one's social standards and tries to avoid another person's censure, while still addressing subject matter that would otherwise be offensive. "With irony, one accepts the cultural norms, and, at the same time, one violates them."[34]

A second use of irony may be seen as "safeguarding private space."[35] According to Anolli et al., irony is "useful for the protection of one's personal space and one's privacy. Irony, in fact, can be used not only as a device to evade social censor, but also as a planned action aimed at maintaining dignity, restraint, and demeanor."[36] Irony allows the artist or communicator to avoid the risk of self-exposure, much like wearing dark glasses allows a person to examine or look at people or situations without others knowing where he or she is looking. In a similar way irony allows one to "discuss dogmas, simplify problems, and handle with cold attachment what they passionately feel" without the risk of self-exposure.[37] Irony is especially useful in dealing with sensitive relational or emotional content. In this way irony can be understood as performative in that it relies on a *public* display that is different from what is happening *privately*. Kierkegaard (writing as his pseudonym Johannes de Silentio) talks about the irony of one who fasts from food. Kierkegaard reminds us that Jesus

---

32. Anolli et al., "Behind Dark Glasses," 82.
33. Anolli et al., "Behind Dark Glasses," 82.
34. Anolli et al., "Behind Dark Glasses," 82.
35. Anolli et al., "Behind Dark Glasses," 83.
36. Anolli et al., "Behind Dark Glasses," 83.
37. Anolli et al., "Behind Dark Glasses," 83.

commands this indirect and ironic approach when fasting. Essentially he says do not be so direct about it but instead "put oil on your head and wash your face, so that it will not be obvious to men that you are fasting" (Matt 6:17–18). Much the same approach is commanded by Jesus when praying. Here he states that one prays in private rather than public prayer. Both of these illustrations are powerful performative ironic stands to take, both also commanded by Christ.

Finally, "irony is semantic [or artistic] ambiguity: renegotiating meaning."[38] Anolli et al. argue that "the ironic comment is like a skin: it alludes to what is hidden."[39] Because the meaning of an ironic statement or art is ambiguous in that the reader, hearer, or viewer is unsure if the statement or art is meant to be taken as literal or innuendo; that is, should it be understood as criticism or a compliment? Consequently, the meaning must be interpreted. Irony "creates a gap of indeterminacy and ambiguousness, leaving the interlocutor [reader, listener, or viewer] free to follow various paths of meaning."[40]

Functioning as a mask that both hides and reveals, irony "shifts the focus from the literal sense to the metapragmatic framework of interaction."[41] With "irony the intention must be known and not known at the same time."[42] Consequently, it is a powerful tool, both in the arts and in personal or social conversation.

We Have to Think About It

Making an ironic statement does not necessarily mean that the author or speaker wishes to be misunderstood. Söderquist argues that indirect ironic statements are different from those statements directly communicated and they "momentarily hinder immediate, straightforward communication."[43] Still, the artist or communicator may have something he or she wants to communicate. In fact the artist may want to edify the hearer, reader, or viewer through the creative effort.

38. Anolli et al., "Behind Dark Glasses," 84.
39. Anolli et al., "Behind Dark Glasses," 84.
40. Anolli et al., "Behind Dark Glasses," 88.
41. Anolli et al., "Behind Dark Glasses," 91.
42. Anolli et al., "Behind Dark Glasses," 91.
43. Söderquist, "Irony," 346.

Regarding Kierkegaard's use of irony, Söderquist states, "Whatever else is going on, it is safe to say that the author behind this gallery of characters is not simply and directly saying what he means, and the intent of the author—if we assume that it makes sense to insist on discovering it—remains hidden."[44]

Kierkegaard's indirect approach to art and communication forces the reader or hearer "to deal with the fact that there is no author directly speaking his mind, and this fact more obviously pushes interpretive responsibility back to the reader. Even for those who are optimistic about the possibility of locating something like an authorial intent, the ironic use of pseudonymous masks compels one to check one's interpretive confidence."[45] To come to the point, readers or hearers can never be sure they have constructed the real voice or the essential message of the story or art. "Part of this has to do with the tricky nature of irony itself. As noted above, the most profound forms of irony are not limited to an isolated statement or passage but seem to pervade the entire text."[46] Söderquist argues that "irony is one of those forms of indirect communication that refuses univocal interpretation."[47] Consequently, irony "affirms even as it refutes; it makes a claim and retracts the claim at one and the same time."[48]

Irony Avoids Didactic and Admonishing Tones

Irony may be ambiguous, nevertheless it assists the hearer or viewer to engage with the symbols encountered and to construct his or her own meaning out of these symbols. In doing so, irony presents a contradiction and leaves it to the listening individual to make sense of what he or she hears or perceives. It allows audience members to take responsibility for their lives and the decisions they make—that is, to take the truth personally and subjectively.

Still, ironic communication avoids a didactic or admonishing tone because it is indirect. Initially, at least, it is unrecognizable in that it does not take on the character that one expects; precisely because of this it

44. Söderquist, "Irony," 348.
45. Söderquist, "Irony," 349.
46. Söderquist, "Irony," 350.
47. Söderquist, "Irony," 350.
48. Söderquist, "Irony," 350.

makes no immediate claims. Ironic communication "compels the reader to make and refute those claims him- or herself."[49] Söderquist argues that "irony frees the individual from the unwarranted authority of inherited laws, customs, habits, beliefs, and norms. It creates an open space, unencumbered by the demands of human tradition, and the individual is at least initially forced back into him- or herself."[50]

Söderquist reminds us that Kierkegaard, playing on a passage in the Gospel of John, "argues that the path to selfhood goes through irony: '[irony] is not the truth, but the way.'"[51] For Kierkegaard, irony ultimately can lead one to an authentic interpretation of oneself and one's own history, which "requires a consciousness of the divine other."[52] Kierkegaard argues that a self that lacks narrative stability is not a self at all.

According to Evans, stable irony—as opposed to unstable or unintentional irony—is intentional and frees us from immediacy, which may be the way to help people "see the spiritual significance of human life."[53] Stable irony is "irony endowed with a moral purposiveness."[54] Finally, Evans asserts that for Kierkegaard "irony does not undermine but presupposes the claims of Christian revelation."[55] We now turn to humor, a literary and communication device frequently used by Kierkegaard.

The Use of Humor

Alejandro González states, "for Kierkegaard, humor tensions the strings of human subjectivity, confounding and teasing towards a higher existential sphere that surpasses irony. Humor outstrips irony in its skepticism since, whereas irony focuses on human finitude, humor is anchored in a grasp of human sinfulness."[56]

Evans points out that Kierkegaard saw humor to be linked to the religious life in that it "resides in a deep structure of human existence."[57]

49. Söderquist, "Irony," 352.

50. Söderquist, "Irony," 356.

51. Söderquist, "Irony," 356.

52. Söderquist, "Irony," 360.

53. Evans, "Role of Irony," 79.

54. Evans, "Role of Irony," 79.

55. Evans, "Role of Irony," 80.

56. Gonzalez, "Humor," 176.

57. Evans, "Role of Irony," 81.

He argues that there are two important notions concerning humor. The first is that a fundamental connection exists between humor and human existence, and second, a crucial connection exists between humor and the religious life. This means that humor is not an accidental or inconsequential human characteristic. Evans states, "Quite contrary to the stereotype of the religious life as dour and somber, completely opposed to the carefree wit of the humorist, Kierkegaard holds that the highest and deepest kind of humor is rooted in a life view which is recognizably religious."[58] Humor is made viable by essentially the same characteristics of human life that make the religious life possible.

Kierkegaard understands humor as a theory of incongruity. In this view, "humor arises through some contrast between what we would normally expect and the actual course of our experience."[59] Oscar Parcero Oubinha asserts, "In Kierkegaard, 'the comic' functions primarily as an 'umbrella term' that comprises other concepts more precisely defined, such as irony and humor," as well as jokes, satire, and wit.[60] This explains why Johannes Climacus, Kierkegaard's pseudonymous author of *Concluding Unscientific Postscript to Philosophical Fragments*, suggests that the humorist is a practiced comic, as humor "has the comic *within itself*."[61] Climacus also states, "The tragic and the comic are the same inasmuch as both are contradiction, but *the tragic is suffering contradiction, and the comic is painless contradiction*."[62] Evans asserts that what Kierkegaard really meant by "contradiction" was "'incongruity,' certainly not logical or formal contradiction."[63]

Three Examples of Humor

Terry Lindvall maintains that the comedic is "based on an experienced contradiction or incongruity. The comic resides in this omnipresent category of contradiction. Even the religious individual will have to confront the tension between inwardness and external activity. Something is not

58. Evans, "Role of Irony," 81.

59. Evans, "Role of Irony," 82.

60. Oubinha, "Comic/Comedy," 5.

61. Kierkegaard, *Concluding Unscientific Postscript*, 1:521.

62. Kierkegaard, *Concluding Unscientific Postscript*, 1:514.

63. Evans, "Role of Irony," 83.

right with the world, and Christianity recognizes that."[64] For example, "If a man tries to establish himself as a tavern keeper and fails, this is not comic. However, if a girl tries to get permission to establish herself as a prostitute and fails, which sometimes happens, this is comic—very comic, inasmuch as it contains many contradictions [or incongruities]."[65] Or consider another example of the comic: "If a king disguised himself as a butcher and a butcher happened to resemble the king in a striking way, people would laugh at both of them, but for opposite reasons—at the butcher because he was not the king, and at the king because he was not the butcher."[66] Finally, we have the example of the person who asks:

> "Did you hear Andy preach today?"
>
> "Yes, I did."
>
> "What did you think of the sermon?"
>
> "Well, there were some really good things in it—for example, the Lord's Prayer."[67]

The significance of the polemical in the comic is a necessary element in the communication process. "Thus, faith is blessed with many such incongruities: the infinite God appearing in finite time; joy erupting out of suffering, as birth out of labor; and the most despicable sins being forgiven. Christianity hides its truths in mysteries and paradoxes."[68] Kierkegaard argues that humor, "present throughout Christianity, is expressed in a fundamental principle which declares that the truth is hidden in the mystery . . . which teaches not only that the truth is found in a mystery . . . but that it is in fact hidden in the mystery."[69] Flannery O'Connor's literary fiction, which is a kind of comic realism (both comic and realistic), compels the readers to discover within themselves a kind of mind that is "willing to have its sense of mystery deepened by contract with reality, and its sense of reality deepened by contact with mystery."[70] George Kilcourse comments, "The leaven of O'Connor's humor appears often when she ponders our neglect of ultimate questions and the

---

64. Lindvall, *God Mocks*, 174.

65. Kierkegaard, *Søren Kierkegaard's Journals and Papers*, 2:266.

66. Kierkegaard, *Søren Kierkegaard's Journals and Papers*, 2:267.

67. Kierkegaard, *Søren Kierkegaard's Journals and Papers*, 2:273.

68. Lindvall, *God Mocks*, 174.

69. Kierkegaard, *Søren Kierkegaard's Journals and Papers*, 2:252.

70. O'Connor, *Mystery and Manners*, 10.

consequences of missing the glimpse of truth offered in literature."[71] Thus, humor, jest, and story all prod us to examine our lives and our relation to the infinite. It is a contradiction that causes us to contemplate these kinds of questions using both jest and earnestness.

As argued in chapter 2, more and more of our lives are given over to a mediated reality. Many people within our fragmented society try to escape the isolation or anxiety by turning to a variety of technological idols including video games, social media, cellular phones, etc., to distract themselves from the discomfort they feel. So we try to avoid not only the finite reality and its imperfection but also the suffering that makes up a part of all our lives. González explains, "the humorist recognizes that life and suffering are essentially yoked," and even though the media is like a drug that helps distract us from the stress of living, it does so at the expense of facing the reality of our existence.[72] However, life presents us with the comic as well. Evans states, "Everyone who exists has . . . a sensitivity for the comic just by virtue of existing."[73] Therefore, everyone who takes a moment to contemplate their life "is able to see a contradiction here or there and to smile and laugh at it. Not everyone, however, is able to see and face the fundamental contradiction of her own existence—to smile and laugh over herself."[74] Evans observes, "the humorist intellectually sees what the religious individuals sees. He has a knowledge of the great contradiction which is the heart of the religious life."[75] For both the humorist and the religious individual "life itself is fundamentally a jest."[76]

Kierkegaard discusses the many times humor appears in Christ's own words and ministry. For example,

> There is more joy in heaven over one sinner who repents than over 100 who do not need repentance (now the irony emerges here)*. It is easier for a camel to go through the eye of a needle than for a rich man to enter the kingdom of heaven.
>
> *Since the meaning can never be that there was a single righteous person who did not need repentance. The same

71. Kilcourse, *Flannery O'Connor's Religious Imagination*, 16.

72. Gonzalez, "Humor," 180.

73. Evans, "Role of Irony," 87.

74. Evans, "Role of Irony," 87.

75. Evans, "Role of Irony," 88.

76. Evans, "Role of Irony," 88.

meaning is seriously expressed in the works: Let him who is without sin among you be the first to throw a stone."[77]

A fundamental contradiction clearly appears in each of these examples. Evans states that the "place for humor is provided by the grace of God and the forgiveness which is offered freely in Christ. It is this which makes it possible for the earnest individual to smile at the contradiction between his life and the ideal he sees in Christ."[78]

Lindvall adds that Johannes Climacus, Kierkegaard's pseudonymous character, acknowledges "the comic as a necessary means of 'indirect communication.' It helps to shatter the illusions of the affective poet, the practical businessman, and speculative philosopher. Any thinker who tries to approach the religious question in an inappropriately objective manner is caught in the grip of an illusion that invites the comic, or the satirical, to jolt him or her from stupidity."[79] Stories that awaken us to the contradictions in our lives grab our attention and jar us into facing the mystery of our existence. As such, humor itself embodies a religious perspective.

The fundamental contradiction which is at the heart of all comedy is that God chooses to bless and give life to fallen humanity. "The comedy of God's saving the most unlikely people when they least expect it, the joke in which God laughs with man and man with God."[80] Frederick Buechner suggests that while the tragic is seemingly inevitable "the comic is the unforeseeable" and as such it catches us by surprise.[81] Furthermore, he points out that the comic is always unexpected. Buechner states, "Is it possible, I wonder, to say that it is only when you hear the Gospel as a wild and marvelous joke that you really hear it at all?"[82] Sarah now in her old age is told she will have a child. How could she not laugh? The prodigal son who squanders his father's fortune yet when he returns home, he receives a blessing and a party. What a joke and a joy. Again and again the stories of the Scripture surprise us and shock us with joyous contradictions.

77. Kierkegaard, *Søren Kierkegaard's Journals and Papers*, 2:254.

78. Evans, "Role of Irony," 89.

79. Lindvall, *God Mocks*, 270–71.

80. Buechner, *Telling the Truth*, 73.

81. Buechner, *Telling the Truth*, 57.

82. Buechner, *Telling the Truth*, 68.

Our purpose here was not to exhaust the depths of irony or humor. We have a more modest goal: to introduce the contribution of these two literary devices to storytelling and indirect communication and identify a few more literary devices available to the storyteller. It is the function of irony and comedy to provoke men and women to consider the absolute paradox: Christ. "For the Christian, the grace of God and forgiveness in Christ are found through faith, which is an existential passion with a concrete historical object. His life then becomes a blend of jest and earnestness, a gift and a task. The gift is given with the task, and the task with the gift."[83]

We want only to suggest that artists with Christian concerns need to become more imaginative in their creative work and perhaps to see their art as an attempt to move people toward Christ, a little at a time, realizing that they are part of a process orchestrated by God. We cannot change one person's mind, nor should we try. We are called to invite and introduce people to Christ. We are witnesses (not lawyers) to that which has taken hold of us and in the most profound comical way makes us new. Our lives have become a intermingling of jest and earnestness: a gift and a task. Now let us turn to identify briefly a few other literary devices available to the artist wishing to employ an indirect strategy.

Other Literary Devices

Erik Garrett argues that for Kierkegaard, indirect communication "was an experimental method that employed irony, humor, playfulness, seduction, and even love."[84] Kierkegaard used several literary techniques to resist one-sidedness and closure, or what he calls "dialectical" aspects in his writing. Ferreira points out,

> [Kierkegaard used several] literary strategies and techniques to unsettle us, to perplex us, to cause us to rethink things; he is always asking provocative questions and using unexpected interventions and comparisons, to make us uncomfortable in our security, to de-familiarize us with something we think we are familiar with already, to make problematical the totality, the system, the closed, the finished, the completed, the finalized.[85]

83. Evans, "Role of Irony," 89.

84. Garrett, "Essential Secret," 16.

85. Ferreira, Kierkegaard, 2.

While Christ ministered on earth, he was not always quick to answer every question, but he often responded to a question with a question of his own. This, of course, is another form of indirect communication. This process understands that not everyone who asks a question really wants to hear the truth. Grace is offered to those who really want to hear and see, to those with a heart open to receive the grace of God.

Often Christ would use pictures or stories to provoke his hearers to reflect on some critical issue before him. He would present a story or paint a picture, only to ask, "What is wrong with the story or picture?" Ferreira states that Kierkegaard repeatedly asks his reader "to imagine strange situations, asking what if someone who wanted to achieve X were to do Y, what would you think. He consistently invites the reader to do the work of making judgments or to come up with alternatives. His writings encourage us to appreciate the tension-filled nature of life."[86]

Not only does the indirect artist challenge the reader or viewer, but often the artist may be ambiguous or deceptive in presenting the truth. Gifted artists often use such literary devices as satire, sarcasm, or riddle. Artists using an indirect strategy use these passionate polemics with an underlying measure of compassion, remembering that such tools should always be used for edification. Ferreira reminds us that all of Kierkegaard's "books could have the subtitle he gave to one of them, 'For Upbuilding and Awakening.'"[87]

We have suggested that Kierkegaard intended his writings to provoke the reader to reflection and action. His book *Fear and Trembling*, which we previously referenced, recalls the biblical concept of the fear of God as devotion, found both in the Old Testament as found in passages such as Psalms 11 and 12 and in some New Testament letters by St. Paul, for example, Phil 2:12–13. He wants us to think earnestly about the challenge presented in these passages considering the Abraham and Isaac story. Ferreira reminds us that "the subtitle *a Dialectical Lyric* conjures up the idea of either a contradiction in terms or a tension filled lyric."[88] The pseudonymous author, Johannes de Silentio, is unmistakably "meant to be provocative—a book authored by silence, a message generated in silence about silence."[89]

86. Ferreira, *Kierkegaard*, 2.

87. Ferreira, *Kierkegaard*, 2.

88. Ferreira, *Kierkegaard*, 50.

89. Ferreira, *Kierkegaard*, 50.

Another example of this provocational intent is found in Kierke-gaard's pseudonymous Johannes Climacus, who uses a variety of literary devices (irony, parody, satire)—including casting his writing in the form of a philosophical thought experiment—where he or she must scrutinize a hypothesis. In so doing, Kierkegaard creates a circumstance where his readers are obliged to wrestle with the unusual forms they encounter in the text. Readers are transported repeatedly to topics that may have been neglected or forgotten from earlier readings; and because the reader thought they already had achieved a thorough understanding of them, the topics no longer have the same meaning or force they once had. Nor do they have the proper role they should have in the person's life. The new construct of the topic is intended to be problematic, to create a new awareness of the topic and a reconsideration of its meaning. As Muench explains, "This is communication to the person who already has found the difficulty so very easy to explain. If it so happens . . . that a reader can scarcely recognize in the presented material that with which he was finished long ago, the communication will bring him to a halt."[90] Such a halt can lead to a subsequent opportunity for the reader to struggle to overcome the strange forms they encounter in the book with the aim of the reader becoming aware that he or she has forgotten what it is to exist as a Christian and the struggle allied with such an existence.

A Biblical Example

We find a clear Old Testament example of indirect communication in the book of Ecclesiastes. In many ways, Kierkegaard is like a modern-day writer of Ecclesiastes. The book implies that its author is Solomon, but most scholars doubt this. Like Kierkegaard's pseudonymous works, the Solomonic attribution appears to be a literary convention typical of the wisdom tradition.

More than authorship, the structure of this book is of utmost im-portance in its interpretation, for the book is intentionally enigmatic. In other words, it is intended to be perplexing. Like a riddle, it is meant to disturb us so that we may deeply contemplate its meaning and the topic under consideration.

Ecclesiastes seems frequently disjointed and often cryptic in style, which serves to baffle the reader. It contains apparent inconsistencies that

90. Muench, "Socratic Method," 144.

make it difficult to determine the author's true view. This book, however, presents an astute study and criticism of the human condition. Many detractors of this work—and there have been more than a few—question whether it should be included in the sacred canon. Others mistakenly think that the book exudes a mood predominantly of delusion and despair.

The chosen name of the author, *Qoheleth*, means "the preacher." The name implies a kind of wisdom conveyed by the speaker to those in the outer court, as distinguished from the "hidden wisdom" known only to those who have been given access to the mystery of God. If all this sounds familiar to the student of Kierkegaard, it is because so many similarities exist between this text and his writings.

While challenging to understand, both Ecclesiastes and many of Kierkegaard's works recognize that art can bring us into authentic confrontations with ourselves through indirect means. As Short states, "Art can also aid in penetrating man's emotional prejudices by showing him who he really is; by accurately reflecting his own pretensions, foibles, and anxieties; by setting up before him a mirror where he may see his own inmost part."[91] The New Testament too speaks to the challenge facing men or women who are unspiritual because they do not understand spiritual things. Paul explains that those who are "unspiritual . . . are unable to understand [spiritual truths] because they are spiritually discerned" (1 Cor 2:14). Literary techniques such as riddle, hinting, suggestion, and other devices indirectly communicate in order to address the hardness of one's heart or confront the illusions that stand in the way of taking in spiritual truth, and they ultimately make one capable of living in accordance to such truth.

Conclusion

This concludes our consideration of Kierkegaard's use of story and some of the literary techniques he used to make his hearers capable knowers. In the next three chapters we examine the use of indirect communication by Jesus, C. S. Lewis, and Flannery O'Connor.

91. Short, *Gospel According to Peanuts*, 14.

Section Three

Practitioners of Indirect Communication: Jesus, C.S. Lewis, and Flannery O'Connor

Chapters 7–9

7

Jesus: Parable and Provocation

It seems to me that more often than not the parables can be read as high and holy jokes about God and about man and about the Gospel itself as the highest and holiest joke of them all.

—FREDERICK BUECHNER, *TELLING THE TRUTH*

Introduction

THE GREAT SCHOLAR KNOWN as the Vilna Gaon once asked the Preacher of Dubno,

> "Help me to understand. What makes a parable so influential? If I recite Torah, there's a small audience, but let me tell a parable and the synagogue is full. Why is that?" The *dubner maged* replied, "I'll explain it to you by means of a parable.
>
> Once upon a time Truth went about the streets as naked as the day he was born. As a result, no one would let him into their homes. Whenever people caught sight of him, they turned away or fled. One day when Truth was sadly wandering about, he came upon Parable. Now, Parable was dressed in splendid clothes of beautiful colors. And Parable, seeing Truth, said, 'Tell me, neighbor, what makes you look so sad?' Truth replied bitterly, 'Ah, brother, things are bad. Very bad. I'm old, very old,

and no one wants to acknowledge me. No one wants anything
to do with me.'

Hearing that, Parable said, 'People don't run away from you
because you're old. I too am old. Very old. But the older I get; the
better people like me. I'll tell you a secret: Everyone likes things
to be disguised and prettied up a bit. Let me lend you some
splendid clothes like mine, and you'll see that the very people
who pushed you aside will invite you into their homes and be
glad of your company.'

Truth took Parable's advice and put on the borrowed
clothes. And from that time on, Truth and Parable have gone
hand in hand together and everyone loves them. They make a
happy pair."[1]

I wonder sometimes whether we have forgotten that one of the tellers of Jesus's story insisted that "he did not say anything to them without using parables" (Matt 13:34). Matthew reminds us that Jesus's use
of parables was prefigured in Psalm 78, which declares, "I will open my
mouth in parables, I will utter hidden things, things from of old" (Matt
13:35). Jesus continually used the language of images and metaphor, not
merely to elucidate hidden things, but also to make them come alive.
In his parables, Jesus suggests what the kingdom of God is like, rather
than spelling it out in detail. His parables hint rather than explain. Again
and again he catches his audience by surprise with an unexpected turn
of events in the plot or with the unanticipated appearance of a strange
character.

In this chapter we will discuss Jesus's indirect approach to communication through the use of parables. Specifically, we will look at three
parables Jesus told: "The Rich Fool," "The Good Samaritan," and "The
Sower." Finally, we will discuss what it means to hear the word of God
(the appropriation of the word) and what it means to make the familiar
strange when communicating the gospel.

Jesus the Storyteller

We live in images and we feel our way into our views or beliefs every bit
as much as we think our way into them. We have seen how the indirect
approach focuses more on feelings or images than ideas or doctrine, and
therefore, how it speaks to the imaginative or emotive part of a person.

1. Weinreich, *Yiddish Folktales*, 7.

Therefore, the indirect method contends that human transformation occurs when we are awakened by images that carry deep symbolic force that modify or replace our present structures of knowing and being.

James A. K. Smith asserts the artist with Christian concerns is directed by a vision that "captures our hearts and imaginations not by providing a set of rules or ideas, but by painting a picture of what it looks like for us to flourish and live well. This is why such pictures are communicated so powerfully in stories, legends, myths, plays, novels, and films," rather than in dissertations, instruction manuals, laws, Twitter messages, and monographs.[2] Smith argues that "we are affective before we are cognitive (and even while we are cognitive), visions of the good get inscribed in us by means that are commensurate with our primary affective, imaginative nature."[3]

Parables that interest us succeed as clever stories. They entice us to attend to the narrative and they avoid becoming tedious by their cryptic and brief nature. They avoid unrealistic details that only get in the way of entering the story and they frequently describe startling behavior, but in doing so they never abandon the realm of credibility. Parables invite us to make judgments and interact with the storyteller or story. They tend to invite rather than persuade.

A parable is intended to challenge our previously held convictions or ideas. By design, they involve familiar subjects, but they are not necessarily easy to fully understand. As Harrington suggests, parables follow the conventions of good storytelling: "concision, repetition so as to set up a pattern, and surprise or contrasting ending."[4] As Thomas C. Oden states, they are "like a gift that one first needs to open and then has to figure out what he has to do with it."[5] In this way, the "parable seeks to facilitate a capacity that can only be set in motion by the act of self-discovery, but that capacity may remain dormant unless the self is jolted out of fixed behavioral routines, which the parables profoundly challenge."[6] Because of its unique properties, a good parable cannot be reduced to a simple proposition, nor does it serve as a simple illustration that could be

2. Smith, *Desiring the Kingdom*, 53.

3. Smith, *Desiring the Kingdom*, 53.

4. Harrington, "Gospel According to Mark," 605.

5. Oden, "Introduction," xv.

6. Oden, "Introduction," xv.

omitted from the text or larger story without doing unalterable harm to its meaning.

Robert L. Short asserts that parables are designed to help make seemingly impossible discernment possible; they do this by presenting the people with "riddles" (Prov 1:6) or "dark sayings" (Ps 78:2), calculated to awaken the hearers before they know what is happening to them. The parables "not only arrest attention; they arouse something deep within."[7] For example, "One scholar speaks of the parable's gentle renunciation of force as a kind of subtle seduction: on the one hand it is just a story, offered objectively as an event; on the other, it is a trap. And yet the reader or listener who becomes enmeshed in the story's net, entangled, as it were, in its narrative law, is not held captive to an interpretation. The reader is compelled, rather, to encounter him-or-herself."[8] Above all, parables endeavor to actualize what the author wants to accomplish in the hearer, to assist in the birth of capability.

Jesus was a storyteller. Jesus did not limit his teaching to indirect communication but used both direct and indirect methods to convey his message. Even a cursory glance at the Gospels shows that Jesus availed himself of a variety of literary and communicative devices. But rarely did he say or teach anything without employing parables; they were his primary means of public communication. In this section we will examine his use of parables as a form of indirect communication in order to better understand Jesus's overall communication strategy.

Before we begin, it is important to note Stephen Wright's advice that Jesus is sometimes seen as a patron for those who tell stories and who claim stories as a persuasive and vital vehicles for communication —particularly Christian communication. "There is a danger," Wright suggests, "of superficiality in this, if the range of possible purposes of Jesus's own storytelling is overlooked. Like any rhetorical form, story is not a mere innocent dress in which one can present any message one likes. Message and medium are bound up together. It does something as well as saying something, and through saying something."[9] It is with this in mind that we approach the parables of Jesus.

The parables come to us directly out of literary works—namely the Gospels—that describe Jesus's life and words. These works, likewise,

---

7. Short, *Gospel According to Peanuts*, 16.

8. Hawkins, *Language of Grace*, 13.

9. Wright, *Jesus the Storyteller*, 4.

contain hints into the meaning and reasons why Jesus used parables. Their presence in the sacred text generates a kind of creative pressure that intensifies the meaning of each story. The parables of Jesus are im-age-driven stories. They have a homely familiarity and feature comedy, exaggeration, distortion, and unexpected events that would have caught original audience members by surprise and captured their attention.

Amy-Jill Levine suggests Jesus told parables because they function as "keys that can unlock the mysteries we face by helping us ask the right questions: how-to live-in community; how to determine what ultimately matters; how to live the life that God wants us to live."[10] These short sto-ries serve as Jesus's way of teaching, and they continue to be remembered not just "because they are in the Christian canon, but because they con-tinue to provoke, challenge, and inspire."[11]

The Power of Story and Parable

Jesus knew what so many advertisers today know: the most influential way to teach or inspire another person does not depend on the use of statistical data or an answer sheet, but rather "from narratives that re-mind us of what we already knew, but are resistant to recall."[12] As Levine states, their influence "comes from stories that prompt us to draw our own conclusions and at the same time force us to realize that our answers may well be contingent, or leaps of faith, or traps."[13]

Stories that influence us feature unforgettable characters that feel both familiar and strange, and they force us to engage our stereotypes even as they confront them. "The parables, if we take them seriously not as historical portraits of real people but as challenges to our stereotypes, help us to locate both our eccentric traits and our excellent talents; they can inspire and humble, challenge and confront."[14]

By its nature a parable contains an element of surprise and the unexpected. As stated earlier, Buechner likens a parable to a "sad and holy joke."[15] Somewhat in jest but with a serious edge, he suggests that

10. Levine, *Short Stories by Jesus*, 275.

11. Levine, *Short Stories by Jesus*, 275.

12. Levine, *Short Stories by Jesus*, 275.

13. Levine, *Short Stories by Jesus*, 275.

14. Levine, *Short Stories by Jesus*, 274.

15. Buechner, *Telling the Truth*, 63.

part of the reason why Jesus seemed unwilling to explain his parables was "because if you have to explain a joke, you might as well save your breath."[16] Levine draws attention to the comic element of many parables when she says, "Jesus knew that the best teachings come from stories that make us laugh even as they make us uncomfortable."[17]

As previously suggested, the Gospels tell us that Jesus said almost nothing "without using a parable" and often his audience did not immediately understand them. Sometime after, "when he was alone with his own disciples, he would explain everything" (Mark 4:33–34). Interestingly, very few of these confidential explanations have been preserved for us, and the crowds who heard his stories, like us, were left to figure out for themselves what he meant. We also must find our own meaning.

Levine argues the Gospel writers, in their wisdom, left most of the parables as open narratives to invite us into engagement with them. Each reader will hear a distinct message and may find the same parable leaves multiple impressions over time.[18] The audience needs to suspend assumptions brought to the hearing of the parable and really *listen* to who Jesus is and what he is saying. Often the parables subvert contemporary understandings. Jesus accompanied his telling of parables with a charge for the audience to "listen." Then as now, many people looked for meaning within their comfort zone instead of allowing the provocation of the parable to disrupt their way of seeing things. They did not want his stories to compel them to restructure their beliefs.

Different audiences will inevitably hear different messages in the parables. Wright reasons that limiting the parables as stories to express only one general truth may obscure their form as stories. He states, "since we are dealing here with highly individual speech-forms, it should be obvious that claims to 'know' either Jesus's aims in telling stories or his hearers' responses to them should always be shrouded in modesty."[19] Levine echoes this sentiment when she says, "reducing parables to a single meaning destroys their aesthetic as well as ethical potential. This surplus of meaning is how poetry and storytelling work, and it is all to the good."[20] This does not relegate the parable to a purely private and

16. Buechner, *Telling the Truth*, 63.

17. Levine, *Short Stories by Jesus*, 276.

18. Levine, *Short Stories by Jesus*.

19. Wright, *Jesus the Storyteller*, 47.

20. Levine, *Short Stories by Jesus*, 1.

subjective truth, but rather encourages us to understand the parables "in a suggestive rather than a definitive manner, in recognition of the vast fields of possibility they open up."[21] (imagination)

Due to their unique narrative structure, the parables elicit various interpretations and then it becomes the audience's duty to sort through those interpretive options to find the meaning. Levine writes,

> Too often we settle for easy interpretations: we should be nice like the Good Samaritan; we will be forgiven, as was the prodigal son; we should pray and not lose heart like the importuning widow. When we seek universal morals from a genre that is designed to surprise, challenge, shake up, or indict and look for a single meaning in a form that opens to multiple interpretations, we are necessarily limiting the parables and, so, ourselves. Perhaps we should be "thinking less about what they 'mean' and more about what they can 'do': remind, provoke, refine, confront, disturb."[22]

Even though parables are generally regarded as familiar tales based on common everyday life, something mysterious usually accompanies Jesus's parables (see, for example, Mark 4:11–12 and Matt 13:11–13). The mystery here does not refer to "a special key to unlock a singular meaning. What makes the parables mysterious, or difficult, is that they challenge us to look into the hidden aspects of our own values, our own lives. They bring to the surface unasked questions, and they reveal the answers we have always known, but refuse to acknowledge."[23] This is what Jesus meant by "hearing" and what is meant by remaining open to various interpretations. This kind of listening challenges one to look inside and reflect on one's own life and behavior. To be truly heard, the parables require that we listen with our heart, emotions, and mind—our whole selves. They call us to look inward even as we imaginatively look outward, and in that way they provoke us to consider our inward selves.

The parables Jesus spoke to his audience immediately invited people to use their imagination. This imaginative element to his stories encouraged listeners to complete the meaning of the story. People think through images, and a parable is a potent way to ignite the imaginative power of the mind to consider self and situations in a new way. Brothers argues

21. Wright, *Jesus the Storyteller*, 47.

22. Levine, *Short Stories by Jesus*, 4.

23. Levine, *Short Stories by Jesus*, 3.

that the image-driven and narrative approach "cultivates a shift in consciousness" in those who hear and may result in a change of perception.[24] Of course, Jesus did not leave his audience without clues to help them construct the "imaginative world he was calling them to enter."[25]

Frequently parables ask difficult, uncomfortable questions that make us truly think about our life and the choices we make. For example, "To prepare his followers for the inbreaking, he also asked them to prioritize. What really matters, and what does not? The parables ask us questions. What is our pearl of great price? What would we do were we to find a treasure in the field? What would satisfy us, and what *should* satisfy us?"[26] Here, it seems, Jesus teaches his listeners by challenging them to decide.

As one classic example, "he refers to himself as the 'son of man,' and in so doing he forces his listeners to make a decision."[27] Those who lived in Israel in that day and who heard Jesus refer to himself by this title were immediately confronted with many questions. Is he talking about himself? Did he have in mind something like God's address to Ezekiel, when the Lord said, "Son of man, can these bones live?" Or is he recalling humanity's nearly divine nature and so almost limitless potential (see Ps 8:4–5)? Or is he perhaps alluding to the "Son of man" in Daniel 7:13–14, who was "coming with the clouds of heaven. He approached the Ancient of days and was led into his presence. He was given authority, glory and sovereign power; all peoples, nations, and men of every language worshiped him?" Or is it one of several other meanings known by the people to whom he spoke? Anyone hearing him at that time would most likely wonder if he were making messianic statements about himself. The point is that the purpose of the parables was to engage listeners and encourage them to participate in a dialogue with him, which in turn led to self-reflection and, for some, capability.

So how are we to determine the meaning of Jesus's parables? In his discussion of Jesus as a storyteller, Wright argues that to properly understand the parables, one needs to understand the *literary* dynamics of the stories as Jesus told them, and as the evangelists used them, as well as the *social* context of the stories in the Gospels. Furthermore, he argues that it is helpful to approach the parables through the lens of narrative criticism.

24. Brothers, *Distance in Preaching*, 143.

25. Wright, *Jesus the Storyteller*, 47.

26. Levine, *Short Stories by Jesus*, 277.

27. Levine, *Short Stories by Jesus*, 12.

In examining the stories in this way, he identifies what he calls the "central 'drivers' of a story-plot, character, point of view, and setting."[28] It is not necessary for our purposes to go into detail about these narrative elements except to suggest the following:

1) setting suggests the historical location and circumstances in which the parables were told and retold;

2) the narrative element of identifying and examining the relationship between characters, as well as the social status and nature of the moral choices they make within the parables, are implied;

3) point of view includes at least four planes: phraseological, spatial-temporal, psychological, and ideological; and

4) plot refers to the inner logic of the story which includes the reasons why events take place as they do.[29]

Wright states, "there is a range of rhetorical forms which cannot all be made to 'work' in one way."[30] Therefore, we should not try to make all of Jesus's stories fit into a single shape or pattern, but instead ask questions about the basic features common to all stories. For example, how do we see all our stories fitting into Jesus's stories—how are we further enfolded into his narrative and incorporated into Jesus himself? As Brothers states, "The relevance and meaning of the biblical story is obtained by the self-location of the hearers in the narrative through their identification with its biblical characters."[31]

Wright further explains that approaching the stories through the lens of narrative criticism has the added benefit of bringing out the inherent ambiguity of the texts. For instance, he suggests examining the spatial-temporal elements of the story, which "concerns 'where' the narrator is in relation to a story," is revealing both to its meaning and to how the story works. Is the narrator, for example, constantly alongside a specific character, observing things as that character observes, or does the narrator shift between diverse locations, permitting the audience to eavesdrop on several conversations happening in different locations? Additionally, Wright states, "In the psychological plane, the narrator is inviting hearers

28. Wright, *Jesus the Storyteller*, 37.

29. Wright, *Jesus the Storyteller*.

30. Wright, *Jesus the Storyteller*, 43.

31. Brothers, *Distance in Preaching*, 91.

into a character's inner world, as happens sometimes in Jesus's stories when we 'overhear' someone's interior thought processes."[32]

A delicate balance exists between the storyteller's efforts at drawing in a person and overpowering them with an emotional appeal paired with rhetorical powers. Brothers states that distancing, something close to what Kierkegaard calls *overhearing*, is defined as "a 'psychic' separation, holding hearers 'at bay,' keeping them from 'direct participation.'"[33] This allows them space to hear and evaluate the message for themselves without outside pressure. Such an approach respects the listeners' ability to decide and allows the audience to experience the parable without the direct influence of the storyteller. "Distance," according to Brothers, "involves the psychic, aesthetic, spatial, and critical relationship" between the storyteller or story and the audience.[34]

Not surprisingly, this literary device, used so often in the parables, is exactly the kind of method suggested by Kierkegaard (discussed later in this chapter). One effect distancing has on the audience is that it allows people to hear the strange rhetoric of the story as a speech-act from one not directly trying to persuade, or reveal, or promise, or warn. Rather, the story invites keen observation and reflection. Wright asserts that "the essential element in all the stories is the way in which they invite reflection on characters. People are presented in them with minimal description but are often recognizable as particular social types."[35]

Despite the distance and indirectness of the parables as found in the Gospels, they are formidable stories that can defamiliarize old ideas, even as they provoke new thought. The stories have a semblance of reality, and even when a character appears to be a clown or a fool, they can cut to the quick. Most of these stories communicate hard lessons, and despite the humor with which many of them are delivered, we tend to resist them. A parable *should* disturb. As Levine states, "If we hear it and are not disturbed, there is something seriously amiss with our moral compass."[36]

The parables of Jesus are typically realistic stories about the first-century world of Palestine, but as Wright informs us, "Realistic stories, however brief, are not translatable into other rhetorical forms without

---

32. Wright, *Jesus the Storyteller*, 56.

33. Brothers, *Distance in Preaching*, 2.

34. Brothers, *Distance in Preaching*, 2.

35. Wright, *Jesus the Storyteller*, 177.

36. Levine, *Short Stories by Jesus*, 282.

loss."[37] To fail to attend to the narrative form, to concentrate only on the facts is to fail to see the veiled or deeper meaning intended by Jesus and the authors of the Gospels.

Jesus's Parables

It may be useful to look at three parables from the Gospel of Luke to understand and illustrate the elements of indirect communication used in telling these stories. As we consider these parables, we will notice each one carries out a double rhetorical function: "On the one hand, it invites a hearer to enter a world in which possible meaning is opened up, not closed down. On the other hand, it has a framework which is not infinitely malleable but has a definite shape."[38] We will not merely concern ourselves only with "what" is being said or the "content" found in the parable. As suggested earlier, we will keep a close eye on "how" the parables are told, on what is called their "performative dimension."

"The Rich Fool" (Luke 12:16–21)

On the surface this seems like a simple and direct story of a wealthy man who saw his business grow beyond his wildest dreams. Unfortunately he hadn't prepared for the extraordinary success of his crops. He therefore had to decide what to do with his newly gained wealth. He responded by tearing down his existing storage facilities and building bigger ones, so he could amass even greater wealth. With this greater wealth secured, he supposed he could enjoy life even more. To this point the story seemed straightforward and innocent enough; but that was all about to change. God appears, questions the man's motives, and then demands the man's life. The stunning ending must have created a flock of questions for the original hearers.

Here we see all the characteristics of a realistic story. A rich man faces the dilemma of his success, as his crops outpaced his ability to store them. The Evangelist allows us to see the inner thoughts of this man and thus reveals him as a man of some insight, yet with no thought of God or others. Barbara E. Reid tells us that the rich man's plan to take his ease and indulge himself in food and drink is "aborted when God interrupts.

---

37. Wright, *Jesus the Storyteller*, 176.
38. Wright, *Jesus the Storyteller*, 89.

This is a shocking moment in the story—no other parable has a direct appearance of God."[39] As a result the hearers and readers are led to a situation "about which they might have mixed emotions of both resentment and envy, and offers, indirectly through the mouth of the character of God, an authoritative perspective on it."[40] Thus, the story leads the hearer or reader to consider the attitudes lying behind such behavior.

Wright points out that Jesus's hearers could look at this situation in at least two ways. First, this man clearly was one of the elites who made life so difficult for many of the hearers. Second, he "was a man whom God seemed to have blessed, and wasn't this the sensible course to follow for such a one? Wasn't this a state in which to aspire?"[41] The strength and vividness of this parable rests in the narrative invitation to imagine it. As Reid comments, "Having begun with a question about reporting an earthly inheritance, the parable shifts to the realm of heavenly inheritance."[42]

"The Good Samaritan" (Luke 10:25–37)

The parable of the good Samaritan certainly provoked thought in those who first heard it. This parable, like the story of the rich fool, began with someone asking Jesus a question. He answered, as he so often did, by asking his own questions. Jesus had no interest in casually disseminating information, but truly wanted to engage the other person.

In this case he engaged a lawyer in a dialogue that would cause the man to seriously reflect on his own life. The parable would not allow him merely to embrace an easy answer or engage in a purely mental exercise. As we have continually rehearsed, knowledge or good intentions can sometimes produce the illusion of a Christian life, when in fact, all we have is knowledge without capability. Jesus wanted followers keenly interested in obedience and living the truth, not those who wanted only undemanding answers or who wanted to discuss the truth without giving any thought to how they ought to live. Truth without consequences betrays a life lived in untruth. It is one thing to know the truth, or think one knows the truth; it is another to live in truth.

39. Reid, *Parables for Preachers*, 139.
40. Wright, *Jesus the Storyteller*, 111.
41. Wright, *Jesus the Storyteller*, 112.
42. Reid, *Parables for Preachers*, 140.

An encounter with a lawyer led up to the telling of the parable and the discussion that followed. The story gives us a glimpse into the real intention of the lawyer. The lawyer was far more interested in testing Jesus than in asking a real question that might have consequences for his own life. Jesus responded with a few questions of his own. Clearly the lawyer was well educated and prepared to respond intelligently, but Jesus's questions quickly took the lawyer to a place he was not prepared to go.

In attempting to justify himself, the lawyer asked a follow-up question, which Jesus answers with a parable. The parable illustrates the kind of life God requires for those who really want to be one's neighbor. The lawyer came to Jesus supposedly seeking to know how to inherit eternal life, a question to which he already knew the answer. Soon, however, he found out the magnitude of God's love for one who has truly inherited eternal life.

In response to the question, "Who is my neighbor?" Jesus tells the parable about the good Samaritan. The story has three main characters and starts out with Jesus describing a crime scene where some robbers attack an unidentified man. The man is beaten, stripped of his clothes, and left for dead. Like so many stories or jokes, three people pass by. The first two are identified as a priest and a Levite. Jesus's unforgettable description of these two types of characters would have sounded immediately familiar to his audience. Wright suggests that almost "any ordinary Jew listening to the story might have indulged in knowing laughter at the behavior of these leading functionaries. Priests and Levites would be held in low esteem, because beneath their outward cultic robes their more important practical function was as agents of Rome."[43]

Of course, some may have felt sympathetic toward these two religious leaders, as many of the hearers would have wanted to avoid the danger that came with getting involved in such a risky situation. All that to say, these two religious leaders may not have been viewed as the villains some might suppose.

The introduction of the Samaritan into the story likely would have caused the hearers' anticipation to rise. They would have thought, *where is this story going?* As Wright suggests, "'Priest, Levite and ordinary faithful Jew' would have made more sense than 'priest, Levite and Samaritan.'"[44]

---

43. Wright, *Jesus the Storyteller*, 106.
44. Wright, *Jesus the Storyteller*, 108.

200 HIDE AND SEEK

This jarring revelation creates suspense, as the hearers wait to learn the fate of the injured man and how the hated Samaritan will act.

As the plot of the story switches from the religious leaders to the Samaritan, the structure of the story changes as well. Levine observes that "as spare as the earlier descriptions of priest and Levite were, the text now lavishes attention on the Samaritan's actions."[45] When the Samaritan is confronted with the badly beaten man, he is moved to action, which is described by a sequence of twelve verbs: "'He came' . . . 'he saw' . . . 'he was moved with pity'" and so on.[46] Furthermore, the Samaritan not only took care of the victim, but he provided for the man's continuing care. His concern for the wounded man is clearly shown in the words spoken to the innkeeper the next day: "Look after him," he said, "and when I return, I will reimburse you for any extra expense you may have" (Luke 10:35). Wright explains that, "this detailed concentration on the figure of the Samaritan portrays the nature of love for one's neighbor more eloquently than any abstract statement of principle could possibly do."[47] The failure to identify the robbers or victim in this story keeps the attention on the Samaritan's actions.

Of importance is the difference between the Samaritan and his two predecessors in their approach to the wounded man. It seems the priest and Levite spotted the man before they reached him and so decided to keep their distance (vv. 31–32). The Samaritan, however, when he came upon the man, immediately moved to act on his behalf (v. 33). "That," Wright states, "is the moment of truth: would the Samaritan check the body for more spoils, or beat a hasty path over or up the road, or what?"[48] Levine reminds us that to understand the parable as its original audience did, we need to think of Samaritans less as oppressed-but-benevolent figures and more as the enemy: "as those who do the oppressing."[49]

It would not be hard to imagine that the Jewish audience addressed by Jesus would feel predisposed against the Samaritan: "Whoever might be expected as a 'foil' to the priest and Levite, it is not a Samaritan!"[50] The audience did not at all anticipate such a story of tender, persistent love.

---

45. Levine, *Short Stories by Jesus*, 95.

46. Wright, *Jesus the Storyteller*, 107.

47. Wright, *Jesus the Storyteller*, 107.

48. Wright, *Jesus the Storyteller*, 107.

49. Levine, *Short Stories by Jesus*, 96.

50. Wright, *Jesus the Storyteller*, 107.

Each succeeding description of the Samaritan represented an additional effort by the narrator to appeal "to the hearer's sense of all that is truly admirable and human. The response of the lawyer to Jesus's closing question encapsulates this tension exactly. He cannot fail to recognize who the neighbor is, but he cannot bring himself to name him."[51]

Furthermore, Wright reminds us that Jesus did not call the Samaritan "good." In fact, church tradition gave him that title. Jesus as narrator "'shows' but does not 'tell.'"[52] Reid reminds us, "the question is not answered by defining the limits of who is to be regarded as neighbor. Rather, the boundaries delimiting neighbor are shattered when one can accept mercy from another who acts as neighbor."[53]

Wright states it is not impossible for one to imagine that some in the Jewish audience may have identified with the victim in the ditch and may have asked themselves how ready they would be to receive assistance from an adversary. However, "The story itself seems to come from, and invite, a viewpoint that reorders the familiar world of violence and ethnic conflict more deeply."[54] It says, "Whoever is the victim and whoever has the power to help, this is what love looks like: this is what being a neighbor means."[55]

This account suggests parables work best when they are "overheard" (a way of creating "distance"). By not quickly answering the lawyer's question but by turning the question back on him, Jesus provided space or the critical distance necessary for the lawyer to answer his own question. The authors of the Gospels create distance through writing their stories and thereby create an opportunity for a new audience to think through the images and characters found in Jesus's stories. Just like the lawyer, they must decide for themselves the true meaning of the parable. Brothers argues, "distance creates the 'imaginative space' required for the parable to 'do what it may want to do'" for the audience genuinely to hear the story.[56] In this way the parable is more like a drama than a

51. Wright, *Jesus the Storyteller*, 107.
52. Wright, *Jesus the Storyteller*, 108.
53. Reid, *Parables for Preachers*, 116.
54. Wright, *Jesus the Storyteller*, 108.
55. Wright, *Jesus the Storyteller*, 108.
56. Brothers, *Distance in Preaching*, 144.

smoothly formed story. As an art, drama—like religion—"lives in so far as it is performed."[57]

David Brown suggests we can understand the parables of Jesus by trying to understand them as Jesus himself understood them. Through telling these stories, Jesus is indirectly inviting us to act or live in a certain way. He does so, however, with one exception. Brown states, "There is often a sting in the resultant perception, not infrequently involving us in some element of self-critique. For example, one discovers oneself as the resentful elder brother in the parable of the prodigal son."[58]

Brown argues, "a critique is most effective when it is self-made," and this in part explains Jesus's strategy in so often answering a question with a question, riddle, or parable.[59] Jesus had no interest in providing easy answers when what was needed was a change of heart or perspective. The insight gained from the lawyer's conversation with Jesus makes it possible for him to begin a new kind of relationship with others and with Christ, and "thus a new type of relation with the truth."[60]

"The Sower" (Luke 8:5–8)

Far from being simple stories that make Jesus's teaching easy to grasp, parables are meant to make their hearers think or ponder—to ask, "What is happening here?" or "What does this mean?" They are meant to disturb us into the truth. As Reid suggests, "Although Jesus used familiar imagery, the stories remained enigmatic and confusing."[61] Jesus's use of parables was—and is—meant to be both puzzling and challenging, so as to create cognitive dissonance within the hearer and thereby a need to reexamine one's life. Notice that even an unembellished story, such as the one in Luke 8:5–8 about the sower, went over the heads of the disciples. And even when Jesus explained to them the importance of acting on God's Word, there remained much left "undecided for a hearer to ponder, and a whole possible range of 'applications.'"[62] This parable is not an instance of arcane fantasy with no relation to the hearers' world. On

57. Victor Turner as quoted in Brothers, *Distance in Preaching*, 144.

58. Brown, *Discipleship and Imagination*, 365.

59. Brown, *Discipleship and Imagination*, 365.

60. Brown, *Discipleship and Imagination*, 365.

61. Reid, *Parables for Preachers*, 13.

62. Wright, *Jesus the Storyteller*, 95.

the contrary "it dealt with an extremely familiar theme and would have drawn in its hearers to identify with its character."[63] Wright reminds us that this mysteriously simple story appears in all three of the Synoptic Gospels and "would clearly have been open to a range of 'meanings' to its first hearers."[64] The framework of the parable is not infinitely flexible, as it has a definite shape and design that draws us to what is being done just as much as what is being said.

The story of the sower does not present a truth about the timing of God's kingdom as much as it prompts imaginative thought and offers hope. Reid argues, "the parable advances Luke's theme of hearing the word and acting on it," but he also suggests the parable is open to many interpretations.[65] Its interpretation will change "depending on which 'character' is chosen as the focus, it could be the Parable of the Sower; the Parable of the Seed; the Parable of the Soil; or the Parable of the Harvest."[66]

The meaning of this parable, especially the discussion directly following the parable (vv. 9–10), has been especially difficult for many scholars to comprehend. The most disturbing issue is why Jesus seemed to say that the secrets of the kingdom were given to some but not to others. To those others he spoke in parables, quoting Isaiah 6:9—"so that, 'though seeing they may not see; though hearing, they may not understand'" (Luke 8:10). What did he have in mind? Was he purposely trying to keep some people from understanding his message? The comment generates a host of explanations, but perhaps the best is offered by Reid when she suggests,

> Jesus does not speak in parables so that some will not understand; their incomprehension is the result of their choice not to join those who struggle to follow him. The "mysteries" of the reign of God entrusted to those who become disciples are not things that remain incomprehensible, but refers to the paradoxical plan of God, now being revealed in Jesus, that salvation comes through one who is rejected and crucified.[67]

63. Wright, *Jesus the Storyteller*, 96.

64. Wright, *Jesus the Storyteller*, 95.

65. Reid, *Parables for Preachers*, 283.

66. Reid, *Parables for Preachers*, 283.

67. Reid, *Parables for Preachers*, 289.

Here we see Jesus using an indirect approach—a parable—to speak a difficult truth that can be understood only by those willing to receive his message (those with eyes to see or ears to hear). Those who do not really want to follow Jesus and his message will find the truth hidden from them until the time when they are ready to receive it—that is, when they are ready to act on it. As Kierkegaard would remind us, the truth of the kingdom of God can be known and appropriated only by God's self-revelation. This is what Jesus meant in v. 8 when he said, "He who has ears to hear, let him hear." Because the disciples wanted to know the meaning of the parable and were ready to learn, Jesus explains the meaning of the parable to them. We see here that if those receiving or hearing the story truly want to understand what God has to say, a certain condition of the heart and mind is required if the message is to be incarnated or appropriated.

Conclusion

When in a communication event, an object or topic is perceived as familiar or common, it is difficult to communicate anything new about the object or topic since the audience assumes they already know and are familiar with it. Parables are most effective in this type of situation in that they make the common strange by defamiliarizing the object or topic. As Sallie McFague says, a parable attempts to "set the familiar in an unfamiliar context" and in so doing, gives us new insight and allows us to "see our ordinary world in an extraordinary way."[68]

To reiterate, the strength of Jesus's stories, especially his parables, is that they set the familiar in an unfamiliar context. The parable's ability to make strange, or defamiliarize the familiar, acts as a midwife for appropriation. Appropriation of the truth differs from mere application. Appropriation, Kyle A. Roberts tells us, is more personal as it "means making the truth your own; it is the personal assimilation of truth such that it transforms one's self."[69] This chapter argues that knowledge of Christ in conservative Christianity is too often aligned with conceptual beliefs in doctrine while in liberal Christianity Christ is associated with knowing about the historical Jesus or with Jesus as simply a moral teacher. Consequently, either of these views may result in an intellectualizing

68. McFague, *Speaking in Parables*, 4.
69. Roberts, *Emerging Prophet*, 13.

and objectivizing the Christian faith. Instead of regarding Scripture as a living book that communicates the living and active Christ, both conservative and liberal Christians see it as either a fixed set of doctrines or as a declaration of one's ethical duty. But one's personal relationship with Christ that is founded in the actualization of belief is more important than either cognitive understanding or doctrinal knowledge.[70] Scriptural interpretation, thus, is the living, dynamic creation of God in man rather than a disengaged attempt to construct an abstract or detached meaning from an inspired text.

It is in this way that Jesus's parables, like Kierkegaard's centuries later, aimed "not merely at the change of mind but a change of will. Kierkegaard does not tell his parables with the expectation that his readers will experience a casual illumination or fascination, but rather that they might say to themselves, 'Aha! I know how that is and it makes a difference in the way I understand myself and make fundamental choices.'"[71] If the parable is effective, "the spectator becomes the participant, not because they want to necessarily, or simply have 'gotten to the point,' but because they have, for the moment, 'lost control,' or as the new hermeneuts say, 'been interpreted.'"[72]

The essence of the parable is its ability to communicate capability that is the appropriation of knowledge. Parables are not meant to tell, as much as show, how to live and in so doing to bring about new ways of living. They are meant to help the hearer or viewer to see in fresh or new ways. In the next chapter we turn to the fiction of C. S. Lewis to consider the ways he uses the indirect forms of story and myth to communicate truth. Thus, we will explore the various strategies of storytelling he employs in order to "entrap" the reader into self-awareness and spiritual growth.

70. Roberts, *Emerging Prophet*.

71. Oden, "Introduction," xiv.

72. Oden, "Introduction," xiv.

8

C. S. Lewis: Storytelling
and Myth Making

*I, King, have dealt with the gods for three generations of men, and I
know that they dazzle our eyes and flow in and out of one another
like eddies on a river, and nothing that is said clearly can be said
truly about them. Holy places are dark places. It is life and strength,
not knowledge and words that we get in them. Holy wisdom is not
clear and thin like water, but thick and dark like blood.*

—C. S. LEWIS, *TILL WE HAVE FACES*

Introduction

IN A RECENT TED talk, Andres Ruzo explained how he found the
mythical boiling river of the Amazon.[1] This young geothermal scientist
grew up in Peru, listening to his grandfather tell tales about a boiling river
deep in the jungle that was protected by a shaman. As Ruzo grew older he
forgot his grandfather's story. While studying for his PhD at a university
in the United States, however, he remembered the legend and began to
wonder if the boiling river really did exist.

1. Ruzo, *Boiling River*.

During a break in his studies, he returned to his homeland to search for the mythical waters. Eventually he found the river along with the legendary gatekeeper. The shaman gave him permission to study the river on one condition: whatever water he removed to analyze he must return to the river because it came from a sacred source.

Ruzo's discovery of the boiling river proved to be an excellent subject for his dissertation as well as an amazing intellectual puzzle. He acknowledged, however, that he made an additional discovery while searching for the river. He discovered his responsibility to steward myths effectively.

Ruzo closed his TED talk with this unforgettable statement: "We are the ones who draw the line between the sacred and the trivial." For him, the nearly forgotten childhood myth, once remembered and explored, became both myth and fact. Or as C. S. Lewis would say, "Myth became fact." Not that the myth was not a fact already! It had gone unrecognized, or more accurately, it was trivialized by some but kept alive by others and ultimately made known to the outside world. Myth may well be the bearer of truth and a shaman may be the keeper of at least part of that truth.

C. S. Lewis's Indirect Approach

One might question whether C. S. Lewis made a significant contribution to our understanding of indirect communication as most people regard him as a "closet theologian" who wrote didactic, apologetic, and evangelistic works. Quite a few of his writings, however, were thinly veiled stories with religious themes expressed within various forms of fiction. Perhaps we should not so easily dismiss all of Lewis's writings as mere rational apologetics. This chapter will look at Lewis's fictional writings— especially fantasy and myth—with special emphasis on *The Screwtape Letters* and *Till We Have Faces*.

After examining the whole corpus of his writing and noting his development as a writer over the course of his lifetime, one may come to understand much of his fictional work as indirect. Few Christians have captured the public's imagination as deftly as Lewis, and it may be that we need to more fully understand his fictional work and to realize just how much his imaginative works have contributed to our understanding of our relationship with God and to apologetics.

Robert MacSwain suggests that instead of regarding Lewis as an amateur theologian, he might better be "seen (à la Kierkegaard) as a deliberately 'indirect' theologian, as one who works by 'thick description' or evocative images, operating in multiple voices and genres, through which a single yet surprisingly subtle and complex vision emerges."[2] James Como points out that Lewis's later work "places him within a constellation of writers with whom he is not ordinarily associated"[3]—that is with some existential writers such as Walker Percy, who was strongly influenced by the writings of Kierkegaard. Como suggests that Lewis sometimes wrote in the same oblique style as Percy. Finally, Como declares he would liked to have seen Lewis—who had no patience with existentialism—to have written more often in the existential style of the writers who understood "the world to be haunted, that meaning is everywhere, and that we must learn to read the signs."[4]

Although Lewis dismissed with exclamatory impatience the ideas and works of Kierkegaard, Como believes that Lewis really didn't understand Kierkegaard. Lewis's "rejection," writes Como, "may have been preponderantly tonal."[5] Como recognized, for example, that Lewis's description of three kinds of men—those who seek pleasure, others who acknowledge a higher claim upon them, and those who, like St. Paul, understand that "to live is Christ"—very nearly echoes Kierkegaard's taxonomy of aesthetic, ethical, and religious stages of spiritual development.[6] Lewis has much in common with Kierkegaard's "Knight of Faith," rejecting the crowd to follow God whatever the price. Lewis also lived a dialectic that did not find selfhood a given, but rather depended upon reading the signs and making a choice to follow them. Consequently, Lewis may have been closer to Kierkegaard than he (and many scholars) realized.

Como also argues that as Lewis grew as an accomplished writer he relied more heavily on narrative fiction to communicate biblical truth. This imaginative approach is consistent with Kierkegaard's notion of indirect communication, or what Como calls "oblique . . . or veiled

---

2. MacSwain, "Introduction," 8.

3. Como, *Branches to Heaven*, 189.

4. Como, *Branches to Heaven*, 189.

5. Como, *Branches to Heaven*, 198.

6. Como, *Branches to Heaven*, 190.

discourse."[7] Rebecca Hans writes about conversion in two of Lewis's books, *That Hideous Strength* and *Till We Have Faces*, noting that "before an individual can convert to Christianity, he or she must convert out of a previously held ideology."[8] She argues that for Lewis the transformation in an individual often comes through the power of narrative.

Consider for a moment Lewis's letter to Carl Henry, written in 1955 in response to an invitation by Henry asking Lewis to write an article for *Christianity Today*. In his letter, Lewis commented on a change in the direction of his writing. He states,

> I wish your project heartily well but can't write you articles. My thought and talent (such as they are) now flow in different, though I think not less Christian, channels, and I do not think I am at all likely to write more directly theological pieces. The last work of that sort which I attempted had to be abandoned. If I am now good for anything it is for catching the reader un-awares—thro' fiction and symbol. I have done what I could in the way of frontal attacks, but I now feel quite sure those days are over.[9]

This statement may be understood as signaling a move away from a didactic literary approach and toward what some might call "imaginative apologetics."[10] With concern for the strength of narrative or imagination to help in the conversion process, Lewis's words "to catch the reader un-awares" sounds much like Kierkegaard's "attack from behind." Both men wanted to surprise or deceive their readers into reconsidering a truth they had dismissed or undervalued. Lewis's reconsideration of the "fron-tal attack" and turn to more imaginative approaches to communicating faith comes very close to Kierkegaard's understanding of indirect com-munication. Also consider that both Lewis and Kierkegaard believed that in Christ God was hidden, or as Lewis put it, "We may ignore, but we can nowhere evade, the presence of God. The world is crowded with Him. He walks everywhere *incognito*."[11] We recall Hans's suggestion: Lewis's

---

7. Como, *Branches to Heaven*, 190.

8. Hans, "That Hideous Strength," 9.

9. Lewis, *Collected Letters*, 3:651.

10. Davison, *Imaginative Apologetics*.

11. Lewis, *Letters to Malcolm*, 75.

own conversion was in part a realization that the "senses did not have a monopoly on information."[12]

Lewis's Use of Imagination

Although Lewis the literary scholar wrote theological books on apologetics, he may have done his best work in writing fantasy. For him, "writing stories and fantasies is not a negative attempt at escaping from reality, nor a vainly fantastic play of imagination just for fun, but a positive way of participating in the metaphysical reality."[13] Clearly Lewis was a man of imagination as well as a man of reason. Although he wrote several books on apologetics in a clear and rational tone, most of his religious writings were imaginative, and I would argue, indirect. Furthermore, Hans argues that Lewis saw his work as a writer, in part at least, to make ready a person's mind and imagination to grasp the Christian vision of a new life—what Kierkegaard would call the meaning of his or her existence.[14]

In 1954, Lewis wrote about his interest in the imagination in a letter. He stated,

> The imaginative man in me is older, more continuously operative, and in that sense more basic than either the religious writer or the critic. It was he who made me first attempt (with little success) to be a poet. It was he who, in response to the poetry of others, made me a critic, and, in deference of that response, sometimes a critical controversialist. It was he who after my conversion led me to embody my religious belief in symbolical or mythopoeic forms.[15]

The imagination Lewis sees in his own life appears to mirror the creativity that we expect of good writers and artists. For Lewis, however, "imagination" means a lot more than mere creativity. Imagination is the power of intuition to move one into the metaphysical reality of this world and of heaven, and the power to communicate that reality. "It perceives the meaning of the world, expresses that meaning, and enables us to participate in the metaphysical reality."[16] Lewis links the great intuitive

12. Hans, "That Hideous Strength," 14.

13. Honda, *Imaginative World of C. S. Lewis*, xiv.

14. Hans, "That Hideous Strength."

15. Lewis, *Collected Letters*, 3:516–17.

16. Honda, *Imaginative World of C. S. Lewis*, 1.

power of the human imagination to the aesthetic experiences he calls *Sehnsucht* (or "joy"), by which he meant an intense longing, or deep emotional yearning, and through which he was convinced of a transcendent reality. As Honda states, "It [joy] is a sensation of extraordinary, indescribable longing caused by quite ordinary things in life. It is numinous, too, because the very person struck by that longing cannot specify what he really longs for."[17]

It was George MacDonald who introduced Lewis to the world beyond the merely logical and sense perspective. As Lewis remarked, "The quality which had enchanted me in his [MacDonald's] imaginative works turned out to be the quality of the real universe, the divine, magical, terrifying and ecstatic reality in which we all live."[18] In the introduction to an anthology of MacDonald's writings, Lewis reveals how MacDonald had a major influence on his imaginative life: "I have never concealed the fact that I regard him as my master; indeed, I fancy I have never written a book in which I did not quote from him." Lewis adds,

> Nothing was at that time [when he discovered MacDonald] further from my thoughts than Christianity . . . What it [the book *Phantastes*] actually did to me was to convert, even to baptize . . . my imagination. It did nothing to my intellect nor (at that time) to my conscience. Their turn came far later and with the help of many other books and men.[19]

Coincidentally, his confession is remarkably similar to an explanation Kierkegaard might have given of the way indirect communication works on people to bring them into a new appropriation of truth.

Perhaps Lewis had something like this in mind when he created the character Aslan for the Narnia stories. In these stories he presents Aslan as a dangerous but loving lion who sacrifices himself for those who betray him. In these children's tales, Lewis begins to veil and secret the truth, just as one would do with indirect communication. Michael Ward advances a similar sentiment in the preface to his book, *Planet Narnia: The Seven Heavens in the Imagination of C. S. Lewis*, by saying that he hopes his "book reaffirms the worth of implicit communication; not everything that needs to be said needs to be said outright."[20] Lewis clearly expressed

17. Honda, *Imaginative World of C. S. Lewis*, 2.

18. Lewis, *Letters to Malcolm*, xxii.

19. Lewis, *Letters to Malcolm*, xxii.

20. Ward, *Planet Narnia*, xv.

that in writing romance or what he came to call the atmosphere of the story, its inner meaning should be carefully hidden.[21] Ward expresses it this way, "It is instructive to survey the many occasions on which Lewis praised the indirect approach in communication. He believed that success in writing comes about by 'secretly evoking powerful associations'; that expressions should 'not merely state but suggest.'"[22]

For Lewis, this veiling of the truth—even in old stories into which he wanted to breathe new life—came through his use of imagination, "a faculty that leads man to God through the ever-unsatisfied desire."[23] Lewis saw imagination as a power of intuitive perception as well as a power of creation. Moreover, for Lewis, "imagination itself has direct access to divine revelation."[24]

Ward recognizes the difficulty in defining the term imagination, which explains why different scholars or writers define it differently. Nevertheless, Ward provides us with Lewis's definitions of reason, imagination, and meaning, "Reason is 'the organ of truth'; imagination is 'the organ of meaning'; and meaning itself is 'the antecedent condition of both truth and falsehood.'"[25] Therefore, "Before something can be either true or false it must mean,"[26] and imagination is what provides new meaning.[27]

Lewis believed one needed both imagination and reason to communicate truth effectively. Ward suggests Lewis was "not willing to reduce himself or his readers to mere 'thinkers' in a sort of ultra-Cartesian move, which plagues so much inferior apologetics."[28] He understood "before we act or think, we understand meaning, in Lewis's view, and so the provision of meaningful images becomes the hallmark of his apologetic method."[29] That is, we need reason to guide us between the varied meanings presented to our senses.

Lewis makes an important distinction between imaginary and imaginative that may inform our thinking about imagination and its relation to reason. Ward states,

21. Ward, *Planet Narnia.*

22. Ward, *Planet Narnia,* 21.

23. Lewis, *Surprised by Joy,* 23.

24. Honda, *Imaginative World of C. S. Lewis,* 23.

25. Ward, "Good Serves the Better," 62.

26. Ward, "Good Serves the Better," 61–62.

27. Ward, "Good Serves the Better," 61–62.

28. Ward, "Good Serves the Better," 72.

29. Ward, "Good Serves the Better," 72.

Lewis distinguishes between "imaginary" (bad) and "imaginative" (good). Pagan myths, howsoever meaningful, were ultimately untrustworthy as a final guide to life because their meanings were imaginary rather than imaginative. Without the controlling and clarifying effects of reason, imaginative efforts at apprehending God are always apt to lose themselves and turn unreliable or even rotten.[30]

Lewis believed we need both imagination and reason, working together, to communicate transcendence and to build a strong apologetic. Likewise, Mark Edwards Freshwater reminds us, "Lewis never totally rejected either the logical or the imaginative but combined them in defense of a Christianity that he claimed was both, 'myth become fact.'"[31] Jonah Sachs argues that myths are powerful stories that "have persisted in the human consciousness for millennia."[32] Lewis says that myths, which he defines as shared stories that remind us of who we are and how we should act, are made up of "certain patterns" that "will influence [us] enormously."[33] These stories tend to be about reluctant or unlikely heroes (think Dorothy, Frodo, Luke Skywalker, or Katniss Everdeen), "lured into a dangerous quest of self-discovery. Hearing these stories excites and entertains us on a conscious level but also subtly influences our very conception of what is possible in our real lives."[34]

Lewis's Use of Myth

Myth, as a kind of story, provided an important communicative element in Lewis's creative work. In understanding the role of myth in the presentation of truth, Lewis drew on Carl Jung's ideas about primordial images, archetypal patterns, and most importantly, the collective unconscious.[35] Lewis saw the collective unconscious as pre-logical, best expressed through images—not reason. He pointed out the mystery of primordial images found in myths is deeper, and their origin more remote, than most suspect.

30. Ward, "Good Serves the Better," 73.

31. Freshwater, C. S. Lewis, 17.

32. Sachs, Winning the Story Wars, 4.

33. Sachs, Winning the Story Wars, 4.

34. Sachs, Winning the Story Wars, 4–5.

35. Jung, Archetypes.

J. R. R. Tolkien helped Lewis understand the power of myths. Tolkien's interpretation of myth as fragments of eternal truth allowed Lewis to see the truth in what he considered the Christian myth. Freshwater suggests Tolkien's influence in this area impressed upon Lewis that in writing stories, people are not a creators but sub-creators, who may hope to reflect something of the eternal light of God. Furthermore, Tolkien gave Lewis an appreciation for the use of fantasy to portray a deeper level of reality. As Lewis remarked in a review of Tolkien's *The Lord of the Rings*, "One of the main things the author wants to say is that the real life of man is of that mythical and heroic quality."[36] Myth, therefore, is no small thing but is fundamental to the development and nature of our basic identity and to many of the stories we construct.

In Lewis's story *The Pilgrim's Regress*, the pilgrim John, troubled by the mythological nature of Christianity, hears a voice, declaring,

> Child, if you will, it is mythology. It is but truth, not fact: an image, not the very real. But since they do not know themselves for what they are, in them the hidden myth is master, where it would be servant: and it is but of man's inventing. But this is My inventing, this is the *veil* under which I have chosen to appear even from the first until now. For this end I make your senses and for this end your imagination, that you might see My face and live. What would you have? Have you not heard among the Pagans the story of Semele? Or was there any age in any land when men did not know that corn and wine were the blood and body of a dying and yet living God?[37]

Lewis's view of myth as expressed in this passage seems to suggest that truth is veiled, much as Kierkegaard believed truth sometimes needed to be veiled and indirect. Herein Lewis clearly suggests an inference of hiddenness or indirectness in myth.

Tolkien further explained that not only abstract thought, but a person's imaginative creations "must originate with God, and must in consequence reflect something of eternal truth. In making a myth, the story teller or 'sub-creator' . . . is actually fulfilling God's purpose and reflecting the splintered fragment of the true light. Pagan myths are, therefore, never just 'lies'; there is always something of truth in them."[38]

---

36. Quoted from Freshwater, *C.S. Lewis*, 21.

37. Lewis, *Pilgrim's Regress*, 171.

38. Freshwater, *C.S. Lewis*, 36.

In a 1931 letter to his friend Arthur Greeves, Lewis describes what he learned from talking to Tolkien. Lewis understood that both pagan mythology and Christianity can view the underlying component of myth as a common element between them. According to Lewis, he came to see that "the Pagan stories are God expressing Himself through the minds of poets, while in Christian stories God is expressing Himself through what we call 'real things.'"[39] For Lewis "something more fundamental, more 'rock-bottom' than the ability to derive information through the senses must exit," and that something comes through myth or fantasy.[40]

These stories or true myths therefore are interpretations of concepts and ideas from God, which he has imparted in a language more adequate than we can create: the actual incarnation, crucifixion, and resurrection. "In other words, when Divine Truth falls on human imagination, myth is born. Myth puts us in touch with Reality in a more intimate way than by knowing what is merely factual. Myth touches our lives at a deeper level than abstract thought and thus, is the best means of Divine communication."[41]

Lewis suggests, "every myth becomes the father of innumerable truths on the abstract level . . . It is not, like truth, abstract; nor is it, like direct experience, bound to the particular."[42] Furthermore, "The reality found in myth cannot be put into words or grasped by the intellect alone. It must be imagined or experienced."[43] In this way, myth brings a sense of unity and evokes an emotional response, such as awe, enchantment, and inspiration. It therefore allows "us to actually experience reality and grasp eternal truths which might baffle the intellect and confuse the mind."[44]

Lewis's view of myth allows him to believe that our conceptions of God are determined by the images through which his revelation appears. "Finite beings in a finite realm have no absolute knowledge of the Infinite God, only analogies, mythical models, symbols, and abstractions. As Lewis claimed, 'Statements about God are extrapolations from knowledge of other things which the divine illumination enables us to know.'"[45]

39. Lewis, *Collected Letters* 1:977.

40. Ward, *Planet Narnia*, 34.

41. Freshwater, *C.S. Lewis*, 37–38.

42. Lewis, *God in the Dock*, 58.

43. Freshwater, *C.S. Lewis*, 38.

44. Freshwater, *C.S. Lewis*, 39.

45. Freshwater, *C.S. Lewis*, 40.

As we previously alluded, Lewis's later and more imaginative writings were less reasoned but more satisfying than his apologetic books. Because they tapped into his imagination, "his children's stories prove nothing, but they impart a vision of reality that makes most fiction seem drab and feeble by comparison."[46] Likewise, his mythic writing, *Till We Have Faces*—which is challenging to read and difficult to understand—is his most mature and discerning work. The main character in that story, Orual, complains that the gods are hidden and not obvious to those men and women who are looking for them. It is clear that Orual feels the gods have not made themselves evident or available to her and she feels that this situation is unfair and that she will be unfairly judged for the lapse on the part of the gods. Therefore, she complains the gods have been too secretive and elusive. In many ways her complaint echoes the modernist's complaint that God is not obvious or present in the affairs of men.

Lewis believed that people desperately need and cannot live without myth. It defines our humanity and as Hein states, "When true myths are absent, false ones rush in to fill the vacuum."[47] It may be that story, myth, and narrative shape emotions, longings, and hopes; this formative process opens us up to transcendent possibilities. Toward the end of his career, Lewis turned primarily to story, myth, and imagination as a means of communicating moral and spiritual insight. "Myths enable readers to enjoy . . . things of permanent value that they otherwise can only contemplate."[48] Peter J. Schakel states, "Myths provide not just intellectual understanding of the truth but a powerful imaginative experience of it."[49] In reading myth, we should pay attention not so much to what the myth "means" [knowledge] but to the "taste" of reality that it offers: "What flows into you from the myth is not truth but reality (truth is always about something, but reality is that about which truth is)."[50] Lewis explains, "Even assuming (which I most constantly deny) that the doctrines of historic Christianity are merely mythical, it is the myth which is the vital and nourishing element in the whole concern."[51] For Lewis, myth gave life to the people of God.

46. Freshwater, *C.S. Lewis*, 127.

47. Hein, *Christian Mythmakers*, 271.

48. Schakel, "Till We Have Faces," 288.

49. Schakel, "Till We Have Faces," 288.

50. Lewis, *God in the Dock*, 58.

51. Lewis, *God in the Dock*, 56.

Like Kierkegaard before him, Lewis was concerned about those in the church in his day who retained a form of Christian faith while at the same time abandoning many of its essential beliefs. Lewis was disturbed by members of the church who retained the vocabulary of Christianity and distorted the emotions received from it, while quietly dropping several of its crucial doctrines.

Although Lewis used both reason and imagination to communicate truth, he was aware of the limitations and problems associated with what Davison calls the "'natural' account of reason, which is supposed to be shared by all."[52] Lewis dealt with the concerns of modernism and the limits of reason in many of his writings, most notably in *That Hideous Strength*. Lewis saw human intellect as hopelessly abstract but believed that we experience reality in a concrete way—*this* man, *this* pain, *this* pleasure. "While loving the man, bearing the pain, enjoying the pleasure, we are not intellectually apprehending Pleasure, Pain or Personality. When we begin to do so, on the other hand, the concrete realities sink to the level of mere instances or examples; we are no longer dealing with them, but with what they exemplify."[53]

Lewis identified two key ways of knowing in his essay, "Meditation in a Toolshed," a brief but important epistemological work exploring how we come to know or understand. He begins the essay with a metaphor of entering a tool shed and observing a beam of light entering through a crack in the door. In this objective view of the beam, he saw the dust particles floating in the light, but he states, "I was seeing the beam, not seeing things by it."[54] When he moved so that the beam fell on his eyes, "Instantly," he states, "the whole previous picture vanished. I saw no toolshed, and (above all) no beam. Instead I saw framed in the irregular cranny at the top of the door, green leaves moving on the branches of a tree outside and beyond that, ninety-odd million miles away, the sun. Looking along the beam and looking at the beam are very different experiences."[55]

To demonstrate the difference between looking at and looking along, Lewis gives an example of a young man "in love" with a young woman. For him, the world is different when he sees her and is with her. Her voice, her touch, her presence is more precious to him than all the

---

52. Davison, "Christian Reason," 12.
53. Lewis, *God in the Dock*, 57.
54. Lewis, *God in the Dock*, 230.
55. Lewis, *God in the Dock*, 230.

charms of other women. He experiences from the inside a different kind of knowing (that is, "looking along") than a scientist who with all his or her knowledge and experience tries to describe a person in love—an attempt that would take place from the outside. The scientist who is "looking at" the man sees all his behavior as "an affair of the young man's genes and a recognized biological stimulus." Lewis then asks, "Which is the 'true' or 'valid' experience which tells you the most about the thing? And you can hardly ask that question without noticing that for the last fifty years or so everyone has been taking the answer for granted. It has been assumed without discussion that if you want the true account of religion you must go, not to religious people but to anthropologists . . ."[56]

For Lewis the question is easily answered, as people have now "taken for granted that the external account of a thing somehow refutes or 'debunks' the account given from the inside."[57] This is the underpinning of the specifically modern kind of thought. We have been deceived into only "looking at" and are taught to suspect any form of inside experiences. Lewis, however, thinks both ways of knowing are imperfect yet potentially useful. He argues, "We must, on pain of idiocy, deny from the very outset the idea that looking at, is by its own nature, intrinsically truer or better than looking along. One must look both along and at everything."[58]

To resolve this tension, Lewis identifies two types of apprehending reality as "enjoyment" and "contemplation." Ward conjectures that Lewis borrowed these terms from Samuel Alexander's book, *Space, Time, and Deity*. According to Ward, these two terms are the basis for the above mentioned essay "Meditation in a Toolshed," in which Lewis recast Alexander's literary techniques of "Contemplation" and "Enjoyment."[59] Ward explains,

> "Looking along the beam" is what Alexander had called "Enjoyment" (participant, inhabited, personal, committed knowledge) and "looking at the beam" is what he had called "Contemplation" (abstract, external, impersonal, uninvolved knowledge). For Lewis, this distinction was so fundamental that he was prepared to divide conscious knowledge accordingly: "Instead of the twofold division into Conscious and Unconscious, we need a three-fold division: the Unconscious, the Enjoyed, and

56. Lewis, *God in the Dock*, 231.
57. Lewis, *God in the Dock*, 232.
58. Lewis, *God in the Dock*, 233.
59. Ward, *Planet Narnia*, 17.

the Contemplated." Like the ancient Persians who debated everything twice (once when they were sober and once when they were drunk), we should try out every question in both lights, the light of Enjoyment (similar to the French *connaitre*) and the light of Contemplation (similar to the French *savoir*).[60]

Lewis thought that one should enjoy or "look along the beam" of the story so completely that it comprised one's whole imaginative vision. Some scholars today call this transportation.[61] Ward explains that the atmosphere created by the details in the story "is not one of the abstractions of literary criticism, but a description of 'concrete imagination' in practice, the full tasting of a work of art on the imaginative palate."[62] In so doing, we surrender ourselves to and give careful attention to the mood of the story, since the atmosphere of the story "has to be Enjoyed rather than Contemplated, it is in a sense, invisible."[63]

As Lewis looked along the beam, he did not see the toolshed or the beam of light. In the same way, the inner meaning of a story cannot be stated by the author without changing its true meaning. As Ward states,

> It [the inner meaning] has to remain hidden, woven into the . . . story so that it comprises not an object for Contemplation but the whole field of vision within which the story is experienced. The kappa element is more like seeing than it is like something seen. Just as one cannot take out one's eyeballs and turn them round to look back at one's optical organs, so one cannot jump out of this "state of being," this mode of Enjoyment consciousness. It is, by its very nature, though knowable, not explicit.[64]

In this hidden and entertaining way of entering the story and being transported to another place or time through the imagination, one may be seduced into seeing reality in ways not hitherto experienced.

It should be clear by now that this "inside experience" or "looking along" is very similar to what Kierkegaard sees as a subjective encounter or a subjective way of knowing. Both Lewis and Kierkegaard see value in both the objective and the subjective ways of knowing, but it is fair to say that Kierkegaard would emphasize the subjective way of knowing

60. Ward, *Planet Narnia*, 17.
61. For example, see Brown, "Examining Four Processes."
62. Ward, *Planet Narnia*, 18.
63. Ward, *Planet Narnia*, 18.
64. Ward, *Planet Narnia*, 18.

and Lewis may be more balanced in his approach. I argue here that the subjective and the objective ways of knowing, as well as reason and imagination, are important to both men. Later in this chapter we will see examples of subjective knowing found in Lewis's writing.

This, of course, is a dilemma, since according to Lewis, the more clearly one contemplates, the more one cannot experience reality. As Lewis states, "You cannot study pleasure in the moment of the nuptial embrace, nor repentance while repenting, nor analyze the nature of humour while roaring with laughter."[65]

Myth is a partial solution to the "joy/contemplation" predicament. Lewis states, "In the enjoyment of a great myth we come nearest to experiencing as a concrete what can otherwise be understood only as an abstraction. At the moment, for example, I am trying to understand something very abstract indeed—the fading, vanishing of tasted reality as we try to grasp it with the discursive reason."[66] David Downing argues that Lewis's love "of fantasy, myth, and romance" finally "led him to Christianity," and that in his science fiction trilogy, *Out of the Silent Planet, Perelandra,* and *That Hideous Strength,* he tries to enchant his readers "with fantasy worlds of wonder and danger, battlefields of good and evil; then gradually he reveals a correlation between these new, absorbing fantasies and some old doctrines whose familiarity may have bred contempt in his readers, or at lease indifference."[67]

For example, think for a moment about the story of Winnie the Pooh and Rabbit. Pooh invites himself to Rabbit's hole and squeezes into his home. Pooh is a very kind bear but he is weak-willed when it comes to honey. Rabbit offers Pooh a taste of honey and Pooh accepts, but he cannot stop eating the honey until he eats all of Rabbit's supply. Like Pooh, most of our faults are not grand or glorious, but are selfish and self-centered and as often as not we yield to nothing but temptation. When we read this little story (or myth), we do not generally think about human nature or the meaning of the story. Nor are we searching for an abstract "meaning" at all. "If that was what you were doing the myth would be for you no true myth but a mere allegory."[68] As Lewis explains, "You were not knowing, but tasting; what you were tasting turns out to be a universal

65. Lewis, *God in the Dock,* 57.

66. Lewis, *God in the Dock,* 57–58.

67. Downing, *Planets in Peril,* 35.

68. Lewis, *God in the Dock,* 58.

principle. The moment we state this principle, we are admittedly back in the world of abstraction. It is only while receiving the myth as a story that you experience the principle concretely."[69] Therefore, myth is not abstract, like truth, nor is it tied to the specific or the particular, like direct experience.

Lewis argues that "the heart of Christianity is a myth which is also a fact. The old myth of the dying god, without ceasing to be myth, comes down from the heaven of legend and imagination to the earth of history."[70] Becoming a fact in no way thwarts it from being myth, and Lewis speculated that some men have "derived more spiritual sustenance from myths they did not believe than from the religion they professed. To be a Christian one must both assent to the historical fact and receive the myth (fact though it has become) with the same imaginative embrace which we accord to all myths."[71] He continues that one should not feel put off by parallels of the Christian story with other mythical stories, or even to "pagan Christs: they ought to be there—it would be a stumbling block if they weren't."[72] Furthermore, "If God chooses to be mythopoeic—and is not the sky itself a myth—shall we refuse to be *mythopathic*?"[73]

Terry Lindvall argues that Lewis invited his audience to immerse themselves in the images found in his stories and then "to move out of and beyond themselves into another world and object. By denying oneself, a reader is able to meet the truth beyond her or himself, and paradoxically to discover their true self."[74] This is exactly the kind of experience that Kierkegaard would have wanted for his readers. Repeatedly Lewis, like Kierkegaard, argued for the reader to examine himself or herself in order to know one's self.

Furthermore, Kierkegaard created his indirect strategy to arouse a passion in those indifferent to the truth or who knew something of the truth but needed to experience it in a new way—with the proper shock of revelation. Lewis, too, wanted to present stories that, in his words,

> could steal past a certain inhibition which had paralyzed much of my own religion in childhood. Why did one find it so hard

69. Lewis, *God in the Dock*, 58.

70. Lewis, *God in the Dock*, 58.

71. Lewis, *God in the Dock*, 59.

72. Lewis, *God in the Dock*, 59–60.

73. Lewis, *God in the Dock*, 60.

74. Lindvall, "C.S. Lewis' Theory," 468.

to feel as one was told one ought to feel about God or the suf-
ferings of Christ? I thought the chief reason was that one was
told one ought to. An obligation to feel can freeze feelings. And
reverence itself did harm. The whole subject was associated with
lowered voices; almost as if it were something medical. But supposing that by casting all these things into an imaginary world,
stripping them of their stained-glass and Sunday school associations, one could make them for the first time appear in their real
potency? Could one not thus steal past those watchful dragons?
I thought one could.[75]

So, Lewis used the gift of writing to convey his religious views
through various works and in different ways—both direct and indirect.
In so doing, it can be said of Lewis what Ferreira said of Kierkegaard, that
he allowed readers to "discover in those writings things that awaken them
and change their view of life."[76] Like Kierkegaard, Lewis would sometimes infuse satire into his work to convey a message through a comedic
mask as he so successfully did in *The Screwtape Letters.*

Hidden Meanings

Ward suggests Lewis "delighted in hidden meanings."[77] In a letter to Arthur Greeves, Lewis said as much about romance writing: "As is proper
in romance, the inner meaning is carefully hidden."[78] Ward argues that
Lewis could be secretive, and his tendency toward holding secrets reflected his personality. Ward also suggests, "no artist is obliged to unveil his
every strategy and . . . Lewis had long-held views about the importance
of 'hiddenness' in literature."[79]

In his book, *Planet Narnia,* Ward argues that despite those who
suggest *The Chronicles of Narnia* lack "coherence" and contain several
"controversial" elements, he finds that when the stories are seen as "seven
ancient archetypes" they are better "understood within the context of a
coherent imaginative strategy."[80] Ward asserts that in reading the *Chronicles* (and much of Lewis's writings), "it is possible to discern a hidden

75. Lewis, *Surprised by Joy,* 70.
76. Ferreira, *Kierkegaard,* 39.
77. Ward, *Planet Narnia,* xiii.
78. Lewis, *Collected Letters,* 1:216.
79. Ward, *Planet Narnia,* 7.
80. Ward, *Planet Narnia,* 4.

meaning deliberately woven into these seven fairy-tales or romances."[81] Ward further points out that in his *Spenser's Images of Life*, Lewis asserts that Spenser "was drawing on the tradition of neo-platonic thought which deemed it proper that all great truths should be veiled, should be treated mythically (*per fabulosa*) by the prudent. It is for the same reason that the good 'is (usually) hidden' in Spenser and that *Faerie Queene* is 'dangerous, cryptic, its every detail loaded with unguessed meaning.'"[82] Ward states, "One particular element that was hidden or finessed by these techniques was divine presence. 'In the medieval allegories and the renaissance masks, God, if we may say so without irreverence, appears frequently, but always incognito.'"[83] We have a desire for both the seen and the unseen—that which is on the surface and that which lies beneath the surface yet is every bit as real as that which is directly observed by our senses. Stories, through the evocation of the imagination, awaken in us a sense of wonder. They confront us with truth that does not stop at the edges of our physical perceptions but that which delights our sense of transcendent reality—a world alive with flesh and spirit.

Indirect Communication Strategies in Lewis's Fiction

To better understand Lewis's use of indirect communication, I want to examine two of his fictional works. Although Lewis crafted his writing strategy intentionally and consciously chose to use many, if not all, of the indirect literary devices we have noted, he did not intentionally use Kierkegaard's indirect approach. Nevertheless, as we have seen, many of the concerns and issues he faced echoed many of the concerns facing Kierkegaard. In response to these similar challenges—materialism, the rise of secularism, modernism, the lingering vocabulary of Christian faith without the requisite passion or behavior of true faith, the scientific method of knowing accompanied by the weakening role of revelation within the culture—Lewis felt himself drawn to many of the same strategies Kierkegaard employed almost seventy years earlier.

Both Lewis and Kierkegaard were intentional in their efforts to undermine the erroneous beliefs of their communities. Furthermore, in their fictional works they used strategies that were both entertaining and

81. Ward, *Planet Narnia*, 5.

82. Ward, *Planet Narnia*, 19.

83. Ward, *Planet Narnia*, 19.

veiled. In their creative and imaginative writings, they vigilantly labored to undermine false beliefs in order to make people aware and cause them to self-reflect. Ultimately they desired to assist others to be capable of living gracious and truthful lives. While I certainly would not suggest that these men agreed on every point of doctrine or held the same communication strategy, I find it striking that both turned to many of the same strategies (imagination, entertainment, hiddenness, or veiled communication) to communicate truth.

In what follows I intend to illustrate briefly several key elements in Lewis's stories that use the indirect approach. Of interest are such strategies as overhearing, speaking without authority, taking away, hide and seek, and Christ as *incognito*. I illustrate different indirect communication strategies by examining two of Lewis's literary and fictional works: *The Screwtape Letters* and *Till We Have Faces*. In so doing, I hope to show, in part, why these works are so effective. I also wish to draw attention to what we can learn from Lewis's use of these artistic and literary tactics. Como argues, "all of Lewis's fictions are allegorical" and while this may be true, Ward points out that Lewis saw a difference between allegorical and symbolical.[84] The first book we will examine, *The Screwtape Letters*, falls between the allegorical and symbolical; while the second work, *Till We Have Faces*, is much more symbolical.

The Screwtape Letters

The Screwtape Letters, the book that put Lewis on the cover of *TIME* magazine in 1941, is one of his most important works. Lewis wrote this unusual fantasy from the perspective of a senior devil (named Screwtape) who writes letters to a junior devil (named Wormwood), to give advice on how to tempt and manage the humans in his "care." The premise is both engaging and disarming. Who does not want to hear about a devil— even if one does not really believe in spiritual beings?

The cleverly written "letters" allow Lewis to smuggle, in a backwards sort of way, the truth of the Christian life into his story (if these letters can be referred to as a story). The letters tempt readers to look at themselves from a more objective perspective. Just as Kierkegaard overheard a conversation of the grandfather talking to his grandson in the cemetery, so too the reader listens in on an older "uncle" talking to his younger

84. Como, "Mere Lewis," 114.

"nephew." Lewis does not speak directly to the reader; he merely reports, in a fictional context, the content of the letters exchanged between two devils.

As one gets caught up in the narrative and in how Screwtape attempts to mentor his nephew in order to help him subdue his "patient" (the man Wormwood is trying to influence), the reader gets interested in the strategies advanced to deceive the patient. Really though, the reader is the one being deceived. Lewis intends to entice his readers into thinking about things from a demonic point of view, which he hopes will prompt the serious business for the reader of examining one's self.

The irony behind this work of fiction is that the letters purportedly come from a demon who writes to help his pupil corrupt and destroy a man's faith; but in fact, Lewis wrote these letters to prompt his readers to rethink their own lives in order to *strengthen* their faith. The letters are therefore intended to build up and awaken the church. Lewis's primary metaphorical method is what might be called a "mirror of possibility" as a point of self-reflection.

One must be conscious of oneself and have an honest awareness of who one really is. If a sick person labors under the delusion that he is not sick, he first needs to become aware of his true condition. Otherwise, how will he attend to whatever is making him sick? In *The Screwtape Letters*, Lewis wanted to provoke his readers into self-understanding, and then to forewarn them about how they could be deceived into believing a falsehood, especially about themselves.

Emily Griesinger states that the "role of imagination in awakening and sustaining hope has profound implications for literature."[85] Lewis intentionally employed the supernatural and magic in his created fantasy worlds. He and his friend Tolkien both saw the craft and artistry involved in imagining such worlds as a God-given gift that could be used under God's inspiration and guidance to communicate religious experience and truth.[86] In *The Screwtape Letters*, Lewis uses a covert strategy that furthers the principles and values of the Christian life such as bravery, loyalty, honesty, faith, hope, and love.

Through this unusual approach Lewis continually prods his readers to imagine and reconsider who they are and who God is. Griesinger reminds us that "as Cinderellas or Ugly Ducklings or tiny Tom Thumb,

85. Griesinger, "Search for Deeper Magic," 320.
86. Griesinger, "Search for Deeper Magic," 322.

we are ignorant or at times misinformed of our true identity as sons and daughters of the King."[87] Lewis wanted us to remember who we truly are and for whom we are made.

These letters have a double-edged purpose in that they point out possible problems facing the reader and warn the reader of the seriousness of these problems. In an unconventional way these letters promote values and give insight that provide wisdom about who we are, the nature of our world, and how we live in it. They function simultaneously as both entertainment and education, and provide a remarkably useful platform to convey religious beliefs, even as they confront readers with many uncomfortable truths about who they are and how they might not be living up to their divine calling.

Although *The Screwtape Letters* is not a pseudonymous work, the narrator's role ascribed to Screwtape carries a similar pedagogical purpose. Lewis maintains his authorial distance by conversing through an archetypal image that teaches theological values from an inverse perspective. Screwtape becomes the voice of authority, an indirect approach that allows readers to draw their own conclusions. This strategy of indirection through the devil's voice lends strength to how Lewis addresses various issues. His choice to write from a devil's perspective meant that he tells the truth "upside down," and this reversal of meaning catches the reader unaware. Readers must unscramble the meaning themselves, which adds poignancy and subtle power to the book.

Lewis's writing reveals a significant thread of psychological awareness. From one point of view, *The Screwtape Letters* may be a study in the psychology of human temptation. Kath Filmer argues that the archetypal imagery helps convey this message. She states, "What ultimately separates the good from the mundane is that a good story actually does connect. When an archetypal connection is made, the story potentially appeals to a mass audience" and may influence how readers infer a "metaphysical or metaphorical meaning in accordance with or even beyond" what the narrative intends.[88]

Mildred McCollum and Betty Flora note that the combination of the "Arts and the Devil" presents an archetypal literary platform of attraction and engagement: "The Devil, as a symbol of evil and interloper in human affairs, has always been peculiarly interesting to readers and

---

87. Griesinger, "Search for Deeper Magic," 322.

88. Filmer, *Fiction of C. S. Lewis*, 33–34.

exceptionally useful to artists of all kinds . . . He still engages the attention of artists, and he still stirs the imagination."[89] Lewis's devil, however, was more than a clichéd depiction of a demon in red pajamas with a pitchfork.

Screwtape appeals to audiences because his portrayal of evil takes on a gentlemanly tone that could pass for a proper British bureaucrat. Lewis portrays his character as an intensely intellectual devil deeply knowledgeable in the ways of satanic philosophy. Lewis's Screwtape delivers his diabolical expertise through a mellifluous voice, overflowing with soothing and cunning seduction.

Screwtape's authoritative tone contradicts the comedic image of the devil held by many of Lewis's contemporaries. Lewis wanted to undermine the popular image of an amusing, red-legged, and playful devil, and so created his smooth-talking, fiendish businessman-like demon. By recasting the devil as a seductive and narcissistic character who truly had destructive and selfish intent, Lewis helped to defamiliarize the comic prankster image of the devil. In the preface to *Screwtape Letters*, Lewis writes, "I live in the Managerial Age, in a world of 'Admin.' The greatest evil is not now done in those sordid 'dens of crime' that Dickens loved to paint."[90] For Lewis, the greatest evil was not found in "concentration camps" or "labor camps," but in warm, ordered offices with clean carpets and good lighting, run by "quiet men with white collars and cut fingernails and smooth-shaven cheeks who do not need to raise their voices. Hence, naturally enough, my symbol for Hell is something like the bureaucracy of a police state or the office of a thoroughly nasty business concern."[91]

Lewis's devil is comic but serious at the same time, and his deeply flawed character can cause serious personal harm. Lewis wants his readers to see *The Screwtape Letters* as serious comedy. The devil is not all fun and games; he can cause us serious harm. Seeing the devil merely as a comedic figure, if we believe in him at all, makes us far more susceptible to his hurtful ploys. In the seventh letter, Screwtape advises Wormwood:

> I do not think you will have much difficulty in keeping the patient in the dark. The fact that "devils" are predominantly comic figures in the modern imagination will help you. If any faint

89. McCollum and Flora, "Arts and the Devil," 466.
90. Lewis, *Screwtape Letters*, x.
91. Lewis, *Screwtape Letters*, x.

suspicion of your existence begins to arise in his mind, suggest
to him a picture of something in red tights, and persuade him
that since he cannot believe in that (it is an old textbook method
of confusing them) he therefore cannot believe in you.[92]

Lewis infuses Screwtape's letters and characters with irony. Lewis
clearly wants his readers to figure out that he is communicating something
very different from what Screwtape writes; in fact, Lewis's true meaning
runs exactly the opposite of Screwtape's advice. Lewis writes something
as if in earnest (by Screwtape), which is not meant to be taken as earnest
(by Lewis). What Screwtape says in the letters is not what Lewis wants
his readers to understand, but writing in this provocative way challenges
the reader to think and to reconsider what is really meant and how one
should live one's own life. Lewis's message is not immediately clear. These
ironic letters carry latent meaning and tend to convey a significance directly the opposite of what lies on the surface.

The literary devices of irony combine wit, comedy, and satire to
convey a message that produces an innovative means for involvement
and inward reflection. We can see Lewis's use of irony in another letter where he addresses sophistry. The letter advises Wormwood to keep
his "patient" believing that the "historical Jesus" is nothing more than a
moral teacher. Screwtape writes,

We thus distract men's minds from who He is, and what He did.
We first make Him solely a teacher, and then conceal the very
substantial agreement between His teachings and those of all
other great moral teachers. For humans must not be allowed
to notice that all great moralists are sent by the Enemy not to
inform men but to remind them, to restate the primeval moral
platitudes against our continual concealment of them. We make
the Sophists: He raises up a Socrates to answer them.[93]

In using irony Lewis situates his moral philosophy and religious
theology into the discussion between Screwtape and Wormwood. Lewis
employs both wit and comedy through the twisted voice of Screwtape.
The deceptive voice of Screwtape is used as a demonic mask to communicate through jest and earnestness theological advice. In so doing, Lewis
entertains his audience by diverting the force of his words into a sense
quite different from that in which they usually experience yet desire to

92. Lewis, *Screwtape Letters*, 32.

93. Lewis, *Screwtape Letters*, 125.

hear. Lewis deceives his reader by hiding truth behind the demonic and humorous mask of uncle Screwtape.

The indirect approach employed here is used primarily to get people to the place where they can consider the question of their own existence. If a sincere message is strategically positioned within a literary mask of jest, indirect communication functions as a genuine means of offering a reader a useful mirror of inward reflection. In this comic and ironic work, Lewis's imagination merged with his Christian beliefs to engage the hearts and minds of his readers in a "literary manner which blends a critical attitude with humor and wit for the purpose of improving human institutions or humanity."[94] Both satire and humor open new paths to personal insight. Francis H. Buckley provides cogent insight into this process when he states that "the satirist's gift is the ability to point out that which we already know, and to provoke a moral or aesthetic response. He does not discover new vices but uncovers old ones to which we have become inured. He provides no new information, but only reminds us that we already know enough to be shocked had we not resigned ourselves to a contented indifference."[95]

This type of communication strategically incorporates literary devices to mask and mirror the communicator's intent. Filmer acknowledges a consistent theme in Lewis's fictional works when she states, "They are masks, because the convention of fiction is that the author is nowhere fully constituted there; but they are mirrors, too, since the mask provides the security which means paradoxically that much more can be revealed."[96]

Till We Have Faces

Ward argues that Lewis's "interest in masks, self-deception, and the difficulty of achieving identity issued ultimately in what he [Lewis] regarded as his best work, 'Till We Have Faces.'"[97] The book of Job begins much like Till We Have Faces, in that Job asks for a hearing: "But I desire to speak to the Almighty and to argue my case with God" (Job 13:3). In Lewis's myth, the main character, Orual, complains about alleged injustice in the world

94. Schakel, "Seeing and Knowing," 129.

95. Buckley, Morality of Laughter, 50.

96. Filmer, Fiction of C. S. Lewis, 2.

97. Ward, Planet Narnia, 6.

230 HIDE AND SEEK

and desires to make her case against God. Schakel argues that ultimately both Job and Orual must accept that their cases are "refuted not by reason but by the nature of God."[98]

In his story, Lewis retells an old myth about Cupid and Psyche from the *Metamorphoses, or The Golden Ass of Lucius Apuleius Platonicus*, but he tells it with a plot twist. He develops the story in the way he thought it should have been told. In the earliest English edition of the book, Lewis describes his work as "the straight tale of barbarism, the mind of an ugly woman, dark idolatry and pale enlightenment at war with each other and with vision, and the havoc which a vocation, or even a faith, works on human life."[99] No doubt it is Lewis's most complicated and challenging work, and perhaps his most disappointing in terms of sales; nevertheless, he considered it his best work. More recently, many critics seem to agree.[100]

Rather than attempt to give a complete account of every literary tactic in *Till We Have Faces* that follows a strategy of indirect communication, we will briefly cite a few examples. But before doing so, we present a summary of the story.

Schakel tells us that "myths generally have a vague setting, thus creating a degree of universality."[101] This myth is no exception. The story begins with the death of Orual's mother, after which her father, the king of Glome, remarries. The king's new wife quickly gets pregnant but dies after giving birth to a baby girl named Psyche. Orual, her half-sister, quickly becomes the mother figure for Psyche. Orual is intelligent but unattractive while Psyche is stunningly beautiful. Orual clearly loves and is devoted to her half-sister while she neglects her middle sister, Redival (a minor character in Lewis's version of the myth). Under Orual's care, Psyche grows up to become a beautiful young woman, so beautiful that the people of Glome begin to worship her instead of worshiping the local goddess Ungit. This comfortable relationship is interrupted when, during a drought and famine, the country is crippled by a plague. Many people are dying and as things grow worse for the kingdom the priest of Ungit informs the king that a sacrifice must be made to Ungit's son the "Brute"

98. Schakel, "Seeing and Knowing," 86.
99. Quoted in Hooper, *C. S. Lewis*, 243–44.
100. See Hooper, *C. S. Lewis*, 243.
101. Schakel, "Till We Have Faces," 283.

and that Psyche is the only acceptable sacrifice. So, Psyche is left on the mountain exposed to all the elements and bound to a holy tree.

After a short time, Orual goes to bury what is left of Psyche, but instead she finds Psyche alive in a valley across a river, clothed in what looks to Orual as rags. Psyche invites Orual into her palace, but Orual cannot see the palace nor can she see any of the beautiful clothes Psyche says she is wearing. All this, Psyche says, was given to her by her husband, whom she has never seen because he comes to her only at night. Caught in this quandary regarding what to believe, Orual visits Psyche a second time and persuades her half-sister, by threatening suicide, to sneak a lamp into their bedchamber to look at her husband after he falls asleep. Orual assures herself that she is doing this for Psyche's own good, however, by now the reader should recognize that Orual is extremely jealous at being replaced by another in Psyche's life.

Against her better judgment, Psyche lights the lamp and sees the god in all his divine splendor. As she attempts to look at her husband, he catches her gazing at him and admonishes her for her betrayal and sends her into exile. As Orual is watching Psyche leave, she (Orual) has an epiphany and hears Psyche's husband say to her that she too "will be Psyche."

When Orual returns to Glome, she starts to wear a veil to hide her face and feelings from others. Soon after her return, the king dies and Orual assumes his responsibilities. She devotes herself to ruling the country and performing the duties of office. As she does, she becomes more and more the queen (a masculine-like monarch) and less and less Orual (a woman and a person).

Years later she hears a priest in Essur, a nearby country, tell a sacred story about Psyche. At this point Lewis retells the Cupid and Psyche story. Orual recognizes it as her own story—but she believes that the teller got it wrong, since (like Apuleius) he says both sisters visited Psyche, and they could see the place and thus became jealous of Psyche. Orual resolves to write her own explanation of what happened to set the facts straight and to prove how unfair the gods have been to her. In writing her story, however, Orual realizes how self-deceived she has been and how she has in fact misused people, especially Psyche. She determines to escape by committing suicide, but again a god intervenes and stops her. In a series of visions, she "becomes Psyche" by helping Psyche accomplish several difficult tasks given to her. By the end of the story, Orual is taught to think of others, instead of only herself; thus, she dies to self, as the god had said she must.

In this section I argue that Lewis used several literary strategies that can be seen as approaches to indirect communication. Specifically, I will examine his use of two of these strategies: masking and taking away. I will close this chapter with identifying the importance Lewis placed on helping the reader to both think about and feel that something real and something important was at stake in his stories.

Schakel argues that the theme of sacrifice, "'very deep-rooted in Christianity,' . . . brings Christian theology into *Till We Have Faces* in ways that are less direct, but deeper and subtler, than in some of Lewis's earlier stories."[102] Orual is caught in a tension between rational discourse, exemplified in the teaching of the Fox, a Stoic who relies on "Greek wisdom" (reason), and religious belief, brought to the reader through the character of the old priest of Ungit, with his faith and devotion to the goddess. He understands holy things like rituals and sacrifice to pagan deities. Schakel states, "For much of her life Orual denies the existence of the gods or denies their justice and goodness if they do exist. What she eventually must admit is that her resistance to the gods was not an inability to believe in them, but an unwillingness to accept them because she did not want to share Psyche with anyone, not even a god."[103]

Doris Myers argues that *Till We Have Faces* "is an extrapolation from what is known and accepted into what is speculated and imagined. Lewis knows the pagan myths that seem to foreshadow Jesus and accepts the gospel accounts as fact. He calls the Incarnation 'myth become fact.' The speculation begins as Lewis asks where the pagan myths came from."[104] Did the story, in myth form, come in part from history, or was it completely made up out of the mind of Apuleius? Whatever the case, it is fair to say that for Lewis, this myth in a very realistic way foreshadowed the incarnation, the appearance of Christ on earth. It is important that Lewis's story is located in an imaginary country, Glome, sometime before the birth of Christ. In fact there is nothing directly Christian about this story. The name of Christ nowhere appears in the story. Schakel argues, "By setting the story before the time of Christ, Lewis eliminates the

---

102. Schakel, "Till We Have Faces," 290.
103. Schakel, "Till We Have Faces," 285.
104. Myers, *C. S. Lewis in Context*, 190.

possibility of addressing Christianity directly. He hides what is in fact a central theme."[105]

In a way, therefore, this is a pre-Christian story with many elements or themes of Christianity written into the myth: the importance of sacrifice, one dying for the many, the need for worship and moral action, living for others, natural love, and divine love. All these religious themes are placed before the reader, in part, because of the care Lewis took in positioning the story long before Christ lived. The events in Glome, placed before the birth of Christ, anticipate his coming.

Lewis used the major characters in the story to traffic in religious themes. Admittedly, these themes are veiled in such a way that many readers miss them, but those who read carefully can see them quite clearly. As Schakel states, "Lewis used Orual's character to give concrete embodiment to ideas about love . . . which he earlier incorporated into *The Great Divorce* years before and finally into *The Four Loves* (after *'Till We Have Faces* years later)."[106]

Three of the main characters demonstrate clearly three kinds of natural love Lewis articulated in *The Four Loves*: *storge* (affection) as illustrated by Orual's love for Psyche; *philia* (friendship) as demonstrated by Orual's relationship with the Fox; and *eros* (romantic love) as illustrated through Orual's unrequited love for Bardia. All these natural loves are good but can be corrupted. As Lewis makes clear in this story, if natural loves are to remain loves, they must be cultivated with and transformed by a higher love—the work of *agape* (divine love), a selfless love that comes from one's relationship to God. This is the selfless love that Orual finally finds when she is "able to see herself clearly to receive the gift of a higher love."[107] Before she receives the gift of *agape*, Orual's natural loves turn possessive and destructive, and in each case they decline until they cease to be love at all. Lewis embodied all these ideas in literary form in his story.

For much of Orual's life she wore a veil to cover her common looks. As Schakel states, however, "The veil gives her a public identity as the Queen and allows her to bury her personal self: she has no face, no identity, and thus no way to relate genuinely to a god, or to other people. Only when she removes the veil, confronts her true self, and gains a 'face' can

105. Schakel, "Till We Have Faces," 289.
106. Schakel, "Till We Have Faces," 285.
107. Schakel, "Till We Have Faces," 286.

she encounter God without defenses, excuses, or pretenses for 'how can [God] meet us face to face till we have faces?'"[108]

Besides the various times Lewis used the masking strategy in his writing he also used the indirect strategy of taking away or making strange. In this next section I will briefly introduce this strategy and illustrate his use of it in his novel *Till We Have Faces*. Lewis wants to address a difficult question that many of his readers face, but he wants to do so in a way that they do not immediately recognize. Lewis saw the conflict in his day between reason (as the penultimate way of knowing) and revelation (how religious truth is known). He understood that direct, abstract arguments were limited and that he needed to provide concrete—albeit fictional—examples of how to address this issue. He did so by engaging the reader in a story that captured their imagination and emotions.

Schakel explains it this way: "Lewis offers an imaginative experience which gives readers a taste of reality. Orual's defense of her life is, at a deeper level, a search for a hidden God."[109] Plainly Lewis did not see the challenge as a problem of information, argument, and reason, but of emotion, will, spirit, and imagination. *Till We Have Faces* addressed this issue covertly in the form of the two main characters: the Fox, a Greek rationalist, and the pagan priest, who believed in mystery, wonder, and revelation. Throughout the book one can see Orual caught between these two men, or between these two ways of knowing. For the most part, she follows the Fox and shares his reliance on wisdom. His enlightened reason helps to guide her in running the country, but her mind never feels completely settled. Despite her best efforts, she cannot completely forget the brief moment by the river when she saw the palace were Psyche lived. None of Orual's well-reasoned arguments can completely explain what she saw. Despite this, she can bury that small fact away in the back of her mind and hide from it, like she hid from herself and everyone else behind her veil.

Story or myth is the perfect way to deal with the *leitmotif* of the whole work, which Kallistos Ware argues "is the hiddenness of the Divine."[110] The mystery of the Divine in our world and in our relationship to God unsettles the modern mind, and Lewis knowingly dealt with this issue through story. Ward argues that for Lewis the inner meaning

108. Schakel, "Till We Have Faces," 286.
109. Schakel, "Till We Have Faces," 289.
110. Ware, "God of the Fathers," 58.

or divine presence was often hidden or finessed. He states, "It is instructive to survey the many occasions on which Lewis praised the indirect approach to communication. He believed that success in writing comes about by 'secretly evoking powerful associations'; that expressions should 'not merely state but suggest.'"[111]

What makes this story so interesting and engaging is that through these characters and situations, created by Lewis, we are forced to contemplate some of life's deepest and most universal questions: Does God exist? How can we know if he exists? If he does, what is he like? Why do bad things happen? Lewis reflected on these sorts of questions in his apologetic works such as *The Problem of Pain, Mere Christianity,* and *Miracles,* wherein he tried to articulate helpful answers in order to assist his readers in understanding what they needed to know about the Christian faith. Here, however, he introduces these issues through the media of myth. In *Till We Have Faces,* Orual complains that the gods do not show themselves clearly, they do not give signs, and they speak in riddles. As she stands before the palace, she cannot see what Psyche can see. Orual's experience as she searches for the hidden gods is mirrored by Lewis's readers.

Ware explains what he believes to be a strategic and moving moment in the story: "Orual cannot see Psyche's palace (except for a brief and tantalizing moment). 'It's no use, Maia,' says Psyche to Orual. 'I see it and you don't. Who's to judge between us?'"[112] Orual argues that the gods do not show themselves. "'The gods set us riddles,' Orual protests, 'but they give us no answers: Why must holy places be dark places?'"[113] They must be dark, of course, because they deal with the unseen world— a world that is unfamiliar to a fallen, broken, and disabled humanity.

Because holy wisdom is often shrouded in mystery, it is best grasped through imagination and story, as the full measure of holy wisdom lies beyond the grasp of our intellectual abilities. If we are to understand God, we can do so only partially. He is infinite and we are finite. He has all wisdom and we know only in part. We are limited. He is limitless. The full wonder and beauty of his face—his presence—can be known only imperfectly because we are imperfect.

111. Ward, *Planet Narnia,* 21.
112. Ware, "God of the Fathers," 58.
113. Ware, "God of the Fathers," 58.

Many people feel drawn to *Till We Have Faces*, expecting to get answers. The myth, however, does not provide answers, although it does hint at some. Lewis apparently wants to provoke interest in the most important questions and to rouse readers to seek their own answers rather than provide answers for them. Perhaps stories like this one can help readers imaginatively identify with Orual in asking questions in the dark places of the soul, and then maybe they too will learn how to see and act.

Whatever the case, myths assist readers to enjoy things of lasting worth that otherwise they can only contemplate. Lindvall states that "in science fiction novels or fairy tales, one meets something truer than mere empirical fact. By introducing an audience to an imaginary world, Lewis believed that he put them in dialogue with personal and universal mythic truths."[114] As we have seen, "Orual started her journey wanting answers, but in the end, she finds not answers but the reason her doubts and questions were not answered: 'I know now, Lord, why you utter no answer. You are yourself the answer. Before your face questions die away.'"[115]

Job too asks questions of God and seeks an audience with him. Eventually God comes to Job and answers Job "out of the whirlwind" (38:1). He does not reason with Job but assails him with questions that display God's greatness and Job's finitude. Job's final words could fittingly have been Orual's: "I have uttered what I did not understand, things too wonderful for me, which I did not know" (42:3). Both Job and Orual complain of alleged injustice in the universe; both present an argument against God; and both consent that their case is refuted, not by reason but by the very nature of God.

Owen Barfield, one of Lewis's closest friends, once said that Lewis "excelled in laying bare" the "nonsensical foundation beneath most of what most of his contemporaries were taking for granted."[116] Barfield states that Lewis's "simple but infallible *modus operandi* was to step quietly around to the back of his reductionist opponent and trip him up from behind."[117] This strategy seems to have held true for much of Lewis's fictional writing as well, and echoes Kierkegaard's own strategy of "sneaking up from behind." According to Barfield, there were two Lewises: the

114. Lindvall, "C.S. Lewis' Theory," 527.
115. Schakel, "Till We Have Faces," 290.
116. Barfield, *Owen Barfield*, 95.
117. Barfield, *Owen Barfield*, 95.

"atomically rational Lewis" and the "mythopoeic Lewis." And in *Till We Have Faces*, we see the mythopoeic Lewis at his best.[118]

Conclusion

In his book *The Narnian*, Alan Jacobs tells a story of one of Lewis's most famous students, Kenneth Tynan. Tynan, who would become an exceptional dramatist, screenwriter, critic, essayist, and director, was both extremely successful and experimental in his writing, directing, and almost everything else he did. This extraordinary man of the British theater was a person of extremes. He liked to cross the boundaries "from pointedly saying words that were not supposed to be said on BBC television to directing the first all-nude musical, *Oh Calcutta!*"[119] Tynan was a great "character" of his time and remained sexually adventurous all his life. Tynan did not share Lewis's beliefs, yet Lewis continued to mentor and counsel him. As remarkable as it sounds, Tynan was drawn to Lewis and his writings. In one diary entry, Tynan wrote, "I note with interest that W. H. Auden wrote in his last book [that] 'Kierkegaard, Williams, and Lewis guided us back to belief.' (C.S., of course.) Will he finally guide me?"[120] Jacobs declares,

> What matters in all this is that "C. S. L." presents Tynan an imaginative picture of goodness and love to which he is consistently drawn—even when the arguments do not convince him. Nothing else in his life offered him that picture, that vision, and it would have been unsurprising if he had left Lewis behind; yet he could not. The vision remained to beckon him. Tynan clearly felt something that Austin Farrer noted in the homily he gave at Lewis's funeral: "But his real power was not proof; it was depiction. There lived in his writings a Christian universe that could be both thought and felt, in which he was at home and in which he made his reader at home."[121]

Lewis and Kierkegaard shared an earnest desire to communicate the truth of the gospel in the most powerful yet respectful way possible, and both men realized the limits to straightforward, rational arguments for

118. Baumgaertner, *Flannery O'Connor*.

119. Jacobs, *Narnian*, 310.

120. Quoted in Jacobs, *Narnian*, 312.

121. Jacobs, *Narnian*, 312.

that purpose. In response, they turned to more imaginative approaches of communication. Both men sought to present a compelling yet truthful picture of God's presence in order to provide their readers with a choice of how to live. By intellect, intuition, and spirit, Lewis used his art to create imaginative stories full of longing, employing his artistic skills to smuggle in religious truth. Rather than directly confront his readers with arguments and propositions (which he would do, if needed), he often found that he could be more effective by creating imaginative stories of goodness and love—to which so many readers feel drawn.

Lewis was a man of reason and imagination. His stories and writings addressed both the mind and heart. Ultimately he ignited the imagination in such a way as to invite others to take notice of the transcendent truth present within our world. Lewis presents us with imaginative worlds that cause us to see our world in new and challenging ways. As we have seen, woven into *Screwtape Letters* and *Till We Have Faces* are clear examples of indirect communication strategies. In fact, much if not all of his fictional writing could be described as using indirect communication strategies for the purpose of imaginative apologetics. We now turn to a writer, who with clear intent, awakens the reader through various indirect communication strategies, to a severe grace.

9

Flannery O'Connor: Stories as Severe
and Costly Grace

St. Cyril of Jerusalem, in instructing catechumens, wrote: "The dragon sits by the side of the road, watching those who pass. Beware lest he devour you. We go to the Father of souls, but it is necessary to pass by the dragon." No matter what form the dragon may take, it is of this mysterious passage past him, or into his jaws, that stories of any depth will always be concerned to tell, and this being the case, it requires considerable courage at any time, in any country, not to turn away from the storyteller.

—FLANNERY O'CONNOR, *MYSTERY AND MANNERS*

Introduction

A N OLD TESTAMENT PASSAGE from the book of Judges tells an ironic story about the marginalized bastard son, Abimelech, who seizes the royal power that Gideon had refused. After Gideon's death, Abimelech, in order to consolidate power for himself, massacred seventy half-brothers on a single stone (Judg 9:5, 18). The opportunist dies himself when a single stone gets dropped on his head a short time later (v. 53). Before his death, however, Abimelech's younger half-brother, Jotham, rebukes him and satirizes the uselessness of the monarchy that Abimelech had so violently sought. His speech goes like this:

> When Jotham was told about this, he climbed up on the top of Mount Gerizim and shouted to them, "Listen to me, citizens of Shechem, so that God may listen to you. One day the trees went out to anoint a king for themselves. They said to the olive tree, 'Be our king.'
>
> But the olive tree answered, 'Should I give up my oil, by which both gods and man are honored, to hold sway over the trees?'
>
> Next, the trees said to the fig tree, 'Come and be our king.'
>
> But the fig tree replied, 'Should I give up my fruit, so good and sweet, to hold sway over the trees?'
>
> Then the trees said to the vine, 'Come and be our king.'
>
> But the vine answered, 'Should I give up my wine, which cheers both gods and men, to hold sway over the trees?'
>
> Finally, all the trees said to the thorn bush, 'Come and be our king.'
>
> The thorn bush said to the trees, 'If you really want to anoint me king over you, come and take refuge to my shade; but if not, then let fire come out of the thorn bush and consume the cedars of Lebanon!'
>
> Now if you have acted honorably and in good faith when you made Abimelech king, and if you have been fair to Jerub-Baal and his family, and if you have treated him as he deserves—and to think that my father fought for you, risked his life to rescue you from the hand of Midian (but today you have revolted against my father's family, murdered his seventy sons on a single stone, and made Abimelech, the son of his slave girl, king over the citizens of Shechem because he is your brother)—if then you have acted honorably and in good faith toward Jerub-Baal and his family today, may Abimelech be your joy, and may you be his, too! But if you have not, let fire come out from Abimelech and consume you, citizens of Shechem and Beth Millo, and let fire come out from you, citizens of Shechem and Beth Millo, and consume Abimelech!" (Judg 9:7–20)

In exaggerated form, Jotham told a story that engaged his audience and at the same time provided a hidden message his listeners needed to hear. Jotham's parable, filled with satire and more than a little violence, expressed a view of politicians as ridiculous and unreasonable.

Had Flannery O'Connor been within earshot of Jotham that day, she most likely would have approved. Many of her stories have an Old Testament sound to them, full of extreme characters and dark overtones. Due to her careful craftsmanship and knack for connecting with audiences, readers around the world still enjoy her work. In this final chapter we examine a few of her powerful stories. We begin by considering her literary strategy and style. I will argue that her writing style and strategy of communication has much in common with the strategy and approach advanced by Kierkegaard. We then examine one of her last stories, "Parker's Back," to illustrate clearly her indirect approach to communicating grace.

An Incarnational Art

O'Connor states, "We live now in an age which doubts both fact and value, which is swept this way and that by momentary convictions. Instead of reflecting a balance from the world around him, the novelist now has to achieve one from a felt balance inside himself . . . There is no literary orthodoxy that can be prescribed as settled for the fiction writer."[1] Therefore, the writer brings not only an eye for seeing things "as they are" but a writer must write for an audience under the sway of a fragmented and suspicious culture. In this context, writers must exaggerate their characters and plots in order to gain the attention of the reader, challenging them to reevaluate both the facts and values they possess.

For O'Connor fiction writing is an "incarnational art."[2] She saw the mystery of the incarnation as a continuing scandal and affront to modernity. It offends their sensibilities. What she meant by this was that God came in a way and in a manner that was not expected or fully understood by modern humanity. People, even religious people, were appalled not so much at seeing a dying man on a cross, or even the gore of this gruesome event, but by the revelation that this is, in fact, God on the cross. Nothing similar can prepare us for this because nothing similar exists in human experience. Her art, therefore, tried to show the real yet extreme dimensions of the incarnation and God's grace therein. O'Connor calls this "the prophetic voice of the fiction writer." The artist or writer is a realist of distance. "All novelists are fundamentally seekers and describers of the real, but the realism of each novelist will depend on this view of

1. O'Connor, *Mystery and Manners*, 49.
2. O'Connor, *Mystery and Manners*, 68.

the ultimate reaches of reality."[3] This world is troubled by the incarnation which transforms our every action and all of our dealings in life. The incarnation teaches us that God exists in all aspects of life, and our truth must depict reality accordingly.

Prophetic Vision

O'Connor does not see the writer with Christian concerns as an artist who deals only with issues of faith, but as an artist who happens to be a Christian and is looking at anything that allows someone to see the mystery of their existence. This stance enables her to begin by contact with "reality through what can be seen, heard, smelt, tasted, and touch."[4]

She believes that writers and artists of her day privileged a kind of artistic orthodoxy. That is, they "demand a realism of fact" (scientific or historical) which ultimately may "limit rather than broaden" a writer's or artist's scope of reality. Most certainly it shrivels their concern with mystery. She argues that most writers consider "social forces" as the only source of legitimate material they can write about. O'Connor, in confronting this materialistic orthodoxy, maintains that a "novelist with Christian concerns will find in modern life distortions which are repugnant to him, and his problem will be to make these appear as distortions to an audience which is used to seeing them as natural; and he may well be forced to take ever more violent means to get this vision across to this hostile audience."[5]

George Kilcourse maintains that O'Connor's understanding of the mystery of our being is realized imaginatively by encountering it through the senses.[6] Consequently, O'Connor did everything in her power to remove herself and her fiction from mere sentiment, which she felt distanced the reader from reality. Part of the challenge for the writer with Christian concerns is to show "the presence of grace as it appears in nature, and what matters for him is that his faith not become detached from his dramatic sense and from his vision of what is. No one in these days, however, would seem more anxious to have it become detached than those Catholics who demand that the writer limit, on the natural level,

3. O'Connor, *Mystery and Manners*, 40.
4. O'Connor, *Mystery and Manners*, 91.
5. O'Connor, *Mystery and Manners*, 33.
6. Kilcourse, *Flannery O'Connor's Religious Imagination*, 297–99.

what he allows himself to see."[7] Here O'Connor argues for seeing and presenting reality in such a way that it can be made alive to our senses—not sanitizing reality so that the church or Christians are presented in a more favorable light than deserved. An artist's strength is that he or she presents truth in its full range of complexity, and that begins with the artist and the community to which he or she belongs. This is no less true for an artist with religious concerns. Each artist must see the church, individual Christians, and the world as they are and avoid describing some idealized form of the church or the world.

O'Connor warned her readers in 1962 of what she saw as a Manichean influence that she understood as "separating nature and grace," which in so doing crippled our understanding of both.[8] This separation of spirituality or *super*nature from nature is not only precarious theology, but it leads to a false view of life. The separation of nature and grace sacrifices a proper understanding of the real, and in so doing this Manichean spirit will reduce an audience's conception of the supernatural to pious cliché.

A careful examination of writers and media today will identify two obvious but negative forms of this communication fallacy: the sentimental and the obscene. Few artists with Christian concerns have recognized the similarity between these two misleading literary notions. Unfortunately, many in the church abhor the one (obscenity) and often adore the other (sentimentality). This situation, however, hinders the artist who wishes to communicate transcendent truth to an audience that does not share that faith. If we cannot see the flaws in ourselves, how can we be trusted to see clearly or to reliably communicate anything at all? How can the nonbeliever trust the artist with Christian concerns when such an artist overlooks the church's own failings and presents an idealized version of the Christian life? O'Connor often challenged "prevailing notions of existence as shallow and impoverished."[9]

The fiction writer with Christian concerns is completely free to observe the world as it is and show others what he or she sees. O'Connor would argue that to try to tidy up reality is the "sin of pride" and to pass over the evil we see, especially in the church or in the life of a Christian and look only for the good, is false redemption and fallacious

7. O'Connor, *Mystery and Manners*, 147.

8. O'Connor, *Mystery and Manners*, 147.

9. Hawkins, *Language of Grace*, 10.

communication. Open and free observation is founded on the faith that the universe is meaningful.

O'Connor often resorts to violence or the grotesque to communicate her uncompromising vision. She frequently situates her stories in a world that requires her to disturb, shock, and strangely draw the world outside of Christ to the reality found in him. As O'Connor asserts, the fiction writer should be characterized by his or her "prophetic vision," by which she means that authors depend on their imaginations and not their moral faculty.[10] The writer-as-prophet is a realist with a vision of distance, which for her includes both the spiritual and the eternal. Therefore, she does not "hesitate to distort appearances in order to show the hidden truth."[11] "In the novelist's case," O'Connor states, "prophecy is a matter of seeing near things with their extensions of meaning and thus of seeing far things close up. The prophet is a realist of distances, and it is this kind of realism that you find in the best modern instances of the grotesque."[12] For O'Connor, prophetic insight is a quality of the imagination that allows the artist to see through reality to comprehend its proper distance—allowing for "natural incidents" to be seen for what they really are in light of time and eternity. It may be "just" a storm, but in it we may see God working. The prophetic vision recalls people to truths they already know but have chosen to ignore.

"The novelist," writes O'Connor, "must be characterized not by his function but by his vision, and we must remember that his vision has to be transmitted and that the limitations and blind spots of his audience will very definitely affect the way he is able to show what he sees."[13] O'Connor argues that authors who find agreement with the current opinions and beliefs of the age and who advance the accepted values and views of their culture will find it easier to address their audience than those whose writings contradict the prevailing beliefs and attitudes. At the same time O'Connor believes, "there is something in us, as storytellers and as listeners to stories, that demands the redemptive act, that demands that what falls at least be offered the chance to be restored."[14] Furthermore, while the reader looks for this redemptive gesture, what has escaped him or

---

10. O'Connor, *Mystery and Manners*, 179.

11. O'Connor, *Mystery and Manners*, 179.

12. O'Connor, *Mystery and Manners*, 44.

13. O'Connor, *Mystery and Manners*, 47.

14. O'Connor, *Mystery and Manners*, 48.

her is its cost. As O'Connor states, "His sense of evil is diluted or lacking altogether, and so he has forgotten the price of restoration."[15]

"Unless the novelist has gone utterly out of his mind," O'Connor argues, "his aim is still communication, and communication suggests talking inside a community."[16] O'Connor's frustration with the attitudes and beliefs of her contemporary audience became evident in the oft-quoted illustration from her first letter to a young woman referred to as "A." She states, "The moral sense, has been bred out of certain sections of the population, like the wings have been bred off certain chickens to produce more white meat on them. This is a generation of wingless chickens."[17] The church may be somewhat responsible for the decline of its influence in the West, as Heschel explains, "Religion declined, not because it was refuted, but because it became irrelevant, dull, oppressive, insipid."[18] Thomas Merton expresses some of O'Connor's concern when he states, "Where authentic religious concern degenerates into salesman-ship it becomes an affront to the honest perplexities of the vast majority of men. I think, frankly, that you are entitled to be left unbothered by the sheer triviality of so much religious vaudeville."[19]

O'Connor's Audience

Let us examine the audience that O'Connor aims to address in her writ-ings. The audience one hopes to address is crucial to any artist or anyone trying to communicate truth. First, O'Connor believes that the Southern-er's identity is shaped by a distrust of the abstract. Therefore, she strives to make her stories as concrete as possible, while at the same time drawing on the grace of God. Like Kierkegaard's suspicion of the crowd, O'Connor believes that "art never responds to the wish to make it democratic."[20] It is not made for everyone but is written or made to address people in a particular situation and at specific times. As O'Connor states, "It is only for those willing to undergo the effort needed to understand it."[21]

15. O'Connor, *Mystery and Manners*, 48.

16. O'Connor, *Mystery and Manners*, 53.

17. O'Connor, *Habit of Being*, 90.

18. Quoted in Kilcourse, *Flannery O'Connor's Religious Imagination*, 50.

19. Quoted in Kilcourse, *Flannery O'Connor's Religious Imagination*, 84.

20. O'Connor, *Mystery and Manners*, 189.

21. O'Connor, *Mystery and Manners*, 189.

For O'Connor, culture desires easy answers, but trustworthy fiction provides none. She argues that the storyteller provides a strong critique of culture, yet her writing was anything but a direct, frontal, intellectual assault. Her technique is to mask the truth in stories pregnant with meaning and filled with conflict. She does so with an unparalleled mastery, as exemplified in such short stories as "A Good Man is Hard to Find," "The Lame Shall Enter First," and "Parker's Back." These stories draw us in with the unusual and sometimes haunting nature of their characters. The provocative nature of these characters causes us to question their motives and behavior, and in so doing questions our own motives and behavior. Their density forces us out of the abstract and into the reality of their being.

Second, O'Connor recognized that she wrote for an audience that doubted the religious and moral views of the past. She crafted stories of transcendent experiences at a time when people commonly lacked the words to express transcendent truths. Even more, her audience lacked the means to enter and relate to stories that spoke plainly of God, grace, and transcendence. Therefore, she had to work "against the limits of contemporary imagination, both with and against the limitations of the reader."[22] O'Connor believed that we live in a world "which has been increasingly convinced that the reaches of reality end very close to the surface, that there is no ultimate divine source, that the things of the world do not pour forth from God in a double way, or at all."[23] In other words, the visual culture that we now occupy is focused on the superficial, on the surface of things. O'Connor borrowed from St. Augustine the belief "that the things of the world pour forth from God in a double way; intellectually into the minds of the angels and physically into the world of things."[24] For O'Connor, the world we see, observe, and write about is ultimately good because it emerged from a good God.

With regard to the audience's understanding of spirituality, she reasoned that we live in an unbelieving age with a noticeably "lopsided spirituality." Thus, she identified three types of spiritual imbalance: 1) one who recognizes spirit in one's self but does not recognize a spirituality outside of the self, 2) one who recognizes a divine being outside him or herself but does not believe that this being can be known analogically,

---

22. Hawkins, *Language of Grace*, 4–5.

23. O'Connor, *Mystery and Manners*, 157.

24. O'Connor, *Mystery and Manners*, 157.

defined dogmatically, or received sacramentally, and 3) one who can neither believe nor contain himself or herself in unbelief. For O'Connor, "Today's audience is one in which religious feeling has become, if not atrophied, at least vaporous and sentimental."[25]

Ways of Seeing

According to O'Connor, the writer and artist with Christian concerns must be an uncompromising observer of the human experience and of the world. She would argue that "in the modern novel one sees reflected in the story 'the man of our time, the unbeliever, who is nevertheless grappling in a desperate and usually honest way with intense problems of the spirit.'"[26] Ralph C. Wood suggests that for O'Connor, art and faith become congruent ways of seeing—"rather than turning inward in indulgent self-exploration, O'Connor believed that the writer is called to cultivate a Conradian vision focused on everything that is radically other."[27] In other words, the purpose of artful indirection is to restore to us a sense of wonder and mystery. Not that transcendence readily yields to art, but that we are more easily returned to God by means of it. As Joanne Halleran McMullen suggests, O'Connor consciously employed "a profound sense of mystery in a concerted attempt to embed her religious message deeply within the story, creating characters whose destinies remain spiritually debatable but thus available to readers she believed religiously hostile."[28] This approach opened readers to see or reflect on their own life from a new perspective and to wrestle with the meaning of the story. She sought, through her art, to see with a keen sense of the real so that the reader might see the same thing—"so that we might see what she saw, but with our own eyes."[29]

O'Connor is remarkably like Kierkegaard in that she is willing to allow for a certain subjective quality to truth. Wood argues that O'Connor's fiction was a great way for her to tell the truth as she envisioned it, as less a method of reflecting directly upon religious themes and more about the reader asking, how is it with me? "'Self-knowledge,' she declared, 'is a

25. O'Connor, *Mystery and Manners*, 161.

26. O'Connor, *Mystery and Manners*, 158.

27. Wood, *Flannery O'Connor*, 27.

28. McMullen, *Writing Against God*, 142.

29. Elie, *Life You Save*, 471.

great curb to irresponsible self-expression, for to know oneself is, above all, to know what one lacks.'"[30]

O'Connor shares with Kierkegaard a lack of patience with religion that makes no difference in the lives of its followers: "Catholics who receive the weekly sacrament without its making any discernible difference in their lives. 'The Church for them,' she wrote, 'is not the body of Christ but the poor man's insurance system.'"[31] Thus, indirection in art becomes a tool for "relating" faith in a decidedly experiential and existential way. It is not a stretch, then, to conclude that both O'Connor and Kierkegaard typify, for artists working within the communication arts, the potential for maintaining a vibrant kind of Christian existentialism. All readers, including the skeptical, are invited to examine O'Connor's stories and see in her characters, no matter how depraved, the shadow of the life of Christ looming behind them, and in so doing, act accordingly.

O'Connor, Communication,
and the Language of Faith

O'Connor found a lack of moral and religious awareness within her culture. Increasingly, this lack of vision or understanding led to the disuse or lack of accurate naming of the things of God. Hawkins argues that O'Connor's discontent "grew out of an inability to assume (and thereby to share directly) this religious vision of reality with the reader."[32] Those artists or writers who really believed in a moral sense and a religious vision of reality were often misunderstood or ignored by their audience. "What she [O'Connor] faced instead was a seemingly insurmountable problem of communication. How could she portray the transforming action of the divine within human life for people who no longer have a powerful sense of God, much less a world of symbols by which to understand and articulate religious experience?"[33]

The situation facing O'Connor is a formidable problem for any writer or artist wanting to communicate transcendent truth to their generation. How can such an artist address a generation distracted to such a degree that they dismiss the meaning of the religious words and ideas so

30. Quoted in Wood, *Flannery O'Connor*, 26.

31. Quoted in Wood, *Flannery O'Connor*, 30.

32. Hawkins, *Language of Grace*, 1–2.

33. Hawkins, *Language of Grace*, 2.

often used to communicate faith in past generations? Hawkins addresses this issue:

> Deprived of the shared assumptions that allow direct address, O'Connor was bound by the need to find new modes of indirection, strategies of communication that might open the reader to dimensions of life become inaccessible to many and remote to most. In other words, she saw that she had to discover a new language of grace in order to confront the reader with the experience of God, for no matter how current God's mysterious presence among us may be, O'Connor knew that the contemporary Christian writer had inherited a "coin of the realm which has the face worn off it"—what Walker Percy, using a similar metaphor, has called the *devaluation* of the old works of grace.[34]

Just as one should not put new wine in old wineskins, so O'Connor sought new ways to communicate grace to an audience not usually moved by stories using the old religious terms or overused rhetorical strategies. Like Kierkegaard's strategy of taking away (making strange), she created imaginative and exaggerated narratives to revitalize the religious imagination and to put the notion of grace back into circulation.[35] Her stories echoed those found in the Old Testament, and in comparison to modernity's dealings with human weakness and God's mercy—which are often sentimental—Flannery O'Connor eschews sentimentality. As Basselin explains, "God does not appear at the end of her stories and take pity on the poor souls she has crafted . . . Rather, grace or the possibility for grace arrives only through the experience of grotesque limitations; mercy is forged in the fires of suffering."[36] For O'Connor, grace comes from suffering, as illustrated in "A Good Man is Hard to Find" where the grandmother offers grace to the Misfit (a serial killer) who has unveiled the grandmother's own hypocrisy and doubt while having her family murdered. Yet in that severe moment, the grandmother's own realization of kinship with the Misfit allows her to mercifully offer him grace. O'Connor remarked, "The best of my work [sounds] like the Old Testament would sound if it were being written today."[37] Wood, recognizing the intense biblical characterization of O'Connor's narrative fiction, explains, "While O'Connor's pistol-shot sentences do not literally declare, 'Thus

34. Hawkins, *Language of Grace*, 2.

35. Hawkins, *Language of Grace*, 2.

36. Basselin, *Flannery O'Connor*, 2.

37. Quoted in Wood, *Flannery O'Connor*, 159.

saith the Lord,' their directness has a decidedly biblical quality . . . even continued rereading of O'Connor's fiction prompts fear and trembling . . . in the dread that we ourselves will be eviscerated."[38] Wood further states, "while no one's salvation depends on getting Faulkner right, we read O'Connor knowing that the stakes are ultimate."[39]

O'Connor worked hard at creating a language and text that was "hermeneutically 'open.' Thus, we will not be asked to infer a single meaning even though it is often clear enough what the author herself is 'thinking'; we will be asked instead to choose among options and to discover our own religious presuppositions in that choice."[40] The advantage of this approach is that the non-believing reader is not immediately put off by the story but is provoked into considering the meaning (possibly with the help of God). They are jarred, perplexed, or shocked by what they read and not immediately sure what to make of the text and how they ought to respond. In this more stimulating or challenging approach, the reader has time and distance from the material so that the story can work on his or her moral and spiritual sensibility. The reader needs time to process major transformations possibly occurring in his or her own life. Individual transformation is more often a process of small steps and varied insights rather than a onetime "Aha" moment. Her approach caused the reader to stop and think; that is, to think differently about their own religious life.

In one sense, the Bible seems like a very closed book to which nothing may be added and nothing taken away; and yet it is constantly "opening itself up to the contemporary reality of the believer, 'evangelizing' human experience by making each isolated moment or event meaningful in terms of its whole."[41] O'Connor's writing is something like that. The conversion of the reader is not all O'Connor intended, nor can her artistry be reduced to simple moral or religious instruction. Nevertheless, Hawkins argues that her "artistry is both instructive and heuristic; that is, it intends not only to recall the reader to truths forgotten, but also to lead us to discover ourselves in God."[42] Her stories of a man lost in the woods or of a neglected child seeking baptism in a river may be narratives which St. Paul proclaims in Romans as "the renewing of our minds."

38. Wood, *Flannery O'Connor*, 159–60.

39. Wood, *Flannery O'Connor*, 160.

40. Hawkins, *Language of Grace*, 4.

41. Hawkins, *Language of Grace*, 6.

42. Hawkins, *Language of Grace*, 8.

The stories move in two directions at once, backward to the established teachings of Scripture and tradition, and forward to the person making sense out of the stories. In this way the stories have a double movement of remembrance and discovery.

The Special Problem of Mystery

Now let us turn to another problem that confronted O'Connor. How could she speak meaningfully about what Hawkins calls "the struggle to suggest the resonance and depth of human life"?[43] How could she communicate the sense of "mystery" in life "when there is no authoritative story commonly held, no language for the realities that transcend our current theories"?[44]

The issue, as Hawkins states it, involves two questions. "First, how can you speak about the experience of grace without assuming a knowledge (let alone an acceptance) of any religious tradition, and, secondly, how can you speak engagingly about such an experience so as to open the reader to the sense of mystery and transcendence which the spirit of the present age has seemingly inoculated us against?"[45] Hawkins notes, "implicit in the latter half of this question, moreover, is the writer's desire not only to open the reader, but to move him or her in a particular direction."[46]

By taking this approach, O'Connor strives to alter the consciousness of her readers so that once more they may take transcendent truth into account. O'Connor held strong opinions, and this came through in her writing. If she felt something was wrong, she spoke of it as wrong, albeit usually in veiled language. Here lies a danger. Fiction may be seen as simply entertainment or as simply sugar glaze on the pill, a way of getting a meaning across "rather than the creation of a world in which the experience of characters is as dense and ambiguous as our own—a believable world which offers the reader a chance for discovery rather than a lesson to be learned."[47] By employing mystery and the grotesque, O'Connor was able to hold up a mirror to her readers that allowed them to consider

---

43. Hawkins, *Language of Grace*, 10.
44. Hawkins, *Language of Grace*, 10.
45. Hawkins, *Language of Grace*, 10.
46. Hawkins, *Language of Grace*, 10.
47. Hawkins, *Language of Grace*, 10–11.

their own sin and weakness, and in doing so were able to break through their cultural pretenses and lay bare their souls and their own defects.

Elie reminds us that although O'Connor often suggested "that her work's power to shock lay in the violence it dramatized or in the 'strange skips and gaps' of its style," this may not remain as true today as when she wrote.[48] Our culture has shifted to embrace some very violent stories, both written and visual. So her stories, while still shocking, are now more acceptable.

O'Connor's view of fiction is so bound up with her faith that it is impossible to separate them. Her observations about the art of fiction almost amount to a defense of the faith. Although some writers and critics see Christian doctrines as a hindrance to the fiction writer, O'Connor felt this was far from the truth. In *Mystery and Manners*, she argues that dogma "frees the storyteller to observe. It is not a set of rules which fixes what he sees in the world. It affects his writing primarily by guaranteeing his respect for mystery."[49] For O'Connor the proper subject of fiction is the mystery of our ultimate concerns, that is, the divine life and our sharing in it, and the central mystery of the Christian faith, which is that our life for all its horror is "found by God to be worth dying for."[50] As Christians we are often given to "instant answers." But for O'Connor fiction ought not have quick or easy answers. For her, "It leaves us like Job, with a renewed sense of mystery."[51]

As an artist with Christian concerns, O'Connor believed sin destroyed freedom, while the modern reader generally believes sin brings freedom. In developing her understanding of the artist, O'Connor borrowed her definition from Conrad. She states the aim of the artist is to penetrate "the concrete world in order to find at its depths the image of its source, the image of ultimate reality."[52] This, she insists, does not in any way hinder the writer's observation of evil but rather refines it. For O'Connor it is only when the natural world is seen as good that evil become lucid as a caustic influence and a necessary consequence of our freedom. Part of the challenge of the fiction writer with Christian concerns is acknowledging the presence of grace and mystery as it appears

48. Elie, *Life You Save*, 425.

49. O'Connor, *Mystery and Manners*, 31.

50. O'Connor, *Mystery and Manners*, 146.

51. O'Connor, *Mystery and Manners*, 184.

52. O'Connor, *Mystery and Manners*, 157.

in nature, without resorting to using pious clichés, sentimentality, or the obscene.

O'Connor's Writing Approach

"The serious writer," O'Connor argued, "has always taken the flaw in human nature for his starting point, usually the flaw in an otherwise admirable character."[53] O'Connor's writings therefore often dealt with conversion and the change of heart that leads to a change of life when one truly begins to imitate Christ.

In her fiction she intentionally veiled or concealed the truth from audiences so that her readers might find the truth hidden there for themselves. O'Connor explains,

> I have to make the reader feel, in his bones if nowhere else, that something is going on here that counts. Distortion in this case is an instrument; exaggeration has a purpose, and the whole structure of the story or novel has been made what it is because of belief. This is not the kind of distortion that destroys; it is the kind that reveals or should reveal.[54]

The purpose of artist and author is to help an audience recognize the truth. O'Connor states that the novelist today knows he or she needs to bring an audience to a moment of revelation. Because of this the "Catholic novelist is forced to follow the Spirit into strange places and work with forms not necessarily congenial to him."[55]

In her essay, "Some Aspects of the Grotesque in Southern Fiction," O'Connor comments on the role of the artist in using exaggerated symbols to tell stories: "Whenever I'm asked why southern writers particularly have a penchant for writing about freaks, I say it's because we are still able to recognize one. To be able to recognize a freak, you have to have some conception of the whole man, and in the south the general conception of man is still, in the main, theological."[56]

O'Connor prizes the artistic experience as a communicative one that at the heart is deeply incarnational. The artist as an "artist" must adhere to the constraints of time and place. For O'Connor, the wider community

53. O'Connor, *Mystery and Manners*, 167.

54. O'Connor, *Mystery and Manners*, 162.

55. O'Connor, *Mystery and Manners*, 206.

56. O'Connor, *Mystery and Manners*, 44.

of humankind takes precedence over any potential "stone of stumbling" within the community of faith, lest we absent a Christian voice from the larger cultural context. Moreover, human beings share the same fallen world's propensity to misunderstand. For this reason, she suggests, "those writers [and artists] who speak for and with their age are able to do so with a great deal more ease and grace than those who speak counter to prevailing attitudes."[57] Here O'Connor's views on culture and the wider understanding of her theory of the novel come into view.

Indeed, for O'Connor, indirect communication and her use of imaginative literature reveal how one may present alternative views of life concretely and imaginatively as a useful means to suggest that human beings may want to examine their own lives and consider their personal moral responsibility in life. She suggests that if we are to speak to this age, we must start "where human knowledge begins—with the senses—and every fiction writer is bound by this fundamental aspect of his medium."[58] In other words, we begin with the concrete and proceed from there to help the individual reflect on their life and how they are living. Thus, she is "interested in characters who are forced to meet evil and grace and who act on a trust beyond themselves—whether they know very clearly what it is they act upon or not."[59] This, of course, does not sit well with the modern reader, who will probably see this as nonsense. Nevertheless, her work is so enticing and her characters so inventive that most readers who give her stories the proper reading will be captivated.

The kind of writing that interests O'Connor sees life as essentially mysterious, and because of this the writer can slight the concrete just a bit. In so doing, the writer will be "looking for an image that will connect or combine or embody two points; one is a point in the concrete, and the other is a point not visible to the naked eye, but believed in by him firmly, just as real to him, really, as the one that everybody sees."[60]

The writer who feels drawn to the surface or concrete image is interested in it "only as long as he can go through it into an experience of mystery itself. His kind of fiction will always be pushing its own limits outward toward the limits of [transcendence], because for this kind of writer, the meaning of a story does not begin except at a depth where

57. O'Connor, *Mystery and Manners*, 47.

58. O'Connor, *Mystery and Manners*, 42.

59. O'Connor, *Mystery and Manners*, 42.

60. O'Connor, *Mystery and Manners*, 42.

adequate motivation and adequate psychology and the various determinations have been exhausted."[61] This kind of story opens one to explore the meaning of life and the place one has in a universe where all things are mysterious.

In March of 1964, four months before her death, Flannery O'Connor received a copy of C. S. Lewis's *Miracles* from a new friend and correspondent, Cudden Ward Dorrance. O'Conner noted a correspondence between Lewis's Christian novels and her own works of fiction stating, "We both want to locate our characters . . . right on the border of the natural and the supernatural."[62] This narrow ridge between the natural and the supernatural is perhaps where writers with Christian concerns need to locate their characters if they are serious about using the indirect style.

She veiled Christian truth in her fiction by offering it indirectly, imaginatively, and emotionally, full of questions rather than answers. Her approach was to hide theology and the doctrine of original sin within a fearless gaze at the grotesque; to break the heart with yearning for redemption, to create a piercing portrayal of grace, both by its absence and by its curious human incarnations. Gooch notes that O'Conner "had spent her life making literary chickens walk backward" and that "just as her friends had to discern the contours of true suffering between the lines of her funny vignettes and invalidism," so too her stories included an implicit or veiled offer of grace to those most resistant to its presence.[63]

Most, if not all, of O'Connor's stories construct a fiction that powerfully delve into the mystery of human transformation, that beguiles as much as it edifies, that arouses curiosity and longing within the reader. Her stories have aims upon the reader, but they exert their will indirectly and without coercion. O'Connor sees the task of the novelist as making everything, even the ultimate concerns of life, as real, as concrete, and as explicit as possible. She attempts to write for an unbelieving age, yet one which is patently and lopsidedly spiritual. For her the challenge for the novelist who wishes to write about man's encounter with God is simply how he or she can "make the experience—which is both natural and supernatural—understandable, and credible, to his readers."[64]

61. O'Connor, *Mystery and Manners*, 42.
62. Quoted in Gooch, *Flannery*, 359.
63. Gooch, *Flannery*, 373–74.
64. O'Connor, *Mystery and Manners*, 161.

Hawkins argues, "it may be useful in thinking about strategies of indirection to look briefly at a mode of literary discourse which, although very much within the biblical tradition, did not in the beginning share any kind of consensus with its audience. It is a mode of discourse that in fact often anticipates an unconvinced or even hostile reception."[65] That, of course, is the very reason to use this approach. If the same story were written in a direct mode for the same audience, it would most assuredly be rejected or go unnoticed. It is to O'Connor's credit that she can cajole and shock her readers with brutal language, stinging metaphor, and provocative images—and yet the reader just can't put the story aside. She owes the strength of her writing, in part, to stories so indirect that readers initially don't see a clear meaning. Furthermore, her tales can be understood or read in so many ways that readers keep reading and return to the stories again and again. Elie writes that O'Connor "portrays the religious artist who is a kind of radical, pushing past the surface of things to the 'limits of mystery,' portraying characters 'who are forced out to meet evil and grace.'"[66] Elie explains,

> [O'Connor] sought to communicate her vision to the reader as fully as possible. Yet, she tried to make clear that she didn't mean to impose her vision on the reader: "you may think from all I have said that the reason I write is to make the reader see what I see, and that writing fiction is primarily a missionary activity," she said. "Let me straighten this out." Rather, she sought, through art, to see with something like objectivity, so that she and the reader might see the same thing—so that we might see what she saw, but with our own eyes.[67]

Clearly one does not have to believe in Christ to develop an understanding of O'Connor's stories. Although plenty of biblical-type characters populate her stories, one may never have read a word of the Old Testament or be able to identify a single biblical character and will still be able to recognize the importance and meaning of the characters in her stories.

In the story "Revelation," O'Connor creates one of her strongest ironic characters, Mrs. Turpin, who is "'a country female Jacob' . . . a

65. Hawkins, *Language of Grace*, 11.

66. Elie, *Life You Save*, 424.

67. Elie, *Life You Save*, 471.

woman moved 'to shout at the Lord across a hog pen.'"[68] Mrs. Turpin gets insulted and assaulted at the doctor's office by Mary Grace, a young college student, and Mrs. Turpin feels hurt and angry. After leaving the doctor's office and returning home, she goes out to the hog pen to consider the state of her soul. As she stands alone at the hog pen, Mrs. Turpin asks, "What do you send me a message like that for?"[69] She says it in a low, fierce voice, barely above a whisper, but with the force of a shout in its concentrated fury. "How am I a hog and me both? How am I saved and from hell, too?"[70] The story brims with Old Testament illusions (and even a vision of heaven before she leaves the pig pen), but its characters and storyline feel so real that you can still enjoy the story with enthusiasm regardless of the religious themes. The ethical, social, and religious questions are all so interesting, comic, and intertwined that the story captivates the reader. You don't even "have to identify the moment of grace as a 'moment of grace,'" to know something powerful is going on in this story.[71] The revelation is painful and disquieting for Mrs. Turpin. Perhaps, for the first time in her life she begins to question her own view of the world and the people in it. Maybe even her own way of categorizing others is thrown into question. As she wrestles with these questions at the hog pen, the reader also begins to examine his or her way of looking at others.

"Parker's Back"

Now we will look at one of O'Connor's last stories, "Parker's Back," in order to better understand her creative force and indirect style. "Parker's Back" has been described variously as a narrative that "recapitulates the point of view of the iconographer"; "gives us images of beauty in suffering"; offers "grace in an unusual fashion"; depicts "a world where the natural and the supernatural are intermixed"; is "about the encounter of Law and Gospel"; "creates an inarticulate and only dimly conscious protagonist"; and "describes the intrusion of an alien figure upon the relationship of two characters."[72] Elie argues that "Parker's Back" has been

---

68. Elie, Life You Save, 353.

69. O'Connor, Flannery O'Connor, 506.

70. O'Connor, Flannery O'Connor, 506.

71. Elie, Life You Save, 354.

72. Zubeck, "Back to Page One," 99; LeNotre, "Flannery O'Connor's 'Parker's Back,'"

seen as either "a parable of the plight of Christ in the modern world, scorned and beaten senseless by those who purport to follow him," or a story about a domestic quarrel and bar fight.[73] He concludes that "it is a conversion story, which ends with Parker crying like a baby under a pecan tree, answering at last to the Christian name given to him at baptism—Obadiah Elihue—which he has denied for so long. It is a final expression of O'Connor's art of the grotesque, in which she'd distorted the image of Christ himself. So as to restore its power to shock."[74]

If O'Connor succeeds at nothing else, she certainly succeeds at creating a diverse and intense conversation about her couple, O. E. Parker and Sarah Ruth. "Parker's Back" can therefore be read in several ways. Perhaps one useful way of seeing the protagonist is suggested by Michel Feith when he states, "[Parker] is the artist of his own life, transformed by his 'creations.'"[75] Feith continues, "*Parker's Back* can therefore also be read as an artistic Odyssey, from a random collection of tattoos to the final, crowning piece that gives them all coherence, at the same time as it provides the protagonist with spiritual cohesion."[76]

Katherine LeNotre states, "the story presents characters whose beliefs shape their aesthetic sense, and it also shows how aesthetics can, in turn, be a starting point for belief in God."[77] O'Connor creates a faltering and almost incoherent protagonist who seemingly does not possess the command of rational discourse to engage mystery. Edward Kessler suggests that Parker has been running from the unknown since his mother tried to take him to church to save his soul.[78] Nevertheless, Parker first stumbles upon the mysterious, not in a church, but at a fair where he is awakened to wonder by a man tattooed from head to foot—not by the man himself, but by an energy acting through him, an "arabesque of men and beasts and flowers on his skin appeared to have a subtle motion of

408; Cofer, "All Demanding Eyes," 37; Hatch, "Wingless Chickens" 125; Baumgaertner, *Flannery O'Connor*, 64; Kessler, *Flannery O'Connor*, 77; Orvell, *Flannery O'Connor*, 166.

73. Elie, *Life You Save*, 364.

74. Elie, *Life You Save*, 364.

75. Feith, "Stained-Glass Man," 4.

76. Feith, "Stained-Glass Man," 4.

77. LeNotre, "Flannery O'Connor's 'Parker's Back,'" 399.

78. Kessler, *Flannery O'Connor*.

its own."[79] The experience changes him, "but the change cannot be shown except by a metaphor."[80] O'Connor explains it this way:

> Until he saw the man at the fair, it did not enter his head that there was anything out of the ordinary about the fact that he existed. Even then it did not enter his head, but a peculiar unease settled in him. It was as if a blind boy had been turned so gently in a different direction that he did not know his destination had been changed.[81]

Parker's life began to change that day as he encountered the art on the body of the tattooed man—perhaps the first beauty he had ever known. After that experience he began to get his body tattooed, always hoping to recapture the wonder he felt when he first saw the tattooed man. LeNotre reminds us that "Parker takes up his service to beauty by trying to imitate the man he saw at the fair. Tattoos preoccupy his mind to a large degree, since experiencing the transcendence of beauty again becomes his constant goal."[82]

Of course none of his tattoos satisfy him for long, and in his desire to re-experience the wonder he needs to get another and another until his whole body becomes a canvass for tattoos. His life changes in other ways too, in that women seem to like the tattoos. He therefore begins to hang out with them and goes to bars and generally gets into a narcissistic lifestyle that in some ways becomes destructive, until one day he meets Sarah Ruth. Sarah Ruth is his opposite: ugly, cold, legalistic, and she dislikes tattoos. The irony is that Parker's search for the wonder in beauty leads him to someone devoid of beauty.

Elie states that "there is no question that O'Connor cast Sarah Ruth as a Puritan and set her against the sensualist Parker. But if *Parker's Back* is merely a dramatization of a heresy, it is worthless. It is a story, and more than any other O'Connor story, it suggests and sustains many different meanings at once. It is a pattern as complex as the 'perfect arabesque' of Parker's tattooed body."[83] Without really understanding why, Parker marries Sarah Ruth—and as one might expect, it is not an easy marriage. Parker is trying to find a way to get Sarah Ruth to work with him on

79. O'Connor, *Flannery O'Connor*, 513.
80. Kessler, *Flannery O'Connor*, 77.
81. O'Connor, *Flannery O'Connor*, 513.
82. LeNotre, "Flannery O'Connor's 'Parker's Back,'" 403.
83. Elie, *Life You Save*, 363–64.

their marriage and he comes up with the idea of getting a religious tattoo. While bailing hay, Parker tries to decide what kind of tattoo to put on his back, the only place left without a tattoo. Preoccupied with his imaginings, he manages to run the tractor he's driving into a tree, flipping the tractor and setting the tree on fire.

Parker gets caught under the tractor and just manages to escape, but emerges from the burning scene without his shoes, which burn up. Profoundly changed by this experience, Parker heads straight to the city for a new tattoo. The tattoo he chooses—or perhaps it is chosen for him—features the Byzantine Christ with all-demanding eyes. He innocently assumes he can get a tattoo of "God," as if it means nothing. After getting the tattoo, he leaves to buy a pint of whisky, which he drinks in five minutes. He then moves on to a pool hall that he formerly frequented, and soon finds himself accused of "getting religion" because of the tattoo on his back. This angers Parker and a brief fight ensues, resulting in his ejection into the alley behind the pool hall. He finds himself alone and begins to contemplate his life. O'Connor states,

> Parker sat for a long time on the ground in the alley behind the pool hall, examining his soul. He saw it as a spider web of facts and lies that was not at all important to him, but which appeared to be necessary in spite of his opinion. The eyes that were now forever on his back were eyes to be obeyed. He was as certain of it as he had been of anything. Throughout his life, grumbling and sometimes cursing and often afraid, once in rapture, Parker had obeyed whatever instinct of this kind had come to him—in rapture when his spirit had lifted at the sight of the tattooed man at the fair, afraid when he had joined the navy, grumbling when he had married Sarah Ruth.[84]

In this reflective state he decides to go home to Sarah Ruth, as all he really wants to do is please her. Kessler states that "Parker's encounter with mystery both alienates him from his natural self and simultaneously introduces him to a renovated natural world."[85] LeNotre reminds us that "getting tattoos and marrying Sarah Ruth are the only two choices he's ever made that involve voluntary suffering."[86] "The story presents char-

84. O'Connor, Flannery O'Connor, 527.

85. Kessler, Flannery O'Connor, 82.

86. LeNotre, "Flannery O'Connor's 'Parker's Back,'" 404.

acters whose beliefs shape their aesthetic sense, and it also shows how aesthetics can, in turn, be a starting point for belief in God."[87]

Parker begins to change and on the way home he has a brief epiphany. O'Connor writes, "His head was almost clear of liquor and he observed that his dissatisfaction was gone, but he felt not quite like himself. It was as if he were himself but a stranger to himself, driving into a new country though everything he saw was familiar to him, even at night."[88] We see clearly that Parker's search for beauty leads him to a transcendent experience, even if he doesn't know what is happening to him. The Byzantine icon has an existential reality for Parker, quite apart from rational development or abstractions. The encounter with mystery, now etched on his back, affects him profoundly—but as yet, only as a felt power, not as meaning. This beauty, this icon, this presence on his back occasions for him "the beginnings of faith in God through the recognition that he is being seen."[89] Parker has been running from the unknown ever since his mother tried to take him to the revival service years ago, and now it seems the unknown has appeared on his back and taken up residence in his flesh.

LeNotre states, "Parker undergoes the beginnings of conversion on multiple levels—aesthetic, moral, and religious. These three overlapping developments arise in response to an experience of worldly beauty and culminate in the supernatural beauty of Christ."[90] Parker's "only knowledge is the knowledge that he has acted and been acted upon: 'he only knew that there had been a great change in his life, a leap forward into a worse unknown, and that there was nothing he could do about it.'"[91]

Joanne Halleran McMullen explains that O'Connor consciously makes use of "a profound sense of mystery in a concerted attempt to embed her religious message deeply within the story, creating characters whose destinies remain spiritually debatable but thus available to readers she believed religiously hostile."[92] She then "places an image of beautiful

87. LeNotre, "Flannery O'Connor's 'Parker's Back,'" 399.

88. O'Connor, Flannery O'Connor, 527.

89. LeNotre, "Flannery O'Connor's 'Parker's Back,'" 401.

90. LeNotre, "Flannery O'Connor's 'Parker's Back,'" 401.

91. Kessler, Flannery O'Connor, 83.

92. McMullen, Writing Against God, 142.

suffering in front of us and invites us to be transformed by it, to make it a touchtone for our own conversion stories."[93]

At last we see Parker going home to Sarah Ruth, knocking on the door, impatient to reveal to her what he had done to himself. Of course the change is still not complete and Sarah Ruth won't let him in until he says his real name: Obadiah ("worshiper of Jehovah") Elihue ("whose God is He"). He finally confesses his real name: his hidden identity is revealed. As he whispers his true name, Obadiah Elihue feels "the light pouring through him, turning his spider web soul into a perfect arabesque of colors, a garden of trees and birds and beasts."[94] The words echoed here, first described the wonder he felt when he saw the tattooed man, and now imply the fulfillment of Parker's search for wonder.

His newfound state of wonder is soon tested as Sarah Ruth wastes no time in lighting into him. Elie states that "the conclusion of the story is notorious, but its meaning is less than absolute."[95] Sarah Ruth thwarts Parker's plan when he agonizingly discovers that she does not recognize God. O'Connor writes,

> "Another picture," Sarah Ruth growled. "I might have known you was off after putting some more trash on yourself."
> Parker's knees went hollow under him. He wheeled around and cried, "Look at it! Don't just say that! Look at it!"
> "I done looked," she said.
> "Don't you know who it is?" he cried in anguish.
> "No, who is it?" Sarah Ruth said. "It ain't anybody I know."
> "It's him," Parker said.
> "Him who?"
> "God!" Parker cried.
> "God? God don't look like that!"
> "What do you know how he looks?" Parker moaned. "You ain't seen him."
> "He don't look," Sarah Ruth said. "He's a spirit. No man shall see his face."
> "Aw listen," Parker groaned, "this is just a picture of him."
> "Idolatry!" Sarah Ruth screamed. "Idolatry!"[96]

---

93. LeNotre, "Flannery O'Connor's 'Parker's Back,'" 410.

94. O'Connor, *Flannery O'Connor*, 528.

95. Elie, *Life You Save*, 363.

96. O'Connor, *Flannery O'Connor*, 529.

The story concludes with Sarah Ruth beating Parker almost sense-less as large welts form on the face of the tattooed Christ. The ambiguous phrase, "God don't look," which Sarah Ruth uses to describe her under-standing of the Scriptures and art can be taken in one of two ways. The first possible meaning is that "God does not see, or watch human beings, that he does not have an effective place in their lives."[97] The second and more likely meaning, that "No man shall see his face," denies the incar-nation. Whatever the meaning of the phrase, it is clear that with Sarah Ruth's rejection of "the tattooed Christ on Parker's back [she] is denying as well the doctrine of the Incarnation, of the corporeality of God."[98]

LeNotre argues compellingly that what O'Connor wants us to see is "the suffering of Christ from Christ's own point of view, not only by allowing her characters to suffer, but even by allowing her readers to ex-perience a form of imaginative suffering in the very act of reading."[99] Parker's anguish is partially ambiguous as we are not sure if he is suffering because he is rejected by his wife, or because she does not see what has happened to him and that she has rejected Christ. Perhaps now, for the first time, he understands that her strict religious practices and beliefs bring her no closer to the living God.

Brian Gregor, reflecting Kierkegaard's view of art, seems to bring a useful perspective to understanding this final scene. He states, "The truth is hidden under the appearance of its contrary; rather than appearing directly in glory, it is given indirectly, as ugliness, weakness, and shame. The indirect appearance of Christian truth is, of course, a central theme for Kierkegaard, and it guides his critique of art."[100] Apparently, it also found resonance in O'Connor's work.

Sarah Ruth, the biblical literalist, for all her knowledge of Scripture, disciplined ways, and ability to identify sin in others, could not express love, forgiveness, or mercy. O'Connor's prophetic vision does not hesitate to distort appearances in order to show a hidden truth. In *Mystery and Manners,* she states, "Often the nature of grace can be made plain only by describing its absence."[101] And here in the character of Sarah Ruth, we

97. Feith, "Stained-Glass Man," 7.

98. Orvell, *Flannery O'Connor*, 167.

99. LeNotre, "Flannery O'Connor's 'Parker's Back,'" 409.

100. Gregor, "Thinking Through Kierkegaard's Anti-Climacus," 455.

101. O'Connor, *Mystery and Manners*, 204.

see that O'Connor has made known the nature of grace by describing its apparent absence.

We cannot ignore the violence in this story and where it serves a purpose in her work is best understood from a christological perspective. Christians often forget the violence and suffering present in the life of Christ and in the early church despite the fact that "beauty can manifest itself in the midst of violence and tragedy . . . In the drama of the world-story, the violence of climactic action takes its place in the larger aesthetic of a complete play just as Christians see the crucifixion in light of Christ's triumphal resurrection."[102]

O'Connor never wrote another story after this one. She spent most of her adult life in and out of hospitals, suffering and struggling with lupus, an autoimmune disease that had taken the life of her father when she was a teenager. In this story, with her failing and imperfect body, perhaps O'Connor was suggesting that we are all imperfect yet made in the image of God. As Elie states, "We carry God and God's story with us like a second skin. In bed, betrayed by her body, O'Connor made the human body an image of God, to be raised up and glorified."[103]

In "Parker's Back," O'Connor made the image literal, etched into flesh. "Each of us," she insisted, "is an image of God. Our pilgrimages are images of his own."[104] Jordan Cofer contends that the ending clearly "subverts the readers' expectations."[105] It has been argued that biblical allusions to Moses, Jonah, and Paul—seemingly contradictory characters— are seamlessly embedded in the story. And while the story captures the biblical world, it also integrates it "into the modern-day secular story."[106]

Hatch notes that O'Connor's story depicts "a world where the natural and the supernatural are intermixed, where one must deal with both simultaneously."[107] O'Connor believes that moderns, by placing so much emphasis on the material world, have forgotten the world "is permeated by the sacred."[108] She would argue that part of the problem for the writer with Christian concerns is how to depict "the presence of grace

102. LeNotre, "Flannery O'Connor's 'Parker's Back,'" 409.

103. Elie, *Life You Save*, 364.

104. Elie, *Life You Save*, 363–64.

105. Cofer, "'All Demanding Eyes,'" 37.

106. Cofer, "'All Demanding Eyes,'" 37.

107. Hatch, "Wingless Chickens," 125.

108. Hatch, "Wingless Chickens," 129.

as it appears in nature."[109] Readers who believe in only one world—only the world our senses can perceive, a world that does not allow "the eyes" of a tattoo "to look," let alone to speak; in other words, a world without mystery—live in a poor world indeed. Perhaps we now seek from the arts what we once sought from religion. If so, we need the artist with Christian concerns to remind us that art is a way to return to what we have lost. At the end of the story, Parker, now called by his true name, Obadiah Elihue, stands alone, "leaning against a tree crying like a baby." In his sorrow, Parker is forever attached to the demanding image of Christ—"a victim of eyes that will never leave looking at him."[110]

The Function of Art in O'Connor with References to Kierkegaard

Kierkegaard's pseudonym, Anti-Climacus, uses the analogy of "eyes" in relation to art when trying to explain two of the major hindrances both within and without the church that artists with Christian concerns have to face when communicating the transcendent nature of God. Anti-Climacus expresses the danger of detached objectification of Christian art. In doing so he identifies both observation and admiration as a hidden danger to the church and to religious art. Like the work of art on Parker's back of the tattooed Christ with the demanding eyes, so too Anti-Climacus states,

> [T]he Christian truth has, if I may say so, its own eyes with which to see, indeed, it seems to be all eyes. But it would be very disturbing, indeed, it would be impossible, for me to look at a painting or a piece of cloth if I discovered while looking at it that it was the painting or the cloth that was looking at me. And this is the case with the Christian truth; it is Christian truth that is observing me, whether I am doing what it says I should do. See, this is why Christian truth cannot be presented for observation or discoursed upon as observations. It has, if I may say so, its own ears with which to hear; indeed, it seems to be all ears. It listens as the speaker speaks; one cannot speak about it as about an absentee or a merely objective presence, because, since it is from God and God is in it, it is present in a totally unique sense as it is being spoken about, and not as an object. Instead, the speaker

109. Hatch, "Wingless Chickens," 125.
110. McKeon, *Novels and Arguments*, 223.

becomes its object; the speaker evokes a spirit who examines him as he is speaking.[111]

When O'Connor refers to a prophetic vision, she has in mind exactly what Kierkegaard called an "examining presence." The object of art examines us, asking if we are living as we should, if we who are made in God's image are in fact living to imitate, to incarnate, Christ. Art, as a mirror, can judge us in the very act of judging it. "In making our decision about what it is, we reveal and define who we are. Works of art, as Lichtenburg said, '... are mirrors: when a monkey peers into them, no Apostle can be seen looking out.' Art, like Christ, casts us back upon ourselves for a searching decision: 'Who do you say that I am?' they ask."[112] O'Connor's stories are challenging in that as often as not they turn "social expectations upside down and portray grace in what society deems grotesque."[113]

For O'Connor, fiction writers and artists ought to be characterized by their prophetic vision. "Prophecy," she asserts, "which is dependent on the imaginative and not the moral faculty, need not be a matter of predicting the future."[114] Rather, it is a matter of telling the truth. She insists that good fiction writers and artists extend their gaze "beyond the surface, beyond mere problems, until it touches that realm which is the concern of prophets and poets."[115] For writers and artists with Christian concerns, "the prophetic vision is not simply a matter of his personal imaginative gift; it is also a matter of the Church's gift, which . . . is safeguarded and deals with greater matters. It is one of the functions of the Church to transmit the prophetic vision that is good for all time, and when the novelist has this as a part of his own mission, he has a powerful extension of sight."[116]

For O'Connor, the definition of art is a created thing that "is valuable in itself and that works in itself. The basis of art is truth, both in matter and in mode. The person who aims after art in his work aims after truth, in an imaginative sense, no more and no less."[117] The truth she seeks to communicate is not abstract but must be concrete. "Our response to life

111. Kierkegaard, *Practice in Christianity*, 234.

112. Short, *Gospel According to Peanuts*, 10.

113. Basselin, *Flannery O'Connor*, 49.

114. O'Connor, *Mystery and Manners*, 179.

115. O'Connor, *Mystery and Manners*, 45.

116. O'Connor, *Mystery and Manners*, 180.

117. O'Connor, *Mystery and Manners*, 65.

is different if we have been taught only a definition of faith," she writes, "than if we have trembled with Abraham as he held the knife over Isaac. Both kinds of knowledge are necessary, but in the last four or five centuries, Catholics have overemphasized the abstract and consequently impoverished their imaginations and their capacity for prophetic insight."[118]

The artist with Christian concerns must understand that the story or work of art is not simply an object of observation which one can look at in some detached way. Rather, true art that raises Christian concerns is art that in effect looks at or examines us. It is intended to question the reader or viewer and to call them into account. Gregor states as a result, one is "unable to observe Christian truth impersonally. Insofar as I make contact with the genuine claim of Christ, I find myself called into question; I am pulled out of my objectivity and called into subjectivity—not the subjectivity of an epistemic subject-object relation, but the subjectivity of responsibility."[119]

Just as Parker discovered, one can no longer take refuge in detachment, escapist behavior, or thought, but one must be answerable to the prophetic influence found in the art. Gregor explains, "the subject's gaze is met by the gaze of another, resulting in a reversal and 'crossing' of gazes."[120] A crossing of the gazes takes place in which one's deliberate gaze is encountered by another-gaze—the invisible gaze that exasperates my wish to remain the unseen seer who can observe the art or story in detachment. In this way I feel myself known and I am called to answer whatever request it demands of me.

O'Connor never wanted anyone merely to admire her work. Gregor states that to "'admire' Christ; by cultivating aesthetic appreciation, or even by nurturing religious or spiritual feelings, we sidestep the requirement of following Christ. Similarly, art can mirror the desires and expectations that we bring to it, confirming the fantastic projections of our religious imaginations."[121] One's first thought may well be that we should admire Christ, or by extension, any art with religious concerns. But upon careful reflection, we can see that simply to admire a work of art and not allow it to examine us and to call us into question can lead to a very superficial and even gnostic form of faith.

118. O'Connor, *Mystery and Manners*, 202–3.
119. Gregor, "Thinking Through Kierkegaard's Anti-Climacus," 453–54.
120. Gregor, "Thinking Through Kierkegaard's Anti-Climacus," 454.
121. Gregor, "Thinking Through Kierkegaard's Anti-Climacus," 457.

O'Connor's understanding of following Christ had nothing to do with possessing warm, admiring feelings about him, no matter how sincere. To hold a work of art, or even Christ himself, in high esteem, seriously underestimates what Christ calls us to do. He has no interest in acquiring fans, no matter how greatly they admire him. Nor does he want students who simply study him and his teachings. The Christian faith is personal and subjective, and as such we are called to join Christ in what he has started. He calls us to do his bidding. As the prototype, Christ has set the example for us to follow, not just to study. Art calls us to live as Christ lived. Indirect and prophetic art, which sees all of reality, provokes us to act, to be what we profess. Art can counter our gaze and call us to responsibility. O'Connor calls for art that "addresses us as viewers and will not let us rest in detached observation or admiration."[122]

O'Connor's Indirect Communication Strategy

In her essay, "Novelist and Believer," O'Connor argues the writer "knows that he cannot approach the infinite directly, that he must penetrate the natural human world as it is."[123] O'Connor approached her art very deliberately. She understood it was not abstract thought that moved her reader, but that her task was to make everything, even the transcendent, "as solid, as concrete, as specific as possible."[124] She understood that her audience seriously mistrusted artists with religious concerns, and that she not only had to make the story as concrete as possible—and by wit and imagination create interest in her story—but she also needed to veil or deceive her readers into reading a story that would extend the limits of reality into transcendent truth.

She carefully chose her images and her words and employed them precisely within the indirect strategy she chose. She took great care not to make the transcendent dimensions of her story too obvious. As Kessler points out, "To name a mystery, as Sarah Ruth names God, is a verbal act O'Connor avoids for the most part in her fiction. We violate the author's silence by reading into her text what she took considerable pains to

---

122. Gregor, "Thinking Through Kierkegaard's Anti-Climacus," 457.

123. O'Connor, *Mystery and Manners*, 163.

124. O'Connor, *Mystery and Manners*, 155.

exclude," namely the direct naming of God.[125] Kessler references a draft of "Parker's Back" where O'Connor wrote,

> He felt like some fragile thing of nature, turned into an ara-
> besque of colors that only himself and the Lord could see. How-
> ever, in revision she cut out "the Lord" and wrote instead: "He
> felt like some fragile thing of nature, turned into an arabesque
> of colors, a garden of trees and birds and beasts." Direct naming,
> the "plain sense," as Donne calls it, must in O'Connor's indirect
> and metaphoric art bow to the "figurative God." Although the
> author can present the "haphazard and botched" fact of man's
> fallen nature, she can move it toward perfection only by meta-
> phor "one perfect arabesque of color." A lord of her own cre-
> ation, the writer must keep her own secrets.[126]

O'Connor explains that all storytellers have to "create the illusion of a whole world with believable people in it."[127] She describes the important "difference between the novelist who is an orthodox Christian and the novelist who is merely a naturalist," maintaining that "the Christian novelist lives in a larger universe. He believes that the natural would contain the supernatural. And this doesn't mean that his obligation to portray the natural is less; it means it is greater."[128]

O'Connor believes that mystery is essential to our understanding of the world and it comes to us "by way of the senses." Also fundamental to O'Connor's understanding of art is that "Christ didn't redeem us by a direct intellectual act, but became incarnate in human form, and he speaks to us now through the mediation of a visible Church."[129] Our way to engage others in the story of faith as artists and communicators, therefore, is through the senses. Reason plays a part, but should never trump the mystery of faith. Therefore, O'Connor tells us "the novelist is required to open his eyes on the world around him and look. If what he sees is not highly edifying, he is still required to look. Then he is required to reproduce, with words, what he sees."[130]

---

125. Kessler, *Flannery O'Connor*, 83.

126. Kessler, *Flannery O'Connor*, 83.

127. O'Connor, *Mystery and Manners*, 175.

128. O'Connor, *Mystery and Manners*, 175.

129. O'Connor, *Mystery and Manners*, 176.

130. O'Connor, *Mystery and Manners*, 177.

Conclusion

After reading Flannery O'Connor a student once emailed me asking why we need to read stories of a serial killer, a small boy drowned while trying to be baptized in a river, a Bible salesman who seduces a woman and steals her wooden leg, or an old woman confronted by a young college student who throws a book at her and calls her a warthog from hell. What possible good can come from this? These characters have nothing to tell us. And why can't we hear positive stories that end well? Of course, the answer is that before a person is open to hearing the good news, they need to know that they live in a fallen world and that there is a need for and a possibility of transcendence. Many people today feel they are in control of their own lives and they do not need any kind of redemption or help to live good lives.

Comfortable or sentimental stories only move the reader, hearer, or viewer superficially because deep inside each one knows that there is something wrong with the world and that each individual needs some sort of assistance. The indirect communication approach found in the stories of Kierkegaard, Lewis, and O'Connor make it clear that indeed there is something wrong in this world, and that this life is not all there is. These authors provide a sacramental view of life that compels their readers to, in Flannery O'Connor's words, consider the "relationship between the flesh and the spirit."[131] These stories have the power to help readers attend to both the natural and the spiritual forces at work in the world.

What these artists give us is a way to contend with a worldview that reflects reality, not seeing life as easy, comfortable, or effortless. For those who struggle with evil in their own lives—even evil within the church—a different way to approach God is needed. It is necessary for those who do not see this world as flawed; perhaps because they are distracted by the false perception that they do not believe in or need the transcendent power of God. Neither do they see the need to follow a crucified savior that may lead them to forfeit their positions of privilege in order to suffer with or engage with those who are not so privileged. For those driven into despair by cultural or personal elements such as addiction, anxiety, poverty, or ill health, a strong and frank antidote of reality that dismantles these delusions needs to be provided. An indirect narrative that awakens us to these perceptions and provides an opportunity for grace can be a strong antidote to these negative influences in our lives.

131. O'Connor, *Habit of Being*, 365.

Artists are better prepared for creating art in a cultural environment such as ours if they consider both the direct and the indirect approach to creating their art. As we have seen in "Parker's Back," the artist or "prophet is a realist of distances, and it is this kind of realism that goes into great novels."[132] For the Christian, transcendent knowledge is not like a math formula that manifests clearly at every moment. We see through dark glasses, and we always have to squint a little, as our faith in God remains a mystery, at least in part. As O'Connor reminds us, even in the darker places of our lives we find vestiges of God's grace. Here O'Connor says nothing new or different than what Christianity for centuries has maintained. She reminds us that God is present in all of life—God is revealed in the brokenness of the cross just as much as he is in the glory of the ascension.

When communicating our faith, we do best if we admit that we have a limited vision and experience. We have humanity's view, not God's. Still, this doesn't mean that we lack sufficient sight for believing and following Christ. Art and beauty touch on the truth, speaking to us in unknown tongues, penetrating the darkness of our lives, and finally pointing us to Christ. As O'Connor's stories suggest, only through faith can we see God's invisible glory hidden within the visible things of this world.

132. O'Connor, *Mystery and Manners*, 179.

Conclusion

A S A WRITER AND Christian one of Kierkegaard's major concerns was how to assist the people of his day in living a truly Christian life. Many people in Denmark were knowledgeable of the basic tenets and rituals of Christianity, nevertheless they were not able to live a Christian life. Kierkegaard realized that knowledge alone was not enough to live as a Christian ought to live and that something else was needed, that something he called *capability*. Furthermore, he saw that a different communication approach was needed in order to enable others to live as Christians. This new strategy he called *indirect communication*. For him both direct (straightforward) and indirect (veiled) communication were important in order to help others embody Christianity.

The indirect approach draws upon several communication strategies to advance the truth, but this work emphasizes story or narrative as one of the most useful approaches to communicating faith. Strong imaginative stories are aimed at the heart rather than the mind and are a useful antidote to a culture that privileges reason and proposition over imagination and revelation. They allow us to both entertain and educated the reader, listener, or viewer. For Kierkegaard, indirect communication is a useful corrective to the modernist penchant for reason and argument in that it engages the imagination and unhinges old meanings in order that new understandings might emerge.

Such strategies, as demonstrated by Jesus, C. S. Lewis, and Flannery O'Connor, are used to illustrate how indirect communication can be used in storytelling. These stories allow a person to see old truths in a new way, thus enabling the individual to reconsider the stories' purpose and use in their lives. They embody the axiom: don't tell us, show us, and in so doing they invite us to live new lives.

This approach to communication is not simple or easy. It takes time and effort and ultimately invites the individual to embody the truth—not just to know the truth. No matter how imperfectly we may live out our faith, we can never escape the truth that Christianity is meant to be lived.

Today many artists with Christian concerns follow the church's proclivity for direct and straightforward methods of communication. In so doing they are unknowingly following the churches' imbibing of a secular logic that privileges reason and argument. Against this I have argued that effective communication, no matter how true, is much more demanding than just providing information or quoting Scripture. The indirect approach balances this rationalist tendency by leaning heavily on the imagination to provoke and inspire a new of way of being, a new way of perceiving. An imaginative approach might attract hearers who would never consider our well-reasoned "proofs," logical arguments, or parroted doctrines. More than the transference of knowledge, the indirect approach conveys the capability to embody the belief we encounter. Following Kierkegaard, we, as artists and storytellers—and we are all artists and storytellers—can draw on the metaphor of "Hide and Seek" to challenge our audience to take stock of their lives and seek out the truth. Hence, hidden within the indirect approach we discover something more than mere information.

It cannot be overstated that for Kierkegaard our existence is christological, and thus incarnational. In Christ, God is hidden and revealed. There is nothing easy or straightforward about this "absolute paradox." Thus, analogous to Christ's existence, he hid spiritual truth in story, parable, and narrative form so that those who want to know the meaning will need to seriously think and reflect upon his words. It is in this way that Christ hides the truth in order that he, the Truth, may be found and followed. If this is the case, we can no longer act as if we are traffickers of truth. In our so-called postmetaphysical age offering a simple and direct message only exacerbates ideological differences and rival hegemonies. Instead, through an indirect approach, we as storytellers stand as midwives, leading others to the Truth in rich, imaginative, and grotesque ways.

Bibliography

Abercrombie, Nicholas, and Brian J. Longhurst. *Audiences: A Sociological Theory of Performance and Imagination.* London: Sage, 1998.

Abicht, Ludo. "Laughing in and at the Mirror: Jewish Humour and Hassidic Wisdom." In *Humour and Religion: Challenges and Ambiguities,* edited by Hans Geybels and Walter Van Herck, 108–22. London: Continuum, 2011.

"America's Changing Religious Landscape." Pew Research Center, May 12, 2015. http://www.pewforum.org/2015/05/12/americas-changing-religious-landscape/.

Anderson, Raymond E. "Kierkegaard's Theory of Communication." *Speech Monographs* 30 (1963) 1–14.

Anolli, Luigi, et al. "Behind Dark Glasses: Irony as a Strategy for Indirect Communication." *Genetic, Social, and General Psychology Monographs* 128 (2002) 76–95.

Aquinas, Thomas. *Summa Theologica.* Translated by Fathers of the English Dominican Province. London: Burns, Oates and Washbourne, 1920.

Augustine. *The Confessions.* Oxford: Oxford University Press, 2008.

Aumann, Antony. "Kierkegaard on Indirect Communication, the Crowd, and a Monstrous Illusion." in *International Kierkegaard Commentary: Point of View,* edited by Robert L. Perkins, 295–324. Macon, GA: Mercer University Press, 2010.

———. "Kierkegaard on the Need for Indirect Communication." PhD diss, 2008.

Backhouse, Stephen. *Kierkegaard: A Single Life.* Grand Rapids: Zondervan, 2016.

Barfield, Owen. *Owen Barfield on C.S. Lewis.* Middletown, CT: Wesleyan University Press, 1989.

———. *Saving the Appearances: A Study in Idolatry.* New York: Harcourt Brace, 1975.

Barna, George. *The Seven Faith Tribes: Who They Are, What They Believe, and Why They Matter.* Brentwood, TN: Tyndale, 2009.

Barna Group. "Most Americans Take Well-Known Bible Stories at Face Value." Research Release in Leaders and Pastors, n.d. https://www.barna.com/research/most-americans-take-well-known-bible-stories-at-face-value/.

Basselin, Timothy J. *Flannery O'Connor: Writing a Theology of Disabled Humanity.* Waco, TX: Baylor University Press, 2013.

Baumgaertner, Jill Pelaez. *Flannery O'Connor: A Proper Scaring.* Chicago: Cornerstone, 1988.

Berger, Peter L. *The Many Altars of Modernity: Toward a Paradigm for Religion in a Pluralist Age.* Berlin: Walter de Gruyter, 2014.

Boersma, Hans. *Heavenly Participation: The Weaving of a Sacramental Tapestry.* Grand Rapids: Eerdmans, 2011.

Bone, Jennifer Emerling, et al. "Beyond Traditional Conceptualizations of Rhetoric: Invitational Rhetoric and a Move Toward Civility." *Western Journal of Communication* 72 (2008) 434–62.

Bonhoeffer, Dietrich. *The Cost of Discipleship.* New York: Simon and Schuster, 1995.

———. *Life Together: The Classic Exploration of Christian Community.* Translated by John W. Doberstein. New York: Harper & Row, 1954.

Boorstin, Daniel J. *The Image: A Guide to Pseudo-Events in America.* New York: Vintage, 1961.

Bouwsma, Oets Kolk. "Notes on Kierkegaard's 'The Monsterous Illusion.'" In *Essays of O. K. Bouwsma,* edited by Ronald E. Hustwit and J. L. Craft, 73–86. Lincoln: University of Nebraska Press, 1984.

Brockes, Emma. "I Want to Be Famous." *Guardian,* April 19, 2010. https://www.theguardian.com/lifeandstyle/2010/apr/17/i-want-to-be-famous.

Brothers, Michael. *Distance in Preaching: Room to Speak, Space to Listen.* Grand Rapids: Eerdmans, 2014.

Brown, David. *Discipleship and Imagination: Christian Tradition and Truth.* Oxford: Oxford University Press, 2000.

Brown, William. "Examining Four Processes of Audience Involvement with Media Personae: Transportation, Parasocial, Interation, Identification, and Worship." *Communication Theory* 25 (2015) 259–83.

Bruner, Michael. *A Subversive Gospel: Flannery O'Connor and the Reimagining of Beauty, Goodness, and Truth.* Downers Grove, IL: IVP Academic, 2017.

Buber, Martin. *Between Man and Man.* New York: Routledge, 2002.

———. *I and Thou.* Translated by Walter Kauffmann. New York: Simon & Schuster, 1970.

Buckley, Francis H. *The Morality of Laughter.* Ann Arbor: University of Michigan Press, 2003.

Buechner, Frederick. *Telling the Truth: The Gospel as Tragedy, Comedy, and Fairy Tale.* New York: HarperCollins, 1977.

Cambell, David. "Q&A: A Look at What's Driving the Changes Seen in Our Religious Landscape Study." Pew Research Center, 2015. http://www.pewforum.org/2015/05/12/americas-changing-religious-landscape/.

Carlisle, Clare. *Kierkegaard: A Guide for the Perplexed.* New York: Continuum International, 2006.

Cavanaugh, William T. "Consumption, the Market, and the Eucharist." *The Other Journal: An Intersection of Theology & Culture,* April 4, 2005. https://theotherjournal.com/2005/04/04/consumption-the-market-and-the-eucharist/.

Cofer, Jordan. "The 'All Demanding Eyes': Following the Old Testament and New Testament Allusions in Flannery O'Connor's 'Parker's Back.'" *The Flannery O'Connor Bulletin* 6 (2008) 30–39.

Como, James. *Branches to Heaven: The Geniuses of C. S. Lewis.* Dallas: Spence, 1998.

———. "Mere Lewis." *The Wilson Quarterly* 18 (1994) 109–17.

Craddock, Fred B. *As One Without Authority.* St. Louis: Chalice, 1998.

———. *Overhearing the Gospel.* St. Louis: Chalice, 2002.

Cron, Ian Morgan. *Chasing Francis: A Pilgrim's Tale.* Grand Rapids: Zondervan, 2013.

Cross, Andrew. "Neither Either Nor Or: The Perils of Reflexive Irony." In *The Cambridge Companion to Kierkegaard*, edited by Alastair Hannay and Gordon Daniel Marino, 125–53. Cambridge: Cambridge University Press, 1998.

Crouch, Andy. *Culture Making: Recovering Our Creative Calling*. Downers Grove, IL: InterVarsity, 2008.

Cunningham, Richard B. *C. S. Lewis: Defender of the Faith*. Louisville: Westminster John Knox, 1967.

Daise, Benjamin. *Kierkegaard's Socratic Art*. Macon, GA: Mercer University Press, 1999.

Davison, Andrew. "Christian Reason and Christian Community." In *Imaginative Apologetics: Theology, Philosophy and the Catholic Tradition*, edited by Andrew Davison, 12–28. Grand Rapids: Baker, 2011.

———. *Imaginative Apologetics: Theology, Philosophy and the Catholic Tradition*. Grand Rapids: Baker, 2011.

Detweiler, Craig. *IGods: How Technology Shapes Our Spiritual and Social Lives*. Grand Rapids: Brazos, 2013.

Djikie, Maja, and Keith Oatley. "The Art of Fiction: From Indirect Communication to Changes of the Self." *Psychology of Aesthetics, and the Arts* 8 (2014) 498–505.

Downing, David C. *Planets in Peril: A Critical Study of C. S. Lewis's Ransom Trilogy*. Amherst, MA: University of Massachusetts Press, 1992.

Elie, Paul. "Has Fiction Lost Its Faith?" *New York Times*, December 23, 2012.

———. *The Life You Save May Be Your Own: An American Pilgrimage*. New York: Farrar, Straus and Giroux, 2003.

Elliot, Carl. "A New Way to Be Mad." *The Atlantic*, December 2000. https://www.theatlantic.com/magazine/archive/2000/12/a-new-way-to-be-mad/304671/.

Ellul, Jacques. *The Subversion of Christianity*: Grand Rapids: Eerdmans, 1986.

Eliot, T. S. "Choruses From 'The Rock'-1934." In *T.S. Eliot: Collected Poems 1909–1962*. New York: Harcourt Brace, 1963.

Elrod, John W. *Kierkegaard and Christendom*. Princeton: Princeton University Press, 1981.

Evans, C. Stephen. "The Role of Irony in Kierkegaard's Philosophical Fragments." In *Kierkegaard on Faith and the Self: Collected Essays*, edited by C. Stephen Evans, 67–80. Waco, TX: Baylor University Press, 2006.

Ewen, Stuart. *All Consuming Images: The Politics of Style in Contemporary Culture*. New York: Basic, 1988.

Fassler, Joe. "Lorin Stein on the Power of Ambiguity in Fiction." *The Atlantic*, November 17, 2015. https://www.theatlantic.com/entertainment/archive/2015/11/by-heart-lorin-stein-paris-review-denis-johnson/416181/.

Feith, Michel. "The Stained-Glass Man: Word and Icon in Flannery O'Connor's 'Parker's Back.'" *Journal of the Short Story in English* 45 (2005). http://jsse.revuse.org/447.

Ferreira, M. Jamie. *Kierkegaard*. Oxford: Wiley-Blackwell, 2009.

———. "Surrender and Paradox: Imagination in the Leap." In *Søren Kierkegaard: Critical Assessments of Leading Philosophers*, edited by K. E. Gover and Daniel W. Conway, 142–67. New York: Routledge, 2002.

Filmer, Kath. *The Fiction of C. S. Lewis: Mask and Mirror*. New York: St. Martin's, 1993.

Fisher, Walter R. *Human Communication as Narration: Toward a Philosophy of Reason, Value, and Action*. Columbia: University of South Carolina Press, 1989.

———. "Narration as a Human Communication Paradigm: The Case of Public Moral Argument." *Communication Monographs* 51 (1984) 1–22.

Foss, Sonja, and Cindy L. Griffin. "Beyond Persuasion: A Proposal for an Invitational Rhetoric." *Communication Monographs* 62 (1995) 2–18.

Fraser, Benson P., and William J. Brown. "Media, Celebrities, and Social Influence: Identification with Elvis Presley." *Communication Monographs* 5 (2002) 183–206.

Freire, Paulo. *Pedagogy of the Oppressed*. New York: Herder and Herder, 1970.

Freshwater, Mark Edwards. *C.S. Lewis and the Truth of Myth*. Lanham: University Press of America, 1988.

Gabler, Neal. *Life: The Movie: How Entertainment Conquered Reality*. New York: Vintage, 2000.

Gablik, Suzi. "The Nature of Beauty in Contemporary Art." *New Renaissance* 8 (1998) 1–3.

Galati, Michael. "A Rhetoric for the Subjectivist in a World of Untruth: The Task and Strategy of Soren Kierkegaard." *The Quarterly Journal of Speech* 55 (1969) 372–80.

Ganssle, Gregory E. *A Reasonable God: Engaging the New Face of Atheism*. Waco, TX: Baylor University Press, 2009.

Garrett, Erik. "The Essential Secret of Indirect Communication." *Review of Communication* 12 (2012) 331–45.

Gary, Kevin. "Kierkegaard and Liberal Education as a Way of Life." *Philosophy of Education Archive* (2007) 151–58.

Gonzalez, Alejandro. "Humor." In *Volume 15, Tome III: Kierkegaard's Concepts: Envy to Incognito*, edited by Jon Stewart et al., 175–81. Burlington: Ashgate, 2013.

Gooch, Brad. *Flannery: A Life of Flannery O'Connor*. New York: Little, Brown and Company, 2009.

Grady, Joseph. "The 'Conduit Metaphor Revisited': A Reassessment of Metaphors for Communication." In *Discourse and Cognition: Bridging the Gap*, edited by Jean-Pierre Koenig, 205–18. Palo Alto: Stanford University Center for the Study of Language and Information, 1998.

Green, Garrett. *Imagining God: Theology and the Religious Imagination*. Grand Rapids: Eerdmans Publishing, 1989.

Greene, Graham. *The Power and the Glory*. New York: Penguin Classics, 2003.

Gregor, Brian. "Thinking Through Kierkegaard's Anti-Climacus: Art, Imagination, and Imitation." *Haythrop Journal* 50 (2009) 448–65.

Griesinger, Emily. "The Search for Deeper Magic: J.K. Rowling and C.S. Lewis." In *The Gift of Story: Narrating Hope in a Postmodern World*, edited by Mark A. Eaton and Emily Griesinger, 317–31. Waco, TX: Baylor University Press, 2006.

Grossman, Cathy Lynn. "America's Fastest-Growing Religious Affiliation: 'None.'" *USA Today*, March 9, 2009. https://www.houmatoday.com/news/20090309/americas-fastest-growing-religious-affiliation-none.

Guinness, Os. *Fool's Talk: Recovering the Art of Christian Persuasion*. Downers Grove, IL: InterVarsity, 2015.

Guite, Malcolm. *Faith, Hope and Poetry: Theology and the Poetic Imagination*. Burlington: Ashgate, 2014.

Hans, Rebecca. "That Hideous Strength and Till We Have Faces: C.S. Lewis, Evangelism, and the Role of Story." *Journal of Inkling Studies* 7 (2017) 7–57.

Harrington, Daniel. "The Gospel According to Mark." In *The Jerome Biblical Commentary*, edited by Raymond E. Brown et al., 596–629. Upper Saddle River, NJ: Prentice Hall, 1990.

Harris, Sam. *The End of Faith: Religion, Terror, and the Future of Reason.* New York: W. W. Norton, 2005.

Hatch, Derek. "Wingless Chickens and Desiderium Natural: The Theological Imagination of Flannery O'Connor and Henri de Lubac." *Christian Scholar's Review* 44 (2015) 117–33.

Hauerwas, Stanley, and L. Gregory Jones, eds. *Why Narrative?: Readings in Narrative Theology.* Grand Rapids: Eerdmans, 1998.

Hawkins, Peter S. *The Language of Grace: Flannery O' Connor, Walker Percy, and Iris Murdoch.* New York: Church, 2004.

Hedges, Chris. *Empire of Illusion: The End of Literacy and the Triumph of Spectacle.* New York: Nation, 2009.

Hein, Rolland. *Christian Mythmakers: C. S. Lewis, Madeline L'Engle, J. R. R. Tolkien, George MacDonald, G. K. Chesterton, Charles Williams, Dante Alighieri, John Bunyan, Walter Wangerin, Robert Siegel, and Hannah Hurnard.* Eugene, OR: Wipf & Stock, 2014.

Herrmann, Andrew F. "Kierkegaard and Dialogue: The Communication of Capability." *Communication Theory* 18 (2008) 71–92.

Honda, Mineko. *The Imaginative World of C.S. Lewis: A Way to Participate in Reality.* New York: University Press of America, 2000.

Hooper, Walter. *C. S. Lewis: A Complete Guide to His Life and Works.* New York: HarperCollins, 1996.

Hoskyns, Barney. *Lowside of the Road: A Life of Tom Waits.* New York: Broadway, 2010.

Hughes, John. "Proofs and Arguments." In *Imaginative Apologetics: Theology, Philosophy, and The Catholic Tradition*, edited by Andrew Davison, 3–11. Grand Rapids: Baker, 2011.

Inchausti, Robert Larry. *Subversive Orthodoxy: Outlaws, Revolutionaries, and Other Christians in Disguise.* Grand Rapids: Brazos, 2005.

Irwin, William. "God Is a Question, Not an Answer." *The New York Times*, March 26, 2016. https://opinionator.blogs.nytimes.com/2016/03/26/god-is-a-question-not-an-answer/.

Jacobs, Alan. *The Narnian: The Life and Imagination of C.S. Lewis.* New York: HarperCollins, 2005.

Johnson, Denis. "Car Crash while Hitchhiking." https://www.meredithsuewillis.com/car%20crash.pdf

Jordan, Nassim Bravo. "Irony." In *Volume 15, Tome IV: Kierkegaard's Concepts: Individual to Novel*, edited by Stephen M. Emmanuel et al., 39–44. Burlington: Ashgate, 2014.

Jost, Walter. "On Concealment and Deception in Rhetoric: Newman and Kierkegaard." *Rhetoric Society Quarterly* 24 (1994) 51–74.

Jung, Carl Gustav. *The Archetypes and the Collective Unconscious.* Buenos Aires: Editorial Paidos, 1970.

Keller, Timothy. *Making Sense of God: An Invitation to the Skeptical.* New York: Penguin, 2016.

Kessler, Edward. *Flannery O'Connor and the Language of Apocalypse.* Princeton: Princeton University Press, 1986.

Kidd, Richard, and Graham Sparkes. *God and the Art of Seeing: Visual Resources for a Journey of Faith.* Oxford: Regent's Park College, 2003.

Kierkegaard, Søren. *The Concept of Anxiety: A Simple Psychologically Orienting Deliberation on the Dogmatic Issue of Hereditary Sin.* Edited by Reidar Thomte. Princeton: Princeton University Press, 1981.

———. *Concluding Unscientific Postscript to Philosophical Fragments, Volume 1.* Edited by Edna H. Hong and Howard V. Hong. Princeton: Princeton University Press, 1992.

———. *Fear and Trembling.* Edited by C. Stephen Evans and Sylvia Walsh. Cambridge: Cambridge University Press, 2006.

———. *The Journals of Kierkegaard.* Translated by Alexander Dru. New York: Harper & Row, 1959.

———. *Kierkegaard's Attack Upon "Christendom" 1854-1855.* Translated by Walter Lowrie. Princeton: Princeton University Press, 1968.

———. *Philosophical Fragments.* Translated by David F. Swenson. Princeton: Princeton University Press, 1936.

———. *The Point of View for My Work as an Author: A Report to History, and Related Writings.* New York: Harper & Row, 1962.

———. *Practice in Christianity.* Edited by Edna H. Hong and Howard V. Hong. Princeton: Princeton University Press, 1991.

———. *Provocations: Spiritual Writings of Kierkegaard.* Edited by Charles E. Moore. Maryknoll, NY: Orbis, 2014.

———. *Søren Kierkegaard's Journals and Papers.* 7 vols. Translated by Edna H. Hong and Howard V. Hong. Bloomington: Indiana University Press, 1967.

Kilcourse, George A. *Flannery O'Connor's Religious Imagination.* Mahwah, NJ: Paulist, 2001.

Kinnaman, David, and Gabe Lyons. *UnChristian: What a New Generation Really Thinks about Christianity . . . and Why It Matters.* Grand Rapids: Baker, 2007.

Lane, Belden C. *Story Telling: The Enchantment of Theology.* Presentation on tape. St. Louis: Bethany, 1982.

Langan, Janine. "The Christian Imagination." In *The Christian Imagination: The Practice of Faith in Literature and Writing,* edited by Leland Ryken, 63–80. Colorado Springs: Waterbook, 2002.

Lasch, Christopher. *The Culture of Narcissism: American Life in An Age of Diminishing Expectations.* New York: W. W. Norton, 1991.

L'Engle, Madeleine. *Walking on Water: Reflections on Faith and Art.* New York: Convergent, 2016.

LeNotre, Katherine. "Flannery O'Connor's 'Parker's Back' and Hans Urs von Balthasar on Beauty and Tragedy." *Renascence* 65 (2013) 399–412.

Levine, Amy-Jill. *Short Stories by Jesus: The Enigmatic Parables of a Controversial Rabbi.* New York: Harper Collins, 2014.

Lewis, C. S. *The Collected Letters of C. S. Lewis, Volume 1: Family Letters 1905–1931.* Edited by Walter Hooper. New York: HarperCollins, 2004.

———. *The Collected Letters of C. S. Lewis, Volume 3: Narnia, Cambridge, and Joy, 1950—1963.* Edited by Walter Hooper. New York: HarperCollins, 2009.

———. *An Experiment in Criticism.* Cambridge: Cambridge University Press, 1961.

———. *George MacDonald.* Edited by Walter Hooper. New York: Harcourt Brace Jovanovich, 1966.

———. *God in the Dock.* Edited by Walter Hooper. Grand Rapids: Eerdmans, 1970.

———. *Letters to Malcolm: Chiefly on Prayer.* San Diego: Harvest, 1964.

————. *Mere Christianity*. New York: Harper Collins, 1952.

————. *On Stories: And Other Essays on Literature*. Edited by Walter Hooper. New York: Harcourt Brace Jovanovich, 1966.

————. *The Pilgrim's Regress*. Grand Rapids: Eerdmans, 1933.

————. *The Screwtape Letters*. San Francisco: Harper Collins, 1942.

————. "Sometimes Fairy Stories May Say Best What's to be Said." In *Of Other Worlds: Essays and Stories*, edited by Walter Hooper, 35–38. New York: Harcourt Brace Jovanovich, 1966.

————. *Surprised by Joy: The Shape of My Early Life*. New York: Harper Collins, 1955.

————. *Till We Have Faces: A Myth Retold*. San Diego: Harcourt, 1956.

Lindvall, Terry. "C.S. Lewis' Theory of Communication." PhD diss., University of Southern California Press, 1980.

————. *God Mocks: A History of Religious Satire from the Hebrew Prophets to Stephen Colbert*. New York: New York University Press, 2015.

Lippy, Charles H., and Eric Tranby. *Religion in Contemporary America*. New York: Routledge, 2013.

Loevlie, Elisabeth M. "Faith in the Ghosts of Literature. Poetic Hauntology in Derrida, Blanchot and Morrison's Beloved." *Religions* 4 (2013) 336–50.

MacDonald, George. *The Princess and the Goblin*. New York: Penguin Random House, 2011.

MacSwain, Robert. "Introduction." In *The Cambridge Companion to C. S. Lewis*, edited by Robert MacSwain and Michael Ward, 1–12. Cambridge: Cambridge University Press, 2010.

Malesic, Jonathan. "A Secret Both Sinister and Salvific: Secrecy and Normativity in Light of Kierkegaard's Fear and Trembling." *Journal of the American Academy of Religion* 74 (2006) 446–68.

Masci, David. "Q&A: A Look at What's Driving the Changes Seen in Our Religious Landscape Study." Pew Research Center, May 27, 2015. http://www.pewresearch.org/fact-tank/2015/05/27/qa-a-look-at-whats-driving-the-changes-seen-in-our-religious-landscape-study/.

Maughan-Brown, Frances. "Imagination." In *Volume 15, Tome III: Kierkegaard's Concepts: Envy to Incognito*, edited by Steven M. Emmanuel et al., 195–202. Burlington: Ashgate, 2014.

Mauriac, Francios. "Banquet Speech at the Nobel Banquet at the City Hall in Stockholm, Sweeden [Transcript]." Stockholm, Sweeden, 1952. https://www.nobelprize.org/nobel_prizes/literature/laureates/1952/mauriac-speech.html.

McAdams, Dan P. *The Stories We Live by: Personal Myths and the Making of the Self*. New York: Guilford, 1993.

McCollum, Mildred, and Betty Flora. "Arts and the Devil." *The English Journal* 49 (1960) 464–68.

McFague, Sallie. *Speaking in Parables*. Philadelphia: Fortress, 1975.

McKeon, Zahava Karl. *Novels and Arguments: Inventing Rhetorical Criticism*. Chicago: University of Chicago Press, 1982.

McLennan, Douglas. "Hail the Amateur, Loved by the Crowd." *The New York Times*, June 12, 2011. https://www.nytimes.com/2011/06/12/arts/music/amateur-musicians-and-crowd-sourced-talent-competitions.html?pagewanted=all.

McMullen, Joanne Halleran. *Writing Against God: Language as Message in the Literature of Flannery O'Connor*. Macon, GA: Mercer University Press, 1998.

Milbank, Alison. "Apologetics and the Imagination: Making Strange." In *Imaginative Apologetics: Theology, Philosophy, and the Catholic Tradition*, edited by Andrew Davison, 31–45. Grand Rapids: Baker, 2011.

Modesti, Sonja M. "Invitation Accepted: Integrating Invitational Rhetoric in Educational Contexts." *Current Issues in Education* 15 (2012). https://cie.asu.edu/ojs/index.php/cieatasu/article/view/904.

Muench, Paul. "The Socratic Method of Kierkegaard's Pseudonym Johannes Climacus: Indirect Communication and the Art of 'Taking Away.'" In *Soren Kierkegaard and the World(s)*, edited by Paul Houe and Gordon Daniel Marino, 139–50. Copenhagen: C.A. Reitzel, 2003.

Myers, Doris T. *C. S. Lewis in Context*. Kent: Kent State University Press, 1994.

Myers, Jacob D. *Preaching Must Die!: Troubling Homiletical Theology*. Minneapolis: Fortress, 2017.

Nelson, Benjamin. "Preface to the Torchbook Edition." In *The Point of View for My Work as an Author: A Report to History*, edited by Benjamin Nelson, vii–xviii. New York: Harper & Row, 1962.

O'Connor, Flannery. *Flannery O'Connor: The Complete Stories*. New York: Farrar, Straus and Giroux, 1988.

———. *The Habit of Being: Letters of Flannery O'Connor*. Edited by Sally Fitzgerald. New York: Farrar, Straus and Giroux, 1979.

———. *Mystery and Manners: Occasional Prose*. Edited by Sally Fitzgerald. New York: Farrar, Straus and Giroux, 1969.

Oden, Thomas C. "Introduction." In *Parables of Kierkegaard*, edited by Thomas C. Oden, vii–xviii. Princeton: Princeton University Press, 1978.

Ong, Walter J. *Orality and Literacy*. New York: Routledge, 2012.

Ordway, Holly. *Apologetics and the Christian Imagination: An Integrated Approach to Defending the Faith*. Steubenville, OH: Emmaus Road, 2017.

Orvell, Miles. *Flannery O'Connor: An Introduction*. Jackson: University Press of Mississippi, 1991.

Oubinha, Oscar Parcero. "Comic/Comedy." In *Volume 15, Tome II: Kierkegaard's Concepts: Classicism to Enthusiasm*, edited by Steven M. Emmanuel et al., 5–10. Burlington: Ashgate, 2016.

Pannenberg, Wolfhart. *Revelation as History*. Toronto: Macmillan, 1968.

Paustian, Mark. "The Beauty with the Veil. Validating the Strategies of Kierkegaardian Indirect Communication Through a Close Christological Reading of the Hebrew Old Testament." Diss., Regent University, 2016.

Penner, Myron Bradley. *The End of Apologetics: Christian Witness in a Postmodern Context*. Grand Rapids: Baker, 2013.

Percy, Walker. *The Message in the Bottle: How Queer Man Is, How Queer Language Is, and What One Has to Do with the Other*. New York: Farrar, Straus and Giroux, 1975.

Peter, Dr Laurence J. *Peter's Quotations: Ideas for Our Times*. New York: Bantam, 1977.

Peters, John Durham. "Beauty's Veils: The Ambivalent Iconoclasm of Kierkegaard and Benjamin." In *The Image in Dispute: Art and Cinema in the Age of Photography*, edited by Dudley Andrew, 9–32. Austin: University of Texas Press, 1997.

———. *Speaking into the Air: A History of the Idea of Communication*. Chicago: University of Chicago Press, 1999.

Peterson, Eugene H. "Foreword: Sacramental Theology." In *Sacramental Preaching: Sermons on the Hidden Presence of Christ* by Hans Boersma, vii–xii. Grand Rapids: Baker, 2016.

Possamai, Adam. *Handbook of Hyper-Real Religions.* Boston: Brill, 2012.

Postman, Neil. *Amusing Ourselves to Death: Public Discourse in the Age of Show Business.* New York: Penguin, 1985.

———. *The Disappearance of Childhood.* New York: Vintage, 1994.

Price, Reynolds. *A Palpable God.* San Francisco: North Point, 1997.

Putnam, Robert D. *Bowling Alone: The Collapse and Revival of American Community.* New York: Simon and Schuster, 2000.

Reid, Barbara E. *Parables for Preachers: The Gospel of Luke: Year C.* Collegeville, MN: Liturgical, 2000.

"Religion in Everyday Life." Pew Research Center, April 12, 2016. http://www.pewforum.org/2016/04/12/religion-in-everyday-life/.

Roberts, Kyle. *Emerging Prophet: Kierkegaard and the Postmodern People of God.* Eugene, OR: Cascade, 2013.

Ruzo, Andres. *The Boiling River of the Amazon.* TED Talk, 2016.

Ryken, Leland. *How to Read the Bible as Literature.* Grand Rapids: Zondervan, 1985.

Sachs, Jonah. *Winning the Story Wars: Why Those Who Tell (and Live) the Best Stories Will Rule the Future.* Boston: Harvard Business Review, 2012.

Saeverot, Herner. *Indirect Pedagogy: Some Lessons in Existential Education.* Rotterdam: Sense, 2013.

Sayers, Dorothy L. *The Mind of the Maker.* San Francisco: Harper, 1987.

Schakel, Peter J. "Seeing and Knowing: The Epistemology of C.S. Lewis's 'Till We Have Faces.'" *Seven: An Anglo-American Literary Review* 4 (1983) 84–97.

———. "Till We Have Faces." In *The Cambridge Companion to C. S. Lewis*, edited by Robert MacSwain and Michael Ward, 281–93. Cambridge: Cambridge University Press, 2010.

Schellenberg, J. L. *Divine Hiddenness and Human Reason.* Ithaca, NY: Cornell University Press, 1993.

Schindler, David C. "'Till We Have Facebook': On Christian Existence in the Age of Social Media." *Fellowship of Catholic Scholars Quarterly* 41 (2018) 306–14.

Schultze, Quentin J. *Habits of the High-Tech Heart: Living Virtuously in the Information Age.* Grand Rapids: Baker, 2002.

Sharier, Jason A. "Redefining Interfaith Discourse: Applying Invitational Rhetoric to Religion." *Young Scholars in Writing* 9 (2012) 87–97.

Short, Robert L. *The Gospel According to Peanuts.* Louisville: Westminster John Knox, 1965.

Simon, Herbert A. *Administrative Behavior: A Study of Decision-Making Processes in Administrative Organizations.* New York: Free Press, 1997.

Simon, Richard Keller. *The Labyrinth of the Comic: Theory and Practice from Fielding to Freud.* Tallahassee: University Presses of Florida, 1985.

Smith, James K. A. *Desiring the Kingdom: Worship, Worldview, and Cultural Formation.* Cultural Liturgies 1. Grand Rapids: Baker, 2009.

———. *Imagining the Kingdom: How Worship Works.* Cultural Liturgies 2. Grand Rapids: Baker, 2013.

Söderquist, K. Brian. "Irony." In *The Oxford Handbook of Kierkegaard*, edited by John Lippitt and George Pattison, 344–64. Oxford: Oxford University Press, 2013.

Stark, Rodney. *What Americans Really Believe: New Findings from the Baylor Surveys of Religion*. Waco, TX: Baylor University Press, 2008.

Stout, Daniel A. *Media and Religion: Foundations of an Emerging Field*. New York: Routledge, 2012.

Taylor, Charles. *A Secular Age*. Cambridge: Belnap Press of Harvard University, 2007.

Tietjen, Mark A. *Kierkegaard, Communication, and Virtue: Authorship as Edification*. Bloomington: Indiana University Press, 2013.

Trakakis, Nick. "An Epistemically Distant God? A Critique of John Hick's Response to the Problem of Divine Hiddenness." *Heythrop Journal* 48 (2007) 214–26.

Turnbull, Jamie. "Communication/Indirect Communication." In *Volume 15, Tome II: Kierkegaard's Concepts: Classicism to Enthusiasm*, edited by Steven M. Emmanuel et al., 17–23. Burlington: Ashgate, 2014.

———. "Kierkegaard, Indirect Communication, and Ambiguity." *Heythrop Journal* 50 (2009) 13–22.

———. "Reason." In *Volume 15, Tome V: Kierkegaard's Concepts: Objectivity to Sacrifice*, edited by Steven M. Emmanuel et al, 191–96. Burlington: Ashgate, 2015.

"US Public Becoming Less Religious." Pew Research Center, November 3, 2015. http://www.pewforum.org/2015/11/03/u-s-public-becoming-less-religious/.

Vlastos, Gregory. *Socrates, Ironist and Moral Philosopher*. Ithaca, NY: Cornell University Press, 1991.

Vogler, Christopher. *The Writer's Journey: Mythic Structure for Storytellers and Screenwriters*. Studio City: Michael Wiese Productions, 1998.

Ward, Graham. "Narrative and Ethics: The Structures of Believing and the Practices of Hope." *Literature and Theology* 20, no. 4 (2006) 438–61.

Ward, Michael. "The Good Serves the Better and Both the Best: C.S. Lewis on Imagination and Reason in Apologetics." In *Imaginative Apologetics: Theology, Philosophy and the Catholic Tradition*, edited by Andrew Davison, 59–78. Grand Rapids: Baker, 2011.

———. *Planet Narnia: The Seven Heavens in the Imagination of C. S. Lewis*. Oxford: Oxford University Press, 2008.

Ware, Kallistos. "God of the Fathers: C.S. Lewis and Eastern Christianity." In *The Pilgrim's Guide: C. S. Lewis and the Art of Witness*, edited by David Mills, 53–69. Grand Rapids: Eerdmans, 1998.

Warren, Michael. *Seeing Through the Media: A Religious View of Communications and Cultural Analysis*. Harrisburg, PA: Trinity International, 1997.

Webber, Robert E. *Ancient-Future Faith: Rethinking Evangelicalism for a Postmodern World*. Grand Rapids: Baker, 1999.

———. *The Younger Evangelicals: Facing the Challenges of the New World*. Grand Rapids: Baker, 2002.

Weinreich, Beatrice Silverman, ed. *Yiddish Folktales*. Translated by Leonard Wolf. New York: Schocken, 1988.

Wilder, Amos N. "The Church's New Concern with the Arts." *Christianity and Crisis* 17 (1957). https://www.religion-online.org/article/the-churchs-new-concern-with-the-arts/.

———. *Early Christian Rhetoric: The Language of the Gospel*. Peabody, MA: Hendrickson, 1971.

Williams, Will. "Story-Telling." In *Volume 15, Tome VI: Kierkegaard's Concepts: Salvation to Writing,* edited by Steven M. Emmanuel et al., 101–7. Burlington: Ashgate, 2013.

Wood, Ralph C. *Flannery O'Connor and the Christ-Haunted South.* Grand Rapids: Eerdmans, 2004.

Wright, Stephen I. *Jesus the Storyteller.* London: Ashford Colour, 2014.

Zubeck, Jacqueline A. "Back to Page One in 'Parker's Back': An Orthodox Examination of O'Connor's Last Story." *Flannery O'Connor Review* 8 (2010) 92–116.

Index

Made in the USA
Las Vegas, NV
15 January 2022

41516310R00184